AUTHORS' LIVES : ON LITERARY B
PR 756 B56H66 1990

A10543291001

D1042069

AUTHORS'
LIVES

Other books by Park Honan

Jane Austen: Her Life
Matthew Arnold: A Life
The Book, the Ring, and the Poet:
  A Biography of Robert Browning
  (with William Irvine)

AUTHORS' LIVES

LIVES

*On Literary Biography and
the Arts of Language*

PARK HONAN

St. Martin's Press, New York

Production Editor: David Stanford Burr

Design by Fearn Cutler

Library of Congress Cataloging-in-Publication Data

Honan, Park.
 Authors' lives : on literary biography and the arts of
language / Park Honan.
        p.   cm.
 "A Thomas Dunne book."
 ISBN 0-312-04261-2
 1. English prose literature—History and criticism.
2. American prose literature—History and criticism. 3. Authors,
English—Biography—History and criticism. 4. Authors,
American—Biography—History and criticism. 5. Biography
(as a literary form)
I. Title.
PR756.B56H66 1990
828'.08—dc20   89-77896
                                                                    CIP

First Edition

10 9 8 7 6 5 4 3 2 1

To David and Mary

CONTENTS

PREFACE

—Or Rather, a Few Frank Words to the Reader as to Why It Is Worth His or Her Trouble to Read the Essays in This Book and Get Inside the Mind and Workshop of a Literary Biographer

James Boswell—two centuries after giving us the first (and still the best) modern literary biography in his *Life of Johnson* (1791)—might be surprised by our hunger for biographies today. He might not be impressed by hardback sales figures. Prices rise, and many of us have to borrow costly biographies from libraries, or wait for paperback editions. But—at least—he would open his eyes over the monetary advances some publishers have been willing to pay for new, standard "lives" and admit that we are curious about the careers of authors. A literary biography may not have much scandal, but it can seem to bridge a gap between the author living *then* and the reader living *now*, and tell us about creativity. And so if we want to know about the characters and lives of authors, the patient, canny, experienced biographer has a function and need not be ashamed to be as delighted as a child in the spotlight, say, at a lecture or a party in the local bookshop. Poor soul! He or she has drudged long enough to deserve the illusion of being useful.

The best tribute to the enterprise of literary biography is just that it survives and absorbs attacks upon it. For example, the genre in effect was attacked by Roland Barthes, who had the clarity one might expect of a teacher at the Ecole Pratique de Hautes Etudes in Paris. At the time of his death he was Professor of Literary Semiology—a title he chose himself—at the Collège de France. He believed that writing (of every kind) destroys its own origins, since the subject of it "slips away" from the author—and thus the reader, and the reader alone, "is simply that *someone* who holds together in a single field all the traces by which the written text is constituted."*

Well, if the author's work is a kind of seed that sprouts and blossoms in the reader, and if writing is cut off from the author as soon as it exists, then we can never quite trace connections between the author and his or her work—or fully say why the author wrote or what contributed to the writing. I think that argument is valid, and that one of our best biographers confirmed it when Richard Ellmann wrote in *Golden Codgers: Biographical Speculations* (1973) that "we cannot know completely the intricacies with which any mind negotiates with its surroundings to produce literature."

Barthes struck a blow against overconfidence in our relating of the author's life to the author's works. Another line of French thought strikes rather more deeply at the forms of literary biography, and implies they are false. This challenge is important because it is changing the *shape* of what we do; it arises from a view of human identity which we associate with the late Fernand Braudel, who, as a historian, demoted kings, parliaments, crises, and key dates and shifted the emphasis to common life, geographical space, economics, and social evolution. In Braudel's view—and even implicitly in the view of some social historians who have challenged his premises since his death—it is less valid to claim that men and women make history, than it is to say that history makes men and women. Roger Chartier, among others, would remind us that individuals (at any given time) find multiple ways to react to an environment or to social relationships. But still, it would appear that history is a part of anyone's cause and makeup, a part of anyone's personal identity; and if that is true then history ought to have some centrality in anyone's story in any adequate, realistic biography. We may feel, accordingly, that Dr. Johnson was right to say that the biographer's business is in part to "display the minute details of daily life"—including the life *around* the subject. Henry

---

* See the fine essay by Barthes, "The Death of the Author," in *Image—Text—Music*, trans. Stephen Heath (London: Fontana, 1977).

James wrote that "to live over people's lives is nothing unless we live over their perceptions, live over the growth, the change, the varying intensity of the scene—since it was by these things that they themselves lived." That emphasis on the *scene* is being understood, I think, as we become more alert to the delicacy and flexibility needed in the task of planning to tell as much of the truth about an author's life as we can.

Well, why should you read this book? My own credentials are only those of a practicing biographer—I have written lives of Matthew Arnold and of Jane Austen and helped to complete a life of Browning. But if I am candid enough, you may feel it worthwhile to see what one literary biographer has to say about his trade. To begin *in medias res*, what about the job of writing a "life" or putting pen to paper—or fingers on the word processor? Biographers are praised now and then, as I was not long ago by the British *Independent* ("Park Honan writes enchantingly") with a mad kindness. I am not even sure that that was a compliment. It was kindly meant—but then I have a tale about my clumsiness and almost paralytic inability to write a simple sentence to tell. It isn't exactly that one cannot write. (You see, this sentence is fairly readable, isn't it?) What cramps one is the problem of trying to get a paragraph to reflect accurately the sense of one's historical evidence after one has placed it together and mulled over it, as it were, worming oneself into the sense of two or three diaries, a letter, a book on agricultural progress in Hampshire, two items in the *Hampshire Chronicle*, by day and night. I fall back on my old, sad belief in the terrible rightness of Generals Grant and Haig (butchers of lives), that you must fight it out on the line all winter if you want to achieve your task. In this case, ten or twelve revisions of a chapter may not be enough; I once wrote one biographical paragraph more than seventy times. (The problem, as I saw it, was to do exact justice to an excessive amount of material—my pile of notes would have kept me a foot off the floor if I had sat on it—relating to Browning in the 1880s when he suddenly became a popular poet, and the result is the first two hundred words on page 499 of *The Book, the Ring, and the Poet: A Biography of Robert Browning*.) A biographer never (in my experience) gets anything right in a first, second, or third draft, but ought to revise from the drafts already at hand and may at last get a deeply accurate paragraph. Revise or die. Biographical prose, which reflects historical truth about persons, is the hardest kind of prose to write. Few experiences—among things we can do with pen and paper—are more satisfying, all the same, than rewriting until one is certain that the prose exactly reflects historical evidence one has.

Yet there is a deeper or more subtle challenge in the writing of biography, and one that I have never seen carefully discussed. It is involved in the nature of the present book. I am well aware that two or three of my chapters, or at least "Points" and "Browning and the Lyric Test," will seem somewhat odd or irrelevant to the literary biographer's work (because biographers aren't supposed to be thinking about such matters as punctuation theory, or a poet's idiosyncratic lyric rhythms), but these chapters very much pertain to that work. Writing a good literary biography may involve studying every feature of the subject, every aspect of a poet's or novelist's expressive choices, every feature affecting rhythm, tempo, and tone in the subject's writing; it is not enough to undertake trivial research when (as Joyce might say) one's research ought to be quadrivial. In seemingly infinitely minute matters, there will be revelations enough. Robert Browning the man will not be understood by anyone indifferent to the ways in which he expressed himself in the lyric; and no master of English prose or poetry will be seen with much accuracy by anyone who cannot take an interest in such a seemingly tiny matter as the writer's punctuation, in light of the history of English punctuation theory and practice. Are these microscopic matters? Well, then, polish the lenses of your microscope. It is no less important, I think, to see that one's research into an author's life should take in extremely large matters, such as the history and exact nature of the society in which he or she lived and worked. But—in several chapters of this book—I have emphasized rather minute matters to show that the microcosm is just as essential to investigate as the macrocosm, and partly to suggest that good biographies depend upon the re-formation of the biographer's mind and outlook.

I think that patience in studying small traces of evidence (even a poet's lyric rhythms, or grammatical features of his or her work) has a double function. The biographer begins to acquire a special intimacy with the author. And one also begins the slow and stumbling task of changing oneself, one's outlook, one's orientations, until it is possible at least approximately to think and feel in the distant and lost world of the subject. Whatever one does in the 1990s, it is impossible to think and feel exactly as Jane Austen or as Matthew Arnold thought and felt, and it is well to be on guard against the illusion that one can. Real success in biography is more impossible than we may care to suppose. The subject—Austen or Arnold, the individual who once lived—is so complex and elusive as to remain in partial shadow and to defeat all possible avenues of approach and all of our computerized ways of learning to know and understand, and so, most assuredly, biography is in one sense a poor and failing enterprise. But it need not be a sham. As anyone who has read two or three "lives" of the same subject will know, there are large differences in the quality and extent of our defeats; some biographies of Dickens are more reliable, accurate, well informed, and rewarding to read than others. But mere industry has not produced the relatively good "life" of that author, or any other. Even a modest degree of truthfulness in a reasonably full account of a life has come about because the biographer has been able to enter into a past time with primed understanding and awareness, or with, in effect, a changed nature. This is one reason it takes some years to write a satisfactory work in this genre—none of us likes to be changed; no biographer can transform himself or herself in a year or two so as to write well in detail of a complex consciousness inhabiting the past. It may cynically be said that quickly written, fluent, and superficial studies win literary prizes, and that the public does not know a good biography from a dreadful piece of claptrap; but even as that is said the public's winnowing out is taking place, and I know of no abominable biography that has been cited with praise long after it was first printed. Bad biographies abound, but we do not hear of them a few months after they glitter. Like catsup bottles dropped off a trawler, they sink from sight and we are glad to have no more news of them.

So it is apparent that unusual patience is required, and not simply because one must traipse over countries and barge into libraries. In writing the first detailed account of Matthew Arnold's life, I did many mechanical (and very necessary) things. I made calendars for every week in Arnold's life, wrote chapter outlines, then outlines of the out-

lines; I lived in the Arnolds' summer house Fox How in the Lake
District for two weeks, fished in his streams, climbed English peaks he
climbed, followed his path up the Gemmi Pass above the Rhône in
Switzerland, made a nuisance of myself by asking questions in hotels
where he stayed, visited almost every locale he knew in France, traveled to American libraries, took notes on his letters and school reports
once for thirty-six hours at a stretch because time was short (and had
the luxury of a loaf of bread and a bottle of orange juice—but no rest
for my eyes); in ten years I worked many a night until four or five in
the morning, sorting notes or rewriting; I barged into twenty libraries,
wrote dozens of letters in quest of information, talked to many people
about Arnold, exploited my family, spent what money I had and did
almost everything I (legally) could to get more for my research; and I
read his letters and poems and essays and books all the while, and
acquired thousands of notes and photocopies of source materials, and
never regretted any of this. While such things are happening, an education is going on, an inner change which may be slight, or more
than slight and thus helpful. There is nothing mystical about such a
change and I simply refer to a self-transformation involving a deeper
"understanding," which enables one to move with some confidence
and authority in the subject's world. The transformation is even more
important than the information one mechanically acquires since the
former determines how well one is able to use what one learns. And
the change requires time. Boswell's *Johnson* has excellence partly because Boswell was engaged in a transformation, an "understanding,"
over a period of twenty-one years; he was always a part of Johnson's
larger world but not of Johnson's private one, and a deep change in
Boswell was required of him in order to understand that.

It would be a parody of the matter to say that the biographer
must pore over prosody, or the history of grammar and punctuation,
to write with authority. But insofar as such topics offer insights into
the subject's temperament or skills, they are important. It is worth
attending to the minutiae of evidence—with the patience of a medieval monk in a stone cell—so as to assist the change that will help one
to enter into an alert understanding of any evidence *at all* relating to
one's subject.

Still, there are larger things to discover. What about major research—such as the effort to find letters, diaries, or other primary documents relating to one's subject? After twenty years of that, I must say that I'm not certain how to go about it. All I have learned prepares me only a little for *new* research. But then what little I have concluded is helpful, subversive, and worth telling you, though other biographers may not agree with me and may think this baneful, perverse nonsense, of a kind that must never be said. It is the gist of what I have learned in twenty years' biographical work in the United States, United Kingdom, Switzerland, and France. It is, first, that for the researcher, a living person must be valued as more precious and important than all of the dead who once lived; I may not seem to value the living: I will exploit or neglect my family and friends (I'm not proud of it) in order to carry out fieldwork or typing. Yet I put them all far above research; I am terribly hungry for friends; I seem cold and out of touch all the time; I don't need to be more loved but need to hear words that go through to my backbone—and so it is that the talk of men who are not my old friends is trying for me; I am a heterosexual who prefers, if I have a choice, talk with women or homosexual men because these seem alert to nuances and are more appreciative of intimate chatter. And, I think, the subordination of research to something else, such as a need for intimate friendship, is a requirement for research into life.

How can I illustrate this?

Several times I asked an elderly couple, living not near Jane Austen's home, if they had documents of use to me. No, they had none. One was a direct descendant of eighteenth-century Austens, and it seemed enough that they offered friendship and wanted to see me. It is not hypocritical to say that I expected, or dreamed, of nothing else. A selfish feeling that I was in touch with "Austens" faded away, and my wife and I visited these people because we loved them. I worried that our friendship would be affected by what I was trying to write about Jane Austen but I never felt pressured or inhibited—and, instead, was supplied and freed by our friends' intelligence and gaiety. (Never has anyone in England inhibited my research in twenty years, prohibited the use of any document or told me what or what not to say.) But I was wary; I felt I might perhaps have cut off a finger to please warm, loyal, intelligent people, but not a sentence of my work. One day my wife and I came to spend a weekend with our friends in hopes that we would have a clear day for a walk. Rain came down without relent. On Sunday afternoon, my hostess said in effect, "This may be more troublesome than the rain, but I recall something that was put in the attic when we married long ago. Would you mind helping me look for it?" Upstairs we went. Under old carpets, we found a trunk, and a third or fourth key opened it; it seemed filled to the brim with eighteenth-century holograph letters. Spotting the name Austen on a folded paper with a broken reddish-orange seal, I knelt at the trunk with the idea of taking a note. That was tactless, I soon felt. Putting a hand on my shoulder, my hostess said something like this: "Don't take any notes, Park. I am going to inconvenience you a *little* further. I want you to take this trunk home with you for a few weeks; tell me what is in it." I insisted on itemizing what was in the trunk before I left and on signing my list of items; but off my wife and I went with unpublished holograph letters by three of Jane Austen's brothers, all of her cousin Eliza's surviving letters, a missing and revealing family diary, letters by Jane Austen's mother, letters by Jane Austen's friends, and more still. For six nervous weeks I lived in my house with a good proportion of the surviving Austen family papers; I kept all this in three drawers of a locked filing cabinet. I soon made photographic copies of everything, but would wake at night thinking of fire or of a jet crashing on my house. It was a relief to return the treasures to my friends. (They no longer have the documents, which are slowly being edited and published.) I might say more of the trust of individuals who deserve something other than this anecdote, but I don't cite them here in an anonymous way to illustrate gratitude or my delight in Austen papers, but to suggest that research isn't always predictable or calculable, and that its urgency ought to be subordinated to the urgency of other commitments of feeling, mind, and need.

How we worship the new biographical fact—"new facts"! (My life and soul for new facts!) And so we have since the humanists of the sixteenth century, only we notice that, perhaps, the sanity and balance of Renaissance humanists are a little lost now that Mr. Gradgrind tells us *all* new facts are sacred—and that facts alone justify a biography. Let me pretend a moment: I have before me P. Massinger's new *Samuel Johnson* (Sir Giles Overreach Press, 1998)—I gather it is to be released in 1998 to allow time for publicity—and I notice that this fine, fat book is said to supersede works by "Boswell" and "Bate" and "Wain" because it offers what the blurb writer calls "sensational new facts about pederasty"; it seems (in my imaginary example) that Dr. Johnson once overtipped his laundress's son, and *that* is what justifies a brand new Johnson biography! Yet, of course, key facts *do* come to light. I revere the new fact myself—and see it not as the end of research, but as part of a troublesome beginning.

The discovery of a new fact from the past for a long while never results in an improvement of understanding, but in gross distortion. The new fact glitters and gobbles, or overweens and screens. A good biographer labors to know historical contexts well enough to remove distortions caused by chance discovery, and yet, still, is grateful for what is "new" in its odd power—which I comment on in the chapter "Historical Privilege." As for me, though lazy and perhaps messy, I try to assimilate facts and work with filing systems all the time. I treat a new detail with elaborate, fussy care. Notes about it go into several files and usually into an "outline of chapters"—an outline out of which other outlines are to be made. I have not found a computer that can match my filing methods or analyze incoming data well enough to be of use; I may tomorrow. But I am primitive in this way; I want to contend with the fuss of sorting, so that something may rub off in the process and lodge in my mind.

In seeking information, I am like that laziest of Russians, Oblomov; not being intuitive, I believe in idleness, stasis, and in being lost. How do you know what to look for? A splendid elderly scholar who had collected Matthew Arnold's letters once invited me to his rooms in Virginia. We liked each other, and so, day after day, we arranged to meet for supper here or there, and would return to his rooms and talk perhaps until 1:00 A.M.—almost never about Arnold, but about the war of 1861–65 (of which I know little enough). Perhaps I qualified for the discussion because my mother was born in Baltimore; two of our family had died as Confederate captains—but I am not sure that my host was impressed. He knew a great deal about the years 1861 to 1865 when Arnold was alive; I returned to holograph letters in the morning (on deposit at a nearby library) with a mind more primed to understand Matthew Arnold. My host cared about the man as I did, understood much about him, but the indirections of our talk helped more than any discussion of Arnold would have been likely to do.

I find my own stupidity, self-indulgence, moodiness, and feelings of the moment very helpful. Again, a brief illustration. Wanting to find the green area known as the Forbury where young Jane Austen and her sister attended the now-demolished Abbey School at Reading, and never having seen Reading, I reached the city late one afternoon. I was bored, restless, uneasy; I wished to be in London and had nearly run out of money. Taking a cheap room for the night, I decided to look for the green Forbury in the dark. People I stopped had never heard of it. Walking on and on without a city map, I became lost, and noticed that I had failed to note the street name where my room was. Near midnight, people disappeared from the streets—so I looked miserably for a church or the railway station to doze for the night. By then, it struck me that a child would have had the sense to look for a green field in daylight, and nearly any mortal wouldn't have been so absentminded. I became very depressed. Then I saw an Anglican church with a light and imagined burglars were in it. Walking in slowly, I found the rector—who, lo and behold, knew much about local history and Reading's Forbury. He had data far in advance of anything published on Jane and Cassandra Austen's Abbey School; he not only directed me back to my room, but saved me weeks of research and provided leads to new data about Jane Austen's early education, a topic I was most "in the dark" about. Next morning I set out with exciting new leads, hungry and filled with energy and bliss I can hardly describe; by wandering in the dark (and thanks to my helper) I had come closer to the historical truth about Jane Austen than a large amount of disciplined work would have taken me.

One sees what Carlyle meant when he said research is "Paradiso." Blunders often remain blunders, but one rejoices often over failures, and seldom regrets having pursued topics for weeks or a month with no direct result. One always learns *something*. I usually can't bear to ask for a librarian's help until just before the library is closing for the day. At the India Office at London's south bank, I once learned about the East India Company's secret records (and the activities of Jane Austen's brother Frank) by being distracted by an Indian lady's beautiful sari, and putting the wrong numbers in the wrong places on "call slips." The *wrong* old records of confidential, dusty files of the Regency company minutes were the ones that told the most.

Wandering and blundering—but the writing of an adequate biography depends on more than *that?* Yes, and because the process of learning and planning is complex, I want to take you into the practical workshop of a literary biographer and show you the essence of what goes on—I mean the kind of thinking and approaches that go into the making of a biography that can withstand the test of time.

The pieces in this book explore biographical problems, draw comparisons, or sketch some of the small and larger contexts of my concern with the minds and lives of writers. I take you into my workshop to show you things that one seeking biographer has felt to be relevant while a book was being researched and written. You may think my first chapter much too theoretical or lacking in just that vividness and charm you might expect of someone interested in Jane Austen (but I did not think that I could represent evidence about the Austens fully and well, without exploring the form I was using to do so). You may skip ahead, and find yourself outside what seems to be the province of a biographer of authors. Begin, if you will, with my dialogue on "Shakespeare's Life" at the end—because that touches on some of my main themes. A good biography of an author takes us close to the realities of a creative life, as close as it is possible to be. But part of the reader's pleasure, I think, is in being alert to how the life is told. Just what is the presenter's job? How did he or she prepare for it? How is the life and work of an author to be pictured? All of the time in pages ahead, my aim is to avoid mere theorizing if I can—though I have to deal with theory—and to illustrate the range and flexibility of a biographer's concern with authors' lives.

The first part, "Writing Biographies," concerns *practical* theory and what can be learned from traditions in English literary biography. In the second and third chapters, on Dr. Johnson and Boswell, I say what I think those original giants usefully have to tell us. In "Some Politics" I examine political biographies for comparison—to see what they offer, where they fail or succeed—and in the two following chapters I comment on modern biographical methods.

Part 2, "Working with Jane Austen," involves the matter of influences that helped to form Jane Austen's mind, person, and talent. Part

3, "Victorians and Moderns," ranges from the life and work of a minor (but very revealing) Victorian down to the recent past. I mean to show that a biographer's work and enthusiasms ought to lead into highways and byways. In "Mary Claude's Blue Eyes," I examine the intellectual and artistic importance of a love affair. In "Browning and the Lyric Test," I look into what a poet's verse technique indirectly shows about his temperament. "Points" is about one of the smallest things of interest to a literary biographer—small but important. I refer often in what follows to my own practice or experience to show you where I stand, but everything personal here is meant to illuminate the nature of one immensely delightful kind of writing—literary biography.

ACKNOWLEDGMENTS

All (but one) of the pieces that follow were written while a biography was in progress, and I have revised them to avoid repetition and so that they will be clear in this sequence.

Since some early titles (such as "Biographia Literaria") are not indicative, I have given several of my pieces new titles—but I have not drawn in my horns, or altered any of my insights; and I thank editors and publishers for permission to reprint from texts that originally appeared in their publications.

"Beyond Sartre: Theory and Form in Modern Biographies," is from *New Literary History* 16 (1984–85): 639–51.

"Dr. Johnson's Lives," "The Young Arnold," and part of "Trollope's Life and Trollope's Novels," were originally published in *Contemporary Review* 245 (December 1984: 304–10), 245 (October 1984: 191–98), and 243 (December 1982: 318–23).

"After Boswell" and "David Lodge before *Changing Places*" are from *Novel: A Forum on Fiction* 13 (1979): 304–10, and 5 (1972): 167–73.

"Some Politics" is from a text first published in *Victorian Studies* 16 (1973): 453–61.

"Problems of Literary Biography" is from *Words International* No. 3 (January 1988), 8–13.

"Ellmann as the Author of *James Joyce* and *Oscar Wilde*" is from *Encounter* 71 (July-August 1988), 50–54.

"Richardson's Influence" and "Sterne and the Formation of Jane Austen's Talent" were included in two volumes edited by Valerie Grovesnor Myer and published by Vision Press and by Barnes & Noble, *Samuel Richardson: Passion and Prudence* (1986) and *Laurence Sterne: Riddles and Mysteries* (1984).

"Revolution" was first printed in *University of Leeds Review* 28 (1985/86): 181–95.

"Good Advice" is from the Jane Austen Society *Report* (1989).

"Bulwer" was published in Bulwer Lytton, *Falkland*, edited by Herbert van Thal (Cassell, 1967).

"Browning and the Lyric Test" is from *Browning's Mind and Art*, edited by Clarence Tracy (Oliver and Boyd, 1968: 82–99).

"Points" is taken from *English Studies* 41 (1960): 92–102.

"Arnold, Eliot, Trilling" was included in *Matthew Arnold in His Time and Ours: Centenary Essays*, edited by Clinton Machann and Forrest D. Burt (University Press of Virginia, 1988): 171–82, and a version of "Historical Privilege" was prepared for Baylor University's Centennial Symposium on Robert Browning in September 1989.

"Ginsberg and Kerouac" is from *The Beats: An Anthology of 'Beat' Writing*, edited by Park Honan, © 1987. Reprinted by permission of J. M. Dent & Sons and Weidenfeld and Nicolson, London.

"Kermode on St. Mark" is from "Biographia Literaria" in *Centrum: Working Papers of the Minnesota Center for Advanced Studies in Language, Style and Literary Theory*, 6 (1978): 133–39.

"Shakespeare's Life" is printed here for the first time.

PART ONE

WRITING BIOGRAPHIES

Chapter One

BEYOND SARTRE: THEORY AND FORM IN MODERN BIOGRAPHIES

I

"READ NO HISTORY," advised Disraeli in his novel *Contarini Fleming* in 1832, "nothing but biography, for that is life without theory."

Disraeli's Carlylean view that biographies catch raw facts of life and need not be shaped by theories persists today. Factual narratives about authors' lives are varied in form, and we may feel that since life has only a simple *inevitable* pattern (all are born, grow older, do or fail to do something that may interest later generations, and die), then to impose general rules on the telling of individual life stories would be pointless. As life is multiform so must writing about it be.

"Life without theory" encapsulates what nineteenth-century critics hoped biography, at its purest, would reflect. Carlyle and Arnold,

Sainte-Beuve and Pater are more concerned to say what biographies can do for us than to criticize their forms. Victorians did condemn books that told too much (Froude on Carlyle or Dowden on Shelley) or that seemed pedestrian. Matthew Arnold, for example, believes that the *Life* (1844) of his father, written by that shining ex-Rugby Sixth Former Arthur Stanley, is "in the style of an ordinary religious English middle class biography, with (for my taste) too much detail, and too bourgeois in its character"—but this occurs in a defensive letter to his mother; it is not a public complaint. Victorians take biographical form for granted and view too much "theory" as embarrassing.

Serious writing about biography in our time most often appears in apologies by practitioners. Biographers have been pressed to justify methods because, in one wave after another, disciplines and ideas (often rolling in from the last century), such as sociology, psychology, historicism, scientific positivism, or, more recently, structural anthropology or feminism, have shown older forms and methods to be flawed—or waterlogged, cumbersome, and uninteresting. Sophisticated criticism has had a lethal effect, exposing slipshod methods. Scholes and Kellogg in *The Nature of Narrative* note that a careless demarcation between fact and fiction has enabled biographers to slide (in one book) between realism and romance. Alarmed by the complexity and autonomy of artworks, biographers can no longer rely on simple, sensible Chestertonian comment in writing sections on Keats's poems or Hardy's novels. They are tempted to omit criticism of works or to offer limited factual comments on sources, processes of composition, and the like, details supported by footnotes.

Biographers as a rule are not concerned with theory, but anxious to avoid mistakes. They must not open themselves to charges of subjectivity, psychological improbability, narrowness and naiveté, historical ignorance, or male chauvinism. Yet in avoiding every gaucherie, they may dehydrate their product. It is risky to say what the public thinks of the product, but in reviews in English, American, and French newspapers, one more often finds respect than enthusiasm for academic biographies that commit no egregious errors but fail to suggest the experiences of their subjects in life, and which are respectable but emotionally impoverished and cautious to the point of banality. Scholars complain that the Boswellian tradition, as seen now in the most responsible biographies, has become tepid, or that something is wrong if a two-volume life of Thomas Hardy has no grasp of Hardy's imaginative life or of what is idiosyncratic and valuable in his manners of thinking and feeling. Helen Gardner found that we are unwilling or unable to respect exceptional experiences: we often subordinate a writer's "true achievement to the inquiry into his psyche"—in an "inquiry" which itself may be pedestrian. She leads one to feel that Victorians were truthful, in a way we are not, by exalting through reverence the uniqueness of a fine poet or novelist.

Biographers apologize for their methods (as Gittings and Edel have) but see their craft as one offering practical problems to solve. They are hard-working pragmatists. Let me use myself as an example. In completing William Irvine's work *The Book, the Ring, and the Poet* (1974; my six chapters on Browning's life were mainly finished in 1969), and then in writing *Matthew Arnold: A Life* (1981) and *Jane Austen: Her Life* (1987), I have found an urgent problem to be selection—or exclusion—in connection with organization. The problem is so vast and pokey, involving countless bits of paper, marked-up Xeroxes, and references in microfilms, that it shoulders out theory—or rather forces me to adopt complex filing systems and simple working theories. Much of my "evidence," for example, seems "true." If I added qualifiers in a context, I might use almost any comment on my historical person, or on his or her works, since even the wrongheaded comment is evidence if it shows how one's subject affected someone else. (Arnold is responsible for his critics, and what his critics have said needs to be patiently considered.) If all or most contemporary evidence and subsequent comments about a writer are indicative, then my task is to cull from this mass certain selections of evidence, to evaluate them for accuracy, pertinence, and illustrative use, and to build with them so as to reveal my subject as closely as history (what can be known of the past) permits. Even a false or "wrong" comment may have uses, and I find it hard to predict which kinds of secondary evidence may be revealing. One is tempted to make choices even among one's wealth of primary documents (letters, diaries, journals, notes, someone's memory of what one's subject said) too readily, and thus diminish without intending to. Many biographers in trying to achieve "vitality" only become reductive: André Maurois's *Lélia*

(1952) refers to George Sand's mind and art but seems to show chiefly her love affairs; and Maurois's reductive errors are paralleled in more recent, scholarly lives of George Sand, which discuss her works but fail to suggest much of her artistic, emotional, and intellectual experience—the sense of life as she knew, felt, and lived it or worked within it—which we come close to in her letters. But how is a biographical form to catch those experiences we begin to sense in an author's letters?

II

Two diverging trends in writing about authors illustrate problems of experience and form. The importing of Freudian ideas into the genre helped it to evolve. Freudian ideas gave the biographer an interior viewpoint or inside platform to stand on and point from with a stick. George Painter in his two-volume *Proust* (1959, 1965) could add his own, un-Freudian interior comments to Freudian explanations of his subject's childhood recollections, adolescent rejections, homosexuality, nostalgia, and so on. Some lives demand of the biographer an intelligent interior method: the scheme that takes us within is valuable even if it is hypothetical. Freud gives Painter a discursive advantage and helps him to avoid the hard, brittle rhetoric of an outward academic manner: a biography limited to Bernard Crick's manner in *Orwell* (1980) would make little sense of Proust. (I shall look more closely at the biographical manners of both *Proust* and *Orwell* in pages ahead.)

Sartre's intimacy with his subject has a free-ranging brilliance in *Saint-Genet* of 1952 (one of his own favorite books), which seems now to be an overshadowing prelude to his late study of Flaubert. Both *Genet* and *Idiot of the Family* (1971) have an inward reflective comment that suits the quality of their subject's mind; these books hardly cross, but run around, the stony terrain that literary biographies cross. Instead of letting patient, factual reconstruction obscure a thinking, creating subject, Sartre lends out his mental vitality to animate a mind equal to his own—and lends out his attributes, of course, to that mind in both cases. He subverts truth in interpretation—as Barthes seems to do with Racine, as Todorov notes—by suggesting that the interpretation of a person cannot be true or false, but is only stimulating or poor, rich, or dull. His biographical "truth" lies in an intellectual fecundity which suggests the intense excitement of Genet's creative intellect. Vercors (Jean Bruller) has written *Moi, Aristide Briand: Essai d'Autoportrait* (1981), which Konrad Bieber, who is writing Vercors's authorized biography, could consider as one sign of Vercors's admiration for Sartre. Vercors uses, or at least consults, historical documents to write Briand's autobiography for him. He takes a step beyond Sartre. Briand, like Cromwell, would have been a literary man if he could—his autoportraitist gives eloquence to an inarticulate mind.

These extrabiographical works reflect a pressure on literary biographers to get around what Conrad in *A Personal Record* (1912) calls the pride of documentary history. Their aim is to depict energy—political, intellectual, creative—in the unusual person. They revolt against cluttering effects of factual documentation and plead for intuition in commentary. They are infused with a spirit of delight, mental freedom—and behind them one sees Sainte-Beuve's gaiety in the biographical essay.

But far from Sartre, Barthes, and Vercors one finds biographers who are more nervous than ever about "character" and "interior views"; the most stringent of their predecessors were more relaxed. They exalt objectivity and in apologies can justify slipshod style as a mark of "truth." They illustrate (inadvertently) the limiting effects that the scientific positivism of our day has had upon the interpretation of persons, but they justly complain that our traditional biographies neglect social contexts. In an interesting discussion of Ruth First and Ann Scott's *Olive Schreiner* (1980), Susan Gardner makes a case for attending to social contexts more thoroughly than we have done as she sums up "weaknesses" in traditional biography:

> These would include its stress on personal/picturesque factors rather than socio-cultural conditions; its theatrical detaching of the heroine from her context, which turns history into a colourful static backdrop rather than a continually changing combination of social forces; its confusing naturalistic accuracy

of detail for a more encompassing realism of typicality . . . and thereby using such "period sets" to *over*-distance history from the present, making connections unlikely to be grasped. *

Gardner testifies to a healthy influence of "objective" biographers. By denying "inwardness" can be shown, or claiming it is irrelevant to identity or character, they draw the biographer's eyes outward—to the relevance of history, of sociostructural factors. Objectivists would help us to see widely, to apply analysis and wit to history (as Strachey applied them to the persona of Gordon or of Nightingale) and thus make politics, economics, or a "combination of social forces" do the characterizing and show what produced Olive Schreiner or George Orwell. If this program would be especially fresh and interesting in the life of an inward, private writer such as Emily Dickinson, one might add that our methods *might* be flexible enough (with Schreiner or Dickinson) to accommodate socioeconomic analysis and intuitive comment too. But in suggesting that readers ought to grasp "connections" between a biography's historic past and "the present," Ms. Gardner, I think, has an irrelevant moral motive. Must Tory politics in a life of Shelley be shown as relevant to Mrs. Thatcher? In a preface to her magnificent edition of *The Lisle Letters* (1981) Muriel St. Clare Byrne introduced Henry VIII by comparing him with "tyrants" of the 1930s and thus obscured him. His pride, conceit, and exalted view of himself are set in, and partly determined by, medieval views of kingship and have little to do with modern politics. Anyone who fully explained religious and sociopolitical factors in a Tudor king's life, and in *that* sense overdistanced history from Hitler, would do us a service. Yet readers may extract from biographies anything that is bracing, as Carolyn Heilbrun does from *Olive Schreiner:* "There is only the struggle. . . . Yet the biography of Schreiner does demonstrate that if women make the choice to live, rather than to protect themselves from life, to be the protagonists of their own stories rather than events in the lives of others, they shall, as Simone Weil knew, 'not perish without having truly existed.'"* That is admirable in a review, and

---

* *Hecate: A Women's Interdisciplinary Journal*, 7, No. 1 (1981), 57.
* "Brave Attempts: Sad Frustrations," *Washington Post*, October 26, 1980.

would not be misleading in a biographer's preface, but it is irrelevant
to the selecting of evidence for a life of Schreiner and to the *making* of
a biography. A biographer's guiding motive might be the devoted one
of getting at the historical truth of her subject, and this might involve
more than "only the struggle."

The "objective" school may have irrelevant moral imperatives; and
the biographer who claims that "inwardness" can never be shown or
has nothing to do with human identity only gives up an essential and
delicate task. People have complex inward lives, and the biographer
who won't think of these will be driven to guess at character. (We shall
return to this when we consider principles and practice in a biography
of Orwell.) Objectivists, however, validly argue that our focus on what
is personal has caused us to neglect social, public, or impersonal influences on past lives. But that in itself gives us no reason for paying
less attention to "inwardness," or for not commenting on it freely. It
would be foolish to condemn an English tradition that includes in
Johnson, Carlyle, Arnold, and Strachey precedents in free-ranging
biographical commentary, such as we find in another tradition running from Voltaire and Sainte-Beuve through Sartre and Barthes.

III

For a useful theory of form in biography, we will ask what we *have* to
take from formal traditions—for example, in displaying evidence.

Boswell uses talk and letters for display. Why? Central to the English (and European) tradition since his *Johnson* (1791) has been an
anthropological myth, articulated by Herder, which sees men and
women as self-defining and emphasizes language. According to this
myth a person realizes his or her identity through the spoken and
written word; we in our century take the subject's talk or letters as
prime biographical documents. We value letters for their revealing
subjectivity—and quote them as evidence of an author's private life,
personality, quality of mind. In the experiments of Sartre, just as in
the work of our most extreme proponents of objectivity, the quoted
word is indicative. No one denies the value of the letter.

But few discuss the uses and drawbacks of letters. Consider how they relate to the parameters of experience and the problem of biographical style. A parameter is a variable factor entering into distributions, and one may take it in biography to mean a reaction to life—a reaction that may enter into a few, many, or all of one's subject's experiences. It is not, as I see it, as static as a "trait." For example, Matthew Arnold, age thirty-six in the autumn of 1859, wrote from the Lake District to Arthur Clough: "I could willingly fish all day and read the newspapers all the evening, and so live—but I am not pleased with the results in myself of even a day or two of such life."

Arnold is not in a pet over the weather: he is fond of idleness, yet discontented with it. Since the ease of confession combines with a tension in meaning, his style is a part of this experience with himself. His discontent with and need for idleness is a parameter that may seem Victorian—an affair of conscience and energy (social passion, the urge to finish work) at odds with pastoral laziness. We find a similar tension in Clough, who was impatient with a clerical Oxford he also loved: "I could sometimes be provoked to send out a flood of lava boiling-hot amidst their flowery ecclesiastical fields and parterres."

But a parameter is fixed in value by evidence of the moment. It does not "reveal" anything but what it says, and it is time bound: so far we have no authority to say that Arnold experienced *this* tension at any time other than a day in 1859. Yet he gives us something else to conjure with. This note is not merely ascribable to his meditations on the dismal roar of London in relation to his reading of Lucretius and thinking about the Heraclitean flux:

> The misery of the present age is not in the intensity of men's
> suffering—but in their incapacity to suffer, enjoy, feel at all,
> wholly and profoundly—in their having their susceptibility
> eternally agacée by a continual dance of ever-changing objects,
> and not having power to attach it upon one, to expand it on that
> one, to absorb it in that one: in their being ever learning and
> never coming to a knowledge of the truth . . . in their having
> one moment the commencement of a feeling, at the next
> moment the commencement of an imagination, and the eternal
> tumult of the world mingling, breaking in upon, hurrying away
> all. . . . The disease of the present age is divorce from oneself.

Since we have his 1859 letter about idleness, it is possible to locate something personal in the objectively cast note. In 1859 he experienced a tension, and however mild or bothersome it was, at another date he criticized "the present age" in a manner that refines what he said to Clough after fishing and reading the papers. We have a refinement of his discontent. In his note, he finds *no* state of activity or inactivity satisfying, because he has a sense of half-experiencing what he thinks, feels, or imagines, with a heightened susceptibility to impressions from without. His note, too, is time bound, so we cannot say his "misery" was constant, or if his delight in fixing the disease of modern life in this *aperçu* and finding Lucretius's world echoing in his own did not outweigh his ill spirits. The parameter in alerting us to what is personally applicable in the note, however, saves us from assuming that objectively framed statements have nothing to do with "inward experience." The parameter gives us one way of directing intuition: a delicate, properly controlled use of evidence can guide intuitive insights in a precise, disciplined way, help us to form a correct view of a person, and save us from that outward sterility of comment found in average academic biographies.

Letters can also be guides to style. About prose style in literary biography one may say nothing truer than this: it is worth attention since its effects are crucial. In this genre, style is an integral "fact," as dates and events are, since it becomes part of the portrayed. Character-revealing or -suggesting elements of discourse cling to the person one writes about. If one is vulgar or sentimental in manner, Pope or Hardy becomes so too, and one's authority is lost. The lazy, emotive styles of popular lives are no feebler than hard, mean, retrospective styles of academic biographies—and the latter are all the worse because they are uniform from book to book. If a biography is to portray an individual closely, its prose ought to suit the individual. Letters, as keys to individuality, reveal tones, rhythms, diction, images, and kinds of details and universals the subject had chosen to make himself or herself clear. Without parodying or imitating, it is possible through intimacy with an author's letters to develop a modern middle style— one bridging between history and the present—that has two prime functions: to accommodate naturally evidence such as the subject's letters, and to convey continually a sense of the subject's presence.

It may not please objectivists to think they create illusions of the subject's presence in literary biography, but they could not portray events coherently otherwise. A "Thomas Hardy" will appear throughout almost any intelligible biography written about him. It is in this sense that biography differs the most from historiography, in having one threading link, one developing persona to which "history" and all other personae seem in one sense subordinate, though not necessarily distorted. A style that conveys a coherent sense of Hardy's presence can help the biographer to make close, delicate, pertinent statements about Hardy's personality and mental life. A careless biographical style will distance Hardy so far that opportunities for pertinent comment on his mind, problems, plans, and awareness at a given time in his life are reduced.

IV

But an author's letters "tell" from one viewpoint. That is their drawback. They reinforce the bad tradition of narrating from their viewpoint alone—and they may dictate biographical *content* by suggesting that their own content is all-important.

For example, one thinks of *Jane Austen's Letters* (edited by R. W. Chapman in 1932, and after a second edition and corrections, still containing errors in the 1979 reprinting). Following its lead, biographers have cast Jane Austen as heroine in a tedious, pointless Regency soap opera. They cannot match her light style and wit. But they follow her letters' content and take us from one ball, visit, or family gathering to the next. They fail to examine forces that may have encouraged her talent (these are not in *Jane Austen's Letters*); they tell us little about England's social-class structure, Hampshire's economy, political affiliations of the gentry, or the war that is reflected in *Mansfield Park* and *Persuasion*; nothing about the French Revolution and its ideas; nothing about anti-Jacobinism of the 1790s; nothing about socioeconomic changes after Trafalgar. They send her upstairs with a tear and a laugh to write novels; in her bedroom, but sometimes in the parlor, she is visited by an awesome spook called Genius, who elicits from the biographer some adjectival Lit. Crit. with congratulations, before the poor lady, transferred to College Street in Winchester, cries out none too soon, "I want nothing but death." (It was in reaction to these Lives that Mudrick and Harding told us the lady was full of hatred.) We can say anything vulgar about her we like, as Kipling proved, so long as we keep her in a cottage without ideas. That she had ideas, read papers, followed war news, discussed America, pored over works on the British empire, understood the banking and clerical and naval careers of her brothers, and mastered the social-class structure is evident. Biographers who save her from her Goody Two-Shoes image by claiming with no evidence that she disliked children and her mother won't help us. Clearly, we need to know the England she knew—and too little of it survives in her *Letters*. For Lives of Jane Austen we need many other sources of help.

The single epistolary perspective is a poor guide to form because it keeps us from seeing out, away from an author, into history and social milieux. A Life *can* have contributory viewpoints. Few Lives make much of them, perhaps none sufficiently. In writing of Arnold, I presented evidence from the viewpoint of his wife (when I had diaries and letters for this) and from general viewpoints for Oxford, school inspecting, and some of my subject's travels. I tried to lift my camera's eye over Arnold's head (without losing sight of him) in tracing his evolving ideas and talents in social contexts, but bolder experiments with viewpoints would have suggested even more of his world.

And we need experiments. In literary biography, material presented from "outside" viewpoints must finally illuminate one author, one Arnold or Scott. Yet it is not easy to use social views, sociostructural analysis, or contributory viewpoints relevantly. The large topic or event looms autonomously outside an author's life, yet must be used to help define one life. Artworks pose a special problem. If *Tess* and *Jude* are autonomous, detached from Hardy, how should we treat them? I would think expectations of *Tess's* and *Jude's* readers can be met. Self-contained as the novels may be, readers suspect that Hardy's books are tied to him in countless ways—by as many threads as tied Gulliver—and are curious to know how his religion or philosophy, aesthetic aims, life experiences, locales, time, the people he knew, and his manners of feeling and observing can in any way be "seen" in his books. A biographer's task can be, in part, to show linking threads

that exist, as well as data that can be known about the genesis, composition process, publishing, and reception of a novel. But *Tess* and
Jude also illustrate Hardy's artistic, imaginative, transforming power of
making that which no longer needs his hand or mind and has a "life"
of its own. This, I think, does not justify our treating them in sharply
blocked off sections of "literary criticism" in a biography, but rather as
contributory to our study of him *as* artist. The books are prime biographical material as *evidence* of Hardy's imagination and artistry, and
not as artifacts in a void.

So far, if I have been pressing beyond the limits of what our academic biographers usually say about their craft, I have been assuming
a theory of biography which many of the severe "objective" school
might accept. I assume that a biography needs to portray not only as
accurately, but as closely, as evidence will permit. By attending to
features of a proper biographical style—those features of style that help
to convey a sense of the subject's presence, or exactly what is personal
in the evidence—we can reduce distance in manner. To think about
the properties of biographical narrative and to take pains with form is
not to toy with superficial elegances (as some of our objectivists maintain) but rather to take the opportunity to enhance and sharpen our
accuracy.

V

The most difficult matter to be accurate about in biography is the
emotional life of a historical person: even if diaries and letters show
how a person felt about one topic, they will not for many other topics.
And if we know how Hardy felt about his first wife, or about Dorset
villages and heaths, we have the problem of conveying a sense of his
feelings. Emotive writing is a deadly fault. One may attribute one's
own feelings to the subject, and even if these have restraint, one's
authority, accuracy, and proper detachment are compromised.

But if one conveys a sense of an author who never felt anything, is
one more truthful? Some might say yes, better to omit what is problematic, but this is a comment on methods and not on the nature of
evidence, if we have an author's letters, diaries, or intimate comments

on anything that mattered in life. Biographies that give us the best sense of persons and that we reread contain more than criticism of ideas and works with added accounts of dates, families, schools attended, places visited and the like; they show us how and why an author felt as he or she did, responded to experience, and how the responses affected a career.

Yet accurate conveying of feeling is perilously difficult; if we quote short, intense passages from letters, we deprive them of the context that seems to convey part of the feeling. If we quote whole letters—or at length and often—we break narrative continuity, and also (as in the traditional *Life and Letters*) create such a gap between biographer and subject that the narrative text becomes brittle and distant, as if we were a warden gesturing in a museum or zoo with a pointing stick. It would seem that a coherent sense of the subject's presence in a biographical narrative is needed if we are to convey feelings accurately. We also need to attend to linear and general—or diachronic and synchronic—narrative levels, I think, to make a proper context for emotional evidence.

In writing a literary biography, I must present a "story," a coherent and clear narrative line, and on this linear string I can attach facts that are known about my author for given times. (I will try to do this with a certain concise fullness, as accurately and gracefully as I can.) But at any point I can offer a general or synchronic comment, an analysis of social forces or a remark on my subject's habits, temperament, predilections, which may have no unique relation to the linear moment. In offering evidence about an author's emotional experience, I can at times in the linear discourse supply the biographical, historical facts that represent, in their way, an approximate formula for that experience. Then my general comment about my subject's character or habits of feeling will have part of its proof "behind" it in my chapter. This is what happens in Boswell's *Johnson*, as when in its earlier chapters Boswell presents facts, in a linear story of Johnson's life—about his education or early career, for example—that add up in emotional weight until Boswell reaches a point when his general comment on Johnson's habits of feeling (or character or behavior) will clarify and bring out the emotional significance of what we have been reading about. Professor Bate's *Johnson* (1978) lacks any similar effect, and fails to portray Johnson's emotional experience, because its linear and general narrative levels do not work together. His general comments on Johnson are excellent, but they usually display the biographer's feeling for Johnson rather than Johnson's feelings.

A proper context for emotional evidence may gather in illustrations from an author's formal writing. One need not confuse dramatic feelings of Tess and Jude with Hardy's own in doing this. One has a right to compare what Hardy felt—if there is evidence in letters or private journals—with what an imaginary character felt in different but not wholly unlike circumstances. Further, one may use qualified comments on Hardy's known and evidenced experience to support narrative by advancing it: commentary may narrate.

I have not been saying what a biographer should do, but what can be done in an accurate manner to portray an author's experience closely. Much, in our own time, mitigates against any attempt to portray emotion in a documented way—but we can hardly blame Hardy or George Eliot for not suiting our honored methodologies. The literary biographer may need to discard some of those limiting methods while working for the readers he or she tries to serve; at any rate, the key requirement is that of having patience to devise new, adequate forms for presenting evidence that one comes to know closely. Intimacy with the evidence helps one to achieve confidence for that freedom of interpretive comment which Sartre and his followers (at their best) display. We can hardly use Sartre's methods, but his resourceful intelligence is a beacon.

Chapter Two

DR. JOHNSON'S
LIVES

SOCIAL HISTORIANS of the future will notice that the end of the twentieth century (the late 1980s and 1990s) was a period of nostalgia in which the lasting significance of a year was that it marked the anniversary of an earlier event—the defeat of the Spanish Armada, or the death of a hero. We make arrangements for the Tennyson centenary of 1992, having disposed of the centenaries of Newman, Browning, Arnold, Trollope, Dickens, and others a little earlier. The "centenary" provides us with a figure permissibly enlarged by the authority a long survival after death conveys, so that even Tennyson, dying in 1892 but oddly to be fêted as if he were a living presence in 1992, triumphs over death with a Christlike persuasiveness. The centenary is an enterprise lifting the dead back to life with the potent, unquestionable authority of the calendar, which itself rules over time as it crushes out the living. Who can quibble over the fact that 1990 is, in part, Newman's year, and 1992 Tennyson's? And the calendar prompts us to extol loosely and freely the Great Figure who is dead but suddenly alive again. So it was with the bicentenary of Samuel Johnson's death back in 1984, when the Arts Council in London, as I recall, mounted a fine display in rooms featuring four Johnson portraits by Sir Joshua Reynolds. One of them shows the thick-lipped, nearsighted Johnson poring over a crumpled text as if he might eat it.

But I kept returning to a plaster cast of Johnson's bust and death mask (made by Hoskins and Cruikshank). Johnson has a splayed nose, almost as wide as it is long, above a wide mouth. The pits of the operation that he had for scrofula are seen in the right side of Johnson's neck. Even at his death at seventy-five, he is young looking, muscular, and seemingly arrogant, although in life he was a modest man, with a just sense of his distinction as a critic and lexicographer. He wanted to be called *Mr.* Johnson, and though well aware of social degree and an advocate of "subordination" in society he had peculiarly democratic instincts. In fact he let some of the needy live in his house and seems to have talked on equal terms with the London poor: he had walked the streets at night with the poet Richard Savage and known poverty well enough. I think that the bicentenary tributes to his character and work did no real justice to Johnson the biographer, or to the author of *Lives of the English Poets.* Boswell said of the short pieces and major biographies comprising the *Lives* that they are altogether "the richest, most beautiful, and indeed most perfect production of Johnson's pen."

What turned Johnson into a biographer? He had begun life as a frail ugly duckling but had become physically strong, proud and swaggering at Lichfield. He was jealous of a younger brother and devoted to and half-ashamed of their father, Michael Johnson, who scraped a poor living as a bookseller, though Johnson later exaggerated the family's poverty. Mrs. Johnson, forty at Samuel's birth, was a bustling and insensitive woman who by turns indulged and lightly denied her bright son, lecturing and beating him as she hoped to make him self-sufficient and feared his hulking laziness and quick, easy tongue. "I did not respect my own mother," he told Mrs. Thrale, "and one day when in anger she called me a puppy, I asked her if she knew what they called a puppy's mother." Another boy would have been thrashed for *that*—and there are signs he was indulged. At Pembroke College,

Oxford, he was to study for thirteen months on a legacy his mother could ill afford to give him, after taking over one hundred volumes from his father's bookshop before he left.

The father "was a foolish old man," as Johnson later said of him, "that is to say was foolish in talking of his children." Samuel had loathed his father's caresses, Mrs. Thrale records, "because he knew they were sure to precede some unpleasing display of his early abilities." The bookseller was fifty-two when Samuel was born: Michael Johnson was a large, gaunt, devout and conscientious man, "prone to melancholy" and hen pecked; it is not surprising that he took excessive pleasure in his son's brilliance.

Psychological problems, including the pressures that made him a confident and forceful biographer, were forming during Johnson's years at Lichfield. He did not suffer from a lack of love, but from an excess of clumsily directed parental concern and affection. As an ugly child, acute and quick, he must have viewed himself as less desirable than his brother; and then Mrs. Johnson's hectoring, anxious concern and Mr. Johnson's "foolish" doting pride in Samuel's wit and rapid learning tied him too closely to his parents. Yet our evidence is a little thin. I do not think it shows (what has been claimed) that Johnson suffered from an acute psychological identification with his father. To Johnson, the aging man seemed ineffectual, feeble, and helpless—as his poor business went to ruins and the father who had been elected Sheriff of Lichfield in the year of his son's birth (1709) had trouble in making ends meet. Whether Mrs. Johnson became more strident as her husband faded, we do not know, but life can hardly have been easy in the household.

In poems he wrote at school, in "Festina Lente" and other exercises, Johnson exhibits a polished talent. The poems have the look of mature work, and seem older and wiser than their author then was. Johnson offers moral reminders that strong feeling is deadly, and shows off an extricating violence:

> Orestes plung'd his vengeful dart
> Into his supplicating mother's heart.

Reason calms the "ruffled soul," and may keep one from moving down cliffs precipitately,

Urg'd headlong on by hatred or by love.

All boys enjoy gore, and these lines may have nothing to do with his parents. What is certain is that he felt oppressed by a "foolish" Michael, and a Sarah Johnson he could not "respect," and that, in manhood, he would have chances to review oppression. Although every biographer tries to recreate a factual past that is not his or her own, one may in biography have a chance to gain insight into one's formative years. One may judge one's parents, or implicitly control them in retrospect by reviewing a different but similar psychological past; one may in writing a Life have an opportunity to judge forces that were bewildering in earlier years, or that one was never able to elude or protect oneself from. One re-creates factual versions of childhood, youth, and early manhood, and now with judiciously authoritative correction and comment. I would go further in saying this. Unless the biographer *does* strongly identify with the person he or she writes about, to the extent of finding reminiscent echoes in that different past, the biography is likely to be what Johnson called a "barren and useless" account. What is always required is a penetrating power, but one needs to penetrate with more than the intellect. We cannot understand anyone without loving the person, as Wordsworth would say; we need love or hatred to depict a life interestingly, faithfully, and as fully as possible. In our century with its legacy of scientific positivism we are less likely than eighteenth-century people to value the commitment, feeling, and subjectivity that made Johnson and Boswell excellent biographers. It is a paradox that a biographer who remains at the mercy of feelings is helpless, useless, and prone to the worst errors; he or she must feel, however, in order to overcome feeling and know what to be objective *about*.

Johnson felt pressures of despair acutely in the five-year period after he left Pembroke College. He plunged into depression and lived in a condition of breakdown, anxiety, and lassitude, so that rational analysis convinced him he was losing his mind. He "strongly entertained thoughts of Suicide," John Taylor later remarked of him, and Boswell only with difficulty learned anything of this interval. Johnson would walk from Lichfield to Birmingham and back, thirty-two miles, to try to master himself. I have walked part of the distance on streets of north Birmingham less pleasant than his fields, but not with anything like Johnson's state of mind (I hope), and it seems to me that his long, compulsive walks have to do with his need for external obstacles. He was a man who required years of poverty and struggle, enormous tasks, long challenges, and outward difficulties to retain inward composure. As for his anguished prayers, which it is fashionable to pity, they had good psychological effects for him. His Christian faith allowed for the sin of despair since its premise was that we are sinful all of the time. As a rational faith it helped him to objectify his sufferings confessionally, to remind himself of ideas that were fortifying and applicable to his state of being, and it promised amelioration through grace. He did emerge from five difficult years, at the age of twenty-five, to marry a widow then in her forties, Mrs. Elizabeth Jervis Porter, or his "Tetty." Lucy Porter, his step-daughter, says that Johnson was then "lean and lank, so that his immense structure of bones was hideously striking to the eye, and the scars of scrophula were deeply visible"; he wore his stiff hair parted behind and had "convulsive starts and odd gesticulations, which tended to excite at once surprise and ridicule." Tetty, however, was impressed by him enough to say, "This is the most sensible man I ever saw in my life."

He began seventeen years of marriage as a schoolteacher with three pupils. With one of them, David Garrick, the future actor-manager, he left in 1737 for London, where he arrived with tuppence-ha'fpenny and a letter of credit in his pocket. However shabby his days, they were redeemed by the gaiety and intellectual interest of a cultural capital. "The happiness of London is not to be conceived but by those who have lived in it," he said thirty years later. His years as a Grub Street writer brought him in contact with the underworld and nearly all professions; his inspired hackwork for Edward Cave's *Gentleman's Magazine* forced him to write on medicine, agriculture, chemistry, politics, city life and travel, while he turned out thirteen brief biographical sketches and then half a million words of the journal's *Parliamentary Debates*. For these, often writing at a rate of eighteen hundred words an hour, he imagined himself into the minds of politicians and developed tactics that made him a fine biographer. His "Life of Savage" (1744) shows what he had learned. He accepted his friend Richard Savage's claim of being an illegitimate son of the

Countess of Macclesfield, but tried to tell the truth about his friend's shiftless, violent, plucky career. Evil is located in a mother's barbarity, and we feel for Savage as he stands in the dark before her door hoping to see the parent who rejected him. But "he could neither soften her heart, nor open her hand, and was reduced to the utmost miseries of want, while he was endeavouring to awaken the affection of a mother. He was therefore obliged to seek some other means of support; and, having no profession, became by necessity an author." There is hardly a better plot line in a Dickens novel. Channeling his emotions into Savage's story, the narrator binds ingredients into a controlling framework of general comment on life. Johnson is a lofty chorus, who sees that his task in part is to illuminate the reader's life. His practice accords very well with his theory in the sixtieth *Rambler* essay where he says that a biographer's business is to "display the minute details of daily life" so that they seem meaningful "to every diversity of condition," and the theory, I think, explains why "The Life of Savage" seems fresh and moving. The tactics are excellent in persuading us that nothing recounted is improbable and that the narrator, with such phrases as "it is very reasonable to conjecture" or "nor is it to be doubted," is rational and moderate. The prose is not excessively balanced, and after pitiable details about Savage, about turmoil and murder and self-indulgence and ruin, we have stately paragraphs in which Johnson extracts lessons from what we have beheld.

His sympathy for the individual case makes his morality appealing. Having known a few of his friend's temptations, he is never in a flutter over Savage's wine drinking or prostitutes. When near the end of his life in 1777, at the age of sixty-eight, Johnson came to write the *Lives of the English Poets*, he knew every level of London society from its depths to its upper levels of wealthy actor-managers and investors, Tory and Whig politicians, and aristocratic ladies. Few men with scholarly aims, interested in the etymologies and multiple meanings of words, were ever so fascinated by daily life in a city as Johnson. It seems just as well that he thought of the *Lives* as a "little" task. The proposal relaxed him, so much so that he badly cheated himself by asking only a small fee for his writing. The Martin brothers' Apollo Press in Edinburgh had launched an enormous edition of the English poets, to the alarm of booksellers, who felt that the Scots were invading their special field. To counter the audacity of the Martins, a group of London publishers decided to produce their own elegant edition of the poets; they limited their scope to forty-seven writers dating back to about 1660 and asked Johnson, a famous man, to write a concise account of each author and name his price. He asked for a modest one hundred guineas, swelled the list to fifty-two poets, and gave them 370,000 words.

No publisher in our time has done well with the *Lives*. They ought to be available in paperback: they must be read as a series—and yet who has ever heard of Johnson's Thomas Yalden or David Mallet or Gilbert West, or knows what to do with the 370,000 words? The Yale edition (costly) is issuing the *Lives*, and meanwhile we have Penguin's *Selected Writings* of Johnson with the whole of "Savage" and "Gray" and a few extracts mainly from "Milton" and "Pope." The *Lives* present a difficulty because they are of varying length; some are so short that Johnson was able to write four or five in one week in April 1780, but those of Cowley, Milton, Dryden, and Pope are major biographies. It is rewarding to adjust to brevity and expansion. Written in the century of Pope and Haydn, each of the *Lives* is a variation on a standard pattern—which includes an account of a man's life, comments on his character, and a succinct review of his works with the author in focus. Suffusing this pattern are the wisest comments on life that I have seen in any work in English after Shakespeare. I know of no biography more enthralling than Johnson's *Lives*, unless it is Boswell's *Life of Johnson*.

The first thing one notices is that there are no dullnesses, except for Johnson's few extracts from pedants. Like Pope, he hates tedium, and the gratuitousness of the floating detail: he had said that we are no wiser about Addison when told of the "irregularity of his pulse." How does the biographer avoid tedium, then? First, it would seem, by establishing his own presence, his seriousness and commitment and unflappable interest in moral character. Johnson appears in universal statements that he uses as a touchstone for judging human worth. His second way of being interesting is by not according blame and credit in any simple manner for behavior, but by judging in a dialectic of moral inquiry. One is fascinated to see how this will work out, as in his "Dryden." Dryden attacked his predecessors vengefully, and that was a fault despite his placable nature and warm friendships. But he cannot quite be judged as other men for he was lively, vigorous, intelligent, and achieving. Thus if he was censorious he must be credited for excellence; he had an authoritative right: "he who excels has a right to teach, and he whose judgement is incontestable may, without usurpation, examine and decide." Dryden is a genial man whose arrogance is a bad fault, though an index of high attainment. Johnson in his critical section looks for the man in the poems and finds in the poet an unusually comprehensive mind goaded by bold, large aims: "His compositions are the effects of a vigorous genius operating on large materials" and even treading "on the brink of meaning." We are left with a vision of Dryden's daring mind.

Since he believes that literature is emotive and that unless a work moves us its brilliance fails, he can be harsh on "the metaphysical poets"—whom he grouped and named for the first time—in "Cowley." They never succeeded in "moving the affections," it seems; but what bothers him particularly about Donne and Cowley is that they splinter life, they dissect just as a sunbeam is shattered by a prism. Here Johnson expresses one of the strongest impulses of his own nature, or his need for wholeness and integration. It is typically a demand of the later eighteenth century when the compartmentalization of knowledge had begun. Life, he believed, is impoverished if feelings tell us one thing and our intellect dictates something else; he would not have agreed with T. S. Eliot that the "dissociation of sensibility" began after John Donne. It is seen virulently in Donne himself. Johnson implies that the main effort of modern writing and thinking must be to find those ideas and resources that unite feeling with intellect, yet he is willing to give Donne and Cowley the credit of "surprise" and "elegance" due them.

Johnson is much more virulently prejudiced in the "Life of Swift" since Swift's politics, gloom, Irishness, and misanthropy all grated on him. When hostile to a writer he tended to avoid research and accept the worst reports he knew. Swift becomes an unstable eccentric, so zany and obsessive he took up jogging: "He thought exercise of great necessity, and used to run up and down a hill every two hours." (There was a tradition that at Letcombe he ran up a hill every day before breakfast.) This dreadful jogger failed to read books at all, then devoured them eight hours a day for seven years before writing his "wild" *Tale of a Tub*. His *Gulliver's Travels* befuddled its critics. ("When once you have thought of big men and little men it is very easy to do the rest," Johnson calmly said.) But Johnson's hostility seems to be the price he must pay for being candid, and Swift gathers importance from the assaults on him. Johnson pours them on: "He is querulous and fastidious, arrogant and malignant; he scarcely speaks of himself but with indignant lamentations, or of others but with insolent superiority when he is gay, and with angry contempt when he is gloomy." The importance and interest of Swift are never denied. No modern admirer of Swift can resent Johnson's essay. And I think this is because "Swift" displays the energy, caring, authority, and passion of Johnson's whole commitment to life. We need not like every classic, but we ought to express our verdicts with absolute fidelity in what we write. "Swift," moreover, ought to be read alongside the balanced, intuitive "Life of Pope," the finest of the *Lives*, in which Johnson unconsciously pays tribute to himself. "Pope had likewise genius," he writes, "a mind active, ambitious, and adventurous, always investigating, always aspiring; in its widest searches still longing to go forward, in its highest flights still wishing to be higher, always imagining something greater than it knows, always endeavouring more than it can do."

Chapter Three

AFTER BOSWELL

WITH LOVE, cunning, and a yearning nostalgia James Boswell caused his magnificent *Life of Johnson* to be published in London in 1791 on May 26. The day marked the anniversary of his first meeting with Johnson, just twenty-eight years before. The day of the meeting becomes pivotal in Boswell's biography itself—and essential in its subtle structure.

Can one learn from that structure? I think we have underestimated Boswell's formal achievement and can best appreciate it by having in mind the general European theory that informs his book. To borrow a term from Charles Taylor's *Hegel* (Cambridge University Press, 1975), Boswell's account of Samuel Johnson displays a new romantic anthropology, an "expressivist anthropology," which already had been elaborated in Germany by Herder and Goethe. Boswell's life is not the first English work to make use of this romantic view of human life, but it is the first biography in any language to do so.

With help from various sources I want to isolate and define that new romantic anthropology. When we isolate theory, I think we shall find adequate criteria for modern biographical forms and a working theory of biography. It will be useful to begin with a glance or two at the elderly Goethe, and then with some complaints of Arnold, before we turn to the theory in the eighteenth century and to some of its results.

It is important for biography that while a new romantic view is formulated with optimism in the 1770s, it gets a gloomy, anxious defense later. Goethe, for example, was not always so tranquil in old age as is sometimes supposed. Selfish as he could often be, he took a large view of human events and saw tendencies in Europe's literary culture as forbidding. Underneath the famous rosy serenity in the *Gespräche mit Goethe* (those conversations recorded by Eckermann between 1823 and 1832) is Goethe's despair over the concatenation of urban forces threatening the unique thing that man has been found to be. And, only a few years later, we find an admirer of Goethe and reader of Senancour and Girardin cataloguing all that is "against" us. It isn't perverse of me to approach the new expressivist anthropology through Matthew Arnold, because Arnold indicates some of the real pressure the theory is under in the twentieth century. Arnold is at Thun, in 1849, recovering from an affair with the blue-eyed Mary Claude who was baptized at Friedrichstadt and who has relatives at Geneva; for a summer or two she has been intimate with Arthur and Anne Clough and Matthew and Tom Arnold (of the "Clougho-Matthean set"); and Arnold's letter to Clough reveals impatience with his old friends. He will not think of his brother Tom, "for my dear Tom has not sufficient besonnenheit for it to be any *rest* to think of him any more than it is a *rest* to think of mystics and such cattle." What threatens *Besonnenheit* (deep self-possession)? "Everything," Arnold continues to Clough,

> everything is against one—the height to which knowledge is
> come, the spread of luxury, our physical enervation, the absence
> of great *natures*, the unavoidable contact with millions of small
> ones, newspapers, cities, light profligate friends, moral
> desperadoes like Carlyle, our own selves.

A better list of reasons that we admire and need our large, complete twentieth-century biographies, such as Ellmann's *Joyce* or Bate's

Samuel Johnson, could hardly be devised: biographies bring order to the "height" of accumulated knowledge, celebrate "great" or unusual natures, counteract the insignificance of daily urban life, tell us of our "selves," and offer valid or convincing "moral" exempla. Modern biographical forms (as in Boswell's *Johnson* or Lockhart's *Scott*) arise when Europeans feel that the "height" of knowledge threatens the individual through its enormous extent; and yet "complete" biographies are made possible through the new information explosion (the subject of Arnold's *Empedocles on Etna* as well as his Oxford inaugural "On the Modern Element in Literature") and are a reply to that explosion, the last line of defense in our attempt to humanize what we know. The new weight of knowledge had oppressed Eckermann's elderly Goethe—but not the young, exuberant Goethe, who was the friend and disciple of Gottfried Herder in the 1770s.

Herder (who as Charles Taylor has reminded us was a chief theoretician of the young *Stürmer und Dränger*), in replying to Condillac had proposed in *On the Origin of Language* (1772) a new view of language and a new anthropology: words for Herder do not simply refer but are part of the activity in which man's *Besonnenheit* or (here) his individuating conscious self unfolds. Expressing himself to clarify what he is, man is seen as a creature of self-defining subjectivity. Goethe in the 1770s boldly related that expressivism to the outward cosmos; perhaps he misread Spinoza's idea of the *conatus* or the "impulse" in all things to preserve themselves. At any rate he emphasized man's "purification" or *Läuterung*: for Goethe expression does not just give vent to feelings but may in some sense purify and lift those feelings to a higher form. Thus expressivist man is in league with a kind of evolutionary principle in a pantheistic cosmos, for Goethe in the 1770s, and for pantheists and panentheists in the next half-century too. The *Stürmer und Dränger* were the first thinkers to exalt the artist, specifically, not as an imitator but as a creator.

Expressivist men and women in the eighteenth century were seen as "complete": whereas formerly a person was defined "completely" in relation to a Deity—religious faith was seen to draw out and to help define thoughts, impulses, feelings, everything that a person is—now *authentic words* are all that reveal and explain the psyche. One recalls that in Richardson's *Pamela*, when neither the clergy nor the aristocracy assist the servant girl, she clarifies her situation and realizes herself, to herself, by pouring into a journal-letter her words; her expression (and really not Mr. Williams) is her strongest and final ally. Consisting mainly of the servant girl's seemingly authentic words, *Pamela* has the fullness of expressivist forms. Biography is slow to become expressivist. There is no trace of the mode in Johnson's *Lives of the Poets* that offers quotations from the poets with Johnson's mature insights, but without allowing a Pope or a Savage to draw his own portrait. But, thirty years younger than Johnson and having spent about 270 days with him in twenty-one years, the stenographic and hungrily observant Boswell managed to produce in 1791 the first expressivist biography we have. He has tried to give his subject's authentic talk and has been "extremely careful as to the exactness" of quoted words from other sources, and has shown Johnson "more completely than any man who has ever lived." The *Life of Johnson* bears out the last boast; and any critic, now, who takes Boswell lightly or who envies him for his long acquaintance with Johnson or his abundance of ready-made evidence in all of the notes on the "talk," ought to think of the nightmare of Boswell's dilemma when he began the *Life*. No biographer has faced a greater *formal* problem. We tend to see the problem in the lopsided narrative in the *Life*, but we only feel or "read" its solution: the problem is that while Boswell had masses of evidence for the last twenty-one unformative years of Johnson's life, he had no earlier experience of Johnson and far less fresh evidence for the crucial first fifty-four years. No expressivist theory offered a hint as to how a satisfactory, balanced *form* is to be made out of a gigantically lopsided heap of primary documents; Richardson, in the novel, of course, had been able to invent and to date "authentic" documents to suit a form. Boswell, as Virginia Woolf would say, had to work in the rigid world of past, fixed facts and dated documents; and yet he seems to have observed the double structural principles of just such sentimental novels as Richardson's.

For, clearly, *Pamela* and *Clarissa* have two structures each: in their assembled documents there is a linear structure that tells a story from beginning to end—for example from Pamela's nearly helpless subservience through her virtuous endurance to her rewarding marriage—and there is a second structure, a structure of feeling, which has the

function of making a Pamela clarify herself progressively through situations that evoke her felt responses, including her thoughts. She is not
any girl in unhappiness, terror, doubt, gratitude, or final confident
triumph: in her final confident triumph she is still being exposed as
something rather new to us, as in her almost feminist remarks on
marriage. (To see her as a prototype for the Victorian feminist such as
Harriet Martineau, no doubt, would be as wrong as to dismiss the
political tincture of her replies to the reformed, husbandly Mr. B.
altogether. I only insist that she is not Everygirl, neither in her distress
nor in her time of "reward.")

Now, in the *Life of Johnson* there is similarly a linear narrative,
taking up in this case only a fifth of the book, for Johnson's life up to
May 1763. One criterion of "completeness" in expressivist or modern,
full-length biographies is thus met: in theory it is irrelevant that we
happen to have piles of evidence for the years of the famous older
person and practically none for the youth or childhood of the same
person: we must somehow "see" the biographee from birth to death.
There is—and should be—no fixed rule as to temporal contraction in
biography, but there is an implicit rule that an account of all years is
necessary. Similarly, too, in the *Life of Johnson*, there is a structure of
feeling: this structure will be satisfactory if it operates in such a way as
to reveal the complex multiplicity of the subject's traits, manners of
feeling, ideas, reactions to the world in a gradual and unredundant
unfolding. Boswell's structure of feeling is one of the great achievements of English literature and too complex to be dissected in a few
sentences. My aim is to point to its supreme formal brilliance, and to
the general idea that the long expressivist biography today, in theory
and practice, *succeeds* or *fails* not alone through its accuracy, moderation, authority, and kind and quality of insights, but through its structure of feeling. This always involves a tactic, a scheme of selection,
and a method of handling the relationship between biographer and
biographee.

For example, it will be apparent that a comment about some habit,
trait, or lifelong predisposition of one's biographee may be placed anywhere in a narrative. I, as biographer, may intrude anywhere I like.
Synchrony is always in tension with diachrony in successful narrative;
and further, the normal order of events may be reversed or defied by a

good teller for a good reason. Boswell grasped the principle that accuracy, or fidelity to history, is in no way compromised by narrative
tactics that ride over time, playing with time and even ironically playing with everyone's normal stolid image of the biographee. The narrative of Johnson's first fifty-four years is writhing with tactics, the first
and one of the most delightful being a grand assault on biographers
(Johnson's blessing on this assault is quoted at length) who are a "nau-
seous" tribe lacking in "art" and "intelligence" since they stick to a
"chronological series" and a "mere dry narrative of facts" and to what
is "dull, heavy" because it is in unimaginative "succession." *Tristram
Shandy* is not fiercer in its attack on unreal, rutted, moleish, artificial,
common notions of chronology than is Boswell at the outset. And
though, always ticking away, an abundance of dates reminds us that
the biographer is working entirely and scrupulously within the world
of historic time and is faithful to the *datedness* of events, Boswell
knows that there are a thousand ways to narrate A B C D E.

Carlyle, one Victorian writer of nonfiction who is in Boswell's
league as a narrator, was to present some of a historic revolution in the
future and even the future imperative tenses: we may feel in reading
The French Revolution (1837) in the twentieth century that the mode
of "Go you Jacobins tomorrow out to the reddened cobble-
stones . . . !" is excessive or that we are not yet ready for Carlyle.
Boswell, unlike Carlyle but like Strachey, realized that when we are
alone with a book, a book of fact, we are extraordinarily glad to be
amused. I am not, by the way, in the least sure that Walter Jackson
Bate's admirable *Samuel Johnson* does well to offer a many-sectioned
chapter called "Humour and Wit" toward the end of his book. Are
humor and wit integratedly part of a life, or not? Humor and wit in
any case tend to reduce otherwise jarring or grating effects of synchronic intrusions in the diachronic—a point that Carlyle grasped im-
perfectly and that Sterne and Boswell and, in our own time, a
biographer such as William Irvine understood and exploited.

The long, rich beginning of Boswell's *Life* for all of its effervescence appears to be nearly seamless; but with his intrusions, backward-
sweeping and forward-looking generalizations about his subject, vi-
gnettes of Johnson and confessional exposures of Boswell, we have all
of the preparation we need for the most important point in the *Life's*

intricate structure of feeling. This occurs one-fifth of the way through, in the meeting between Johnson and Boswell in May 1763, which is technically the most "sentimental" section of the book since it is focused on Boswell's chief crisis. This first meeting between biographer and subject seems to be about Boswell's feelings in relation to Johnson's reception of him. As readers we come to it versed in the chief characteristics of the two men. From the point of May 1763 on, we are prepared to relate to Johnson as the biographer does. We are to participate in Boswell's experience of gradually and intimately coming to know his man—in close focus and always more completely, since each new conversation or recounted event tells something that refines our knowledge of Johnson.

Boswell's reportorial language is now and again literal, abstract, metaphoric, or literal and symbolic; and we should note how "style levels" or varieties can accommodate themselves to the needs of the long, expressivist biography. Johnson "walked with me down to the beach," Boswell for example recounts of his departure near Harwich in August 1763. He has by this time introduced legitimate, playful animal metaphors for Johnson as well as the famous participle, "rolling," and now he continues:

> We embraced and parted with tenderness, and engaged to
> correspond by letters. I said, "I hope, Sir, you will not forget me
> in my absence." JOHNSON. "Nay, Sir, it is more likely you
> should forget me, than that I should forget you." As the vessel
> put out to sea, I kept my eyes upon him for a considerable time,
> while he remained rolling his majestick frame in his usual
> manner: and at last I perceived him walk back into the town,
> and he disappeared.

If this has become classic, I am not sure that we have seen that its sentiment alone does not explain its power: its language, I think, is the key to its profound accuracy. If *rolling* makes Johnson's presence palpable, the participle suggests not only nervous anxiety and lonely pain at the parting but a deeper, residual anguish; that effect is qualified in "I perceived him walk back into the town." The action has a symbolic suggestion of Johnson's courage, his return to the "town" that feeds the critical and creative intellect of the man (though "town" echoes much else that has been said about the city).

If we accept an expressivist anthropology, then neither the words of the self-revealing subject, nor the words of the biographer that point out, heighten, and explain the revelations, are to operate simply at a literal level. Expressivism demands that the biographer not only be aware of style but exploit it, all of the resources of language, with great delicacy in order to convey what is personal and factual in the historical evidence we have. The *Life of Johnson*, so fine in its structure of feeling and use of language, reminds us of one thing more. The "document" in biography must be something more than the proving illustration: its first function is to direct imagination. What is notable in Johnson's seemingly authentic talk—the *Life's* major document—is that Boswell so often reminds us that it is not "the whole of what Johnson said" or that it lacks its "original flavour" that as we read it we tend to intuit, pictorialize, and "fill in" to an unusual degree. Not this letter or that defines Charlotte Brontë, but the total of what she ever said and ever wrote defines her, material all but entirely lost; thus any document well used will give a suggestion of much else that it must stand for. No full-length Life, in theory, is adequate unless it suggests that much has been left out and can never be known, and unless it solicits the reader's imagination and help in the biographical act.

It is not possible to employ Boswellian strategies of relationship if, as is usually the case, the biographer has never seen the subject and is removed from a "John Keats" by history and time. I can intrigue nobody for long by telling about my visit to Hampstead and my eye-opening adventures with Keats in the Manuscript Room of the British Library; but in my ontological considerations I shall do well to recall that my purpose is not to scrape up poor Keats's bones or dust. In what does his being consist now? How does he enter my narrative? He exists only in the minds of the living, therefore in my mind; and in no ghoulish or morbid sense my relationship with the historic Keats is my only bridge over the River Styx and the most vital element in my biography. When that relationship has emotional, intellectual, and moral pressure and is considered by me of central importance to my work, I am perhaps ready to write a Life of Keats—or to begin to research it. If that relationship is displaced by anything else, my biography is likely to be a dead thing.

It is because the emotional, intellectual, and moral pressure of a modern writer's relationship with Dr. Johnson is great, and in focus, that Walter Jackson Bate's *Samuel Johnson* (1978) so well succeeds. Certainly this splendid biography is not perfect; Bate's narrative is thin and a little prolix; his commentary is magnificent, but he has never quite learned to integrate commentary and critical exposition with narrative. And (though this does not affect his bright, masterly illumination of his subject) when he forgets his relationship with Johnson and turns advertisingly to *us*, he says strange things such as, "Whatever we experience, we find Johnson has been there before us." How would Wordsworth, Thoreau, Richter, or Novalis react to that? If I've experienced the reverie of a New England Transcendentalist, Johnson hasn't been there before me, and couldn't be, since a vast gap separates those who have felt the full influence of the French Revolution of 1789 and those who (like Johnson) never did. When Mr. Bate says of Johnson, "In this ability to arouse—and sustain—an immediate and permanent trust, no other moralist in history excels or even begins to rival him," I say that I am hearing a provincial note. What are we to make of the long reception of the moralist Seneca in France (which so troubled Vauvenargues)? What happens to the unparalleled moral cogency, the millennium-long reception of the logical, affecting, and trust-inspiring Epictetus, whose *Discourses* recorded by Arrian come at the end of three hundred or more years of Greek Stoic thought? We have no excuse not to know Epictetus, now that his Greek has been rendered by Oldfather in the Loeb edition. We need not argue the degrees of "trust" moralists have inspired; I only say it is preposterous to elevate our beloved Johnson over every "other moralist in history," on any grounds, and worse if no allusion is made to moralists who have won the trust of Europeans for many centuries. It is never the biographer's function to advertise a subject, surely, but rather to keep the emotional, intellectual, and moral relationship with the biographee in focus—to do full and unremitting honor to that, to relate everything to the illumination of a person in history at the other side of the bridge.

Mr. Bate's marvelous, diamond-bright, persuasive general remarks on Johnson are worth almost anything: and he shows us how much the generalized remark in narrative relieves the literalness of the ongoing linear plane in biography. Susanne Langer, commenting on Ernst Cassirer, in "Life and Its Image," gives us a way of thinking about the two planes of biography in terms of the two intellectual functions of language that go on in every sentence:

> For in language we find two intellectual functions which it performs at all times, by virtue of its very nature: to fix the preeminent factors of experience as entities, by giving them names, and to abstract concepts of relationship, by talking about the named entities. The first process is essentially hypostatic; the second, abstractive.

It is peculiar to biography and historiography, but not to fiction, that the hypostatic function of naming is constantly threatening to become so important that the sense of experience in events may be lost. I may need to include so many expository facts or so much naming that I find my narrative a clotted string of evidence. Consider the difference between George Painter's first volume of *Marcel Proust*, which is cluttered in its account, and the second volume, which I think suggests more of Proust's experience for the reason that Proust in later years is more withdrawn and involved with fewer, or less complex, new events; the biographer now brings previous exposition easily to bear on the writing of a reflective 1,240,000-word novel. We may object to Painter's Freudianism or to the difference between controlled statments in *Proust* such as,

> Mme Straus's wit is important, for Proust made it his chief model for the celebrated 'Guermantes wit'

and hypotheses presented as fact, such as,

> there was a rejected part of himself, forever prevented by stronger forces from coming to power, for which the young girls were also substitutes for Marie de Benardaky,

*   *   *

especially as we do not see how Painter has been able to discover evidence for the existence of that early psychic part of himself which Marcel Proust supposedly rejected. But we don't object very strongly. Proust demands a psychoanalytic interpretation. If Mr. Painter sometimes lacks biographical tact he has brought credible ideas fascinatingly to bear on Proust and written one of the more intelligent, compelling biographies of our time. What we see in *Marcel Proust* is that the "abstractive" plane in biography readily assimilates large idea systems, whole theories of psychology, economics, sociology, or history so long as they are brought interestingly and realistically to bear on the illumination of one person.

Certainly the expressivist anthropology, which supposes that a man or a woman is most fully defined through the words he or she chooses to utter or write, was an immense stimulus to biography. (Goethe's amendments to Herder have helped to exalt literary biography.) But the expressivist Life demands more than a linear, one-thing-after-another narrative if we are to see what a person is: it demands an inner structure, with synchronic strategies, so that the reader shall come to understand in a certain truthfully and intelligently planned order the recoverable aspects of a subject's personality and character. (Carlos Baker's *Hemingway* lacks an inner structure; J. E. Neale's political biography *Queen Elizabeth I* is a very brilliant example of an enduring book that has it.) Any biographer's success depends above all on fidelity to the fact—but also on his or her intellectual (and moral) relationship and that increased and altered "understanding" with respect to the subject that I tried to define in my preface. If there is a necessary plane of "naming" in biography, there is also an abstractive plane that readily accommodates itself to explicatory idea systems—as Painter's *Proust* shows. I have alluded to language in remarks on Boswell, and now I want to consider biographical prose a little further in the light of retrospection, the accidental and the contingent, and the historical present.

Since Strachey's time, in the English-speaking countries, academic writers have produced many of our most reliable accounts of authors' careers. A list of our best biographers will by no means be wholly academic but will include Ray, Ellmann, Irvine, Haight, Bate, and perhaps Gill for *Wordsworth* and Super for *Trollope*. (One might add other names.) Professors favor the positive and finite and orderly, and tend to believe (unlike Browning or Eliot or Joyce) that linear narratives can be truthful about human experience. The academy trains one to regard the past with a cool, deliberate, slightly skeptical measuredness. After Sartre protested that the form of the novel was based on a false premise of retrospection, a professor replied to him very firmly.

But academic biographers, favoring what is positive and finite, have tended to remove from biography the unpredictable nature of life. Here our language is limited. We have no single word for the sense of experiencing life not just today, or this hour, but on the moment-to-moment knife edge of time. Life seems to depart as soon as it begins so that there is no stasis and every present is a present that was. Our minds are filled with presents that were and plans, hopes, fears, doubts, worries, determinations, as well as contingent daydreams, plans, hopes, fears, and so forth relating to an unpredictable future. In novels such as *Wuthering Heights* and *A la Recherche* extraordinary strategies are used to initiate us into presents that were and ways of feeling that are not normally our own; and after the complex "beginnings," evocative imagistic language in these novels keeps us on the wave of the felt present of experience. Their "beginnings" are no more complex and crucial than is the long "beginning" of Boswell's *Life*, which prepares us for a sustained illusion of the present. Few biographers have given us anything like the present-ness of Boswell's narrative of the years 1763 to 1784. Henry James in *William Wetmore Story and His Friends* gives a sense of the present by quoting evocative letters and partly by infusing his text with the quivering, sensitive Jamesian presence—which seems to catch everything except W. W. Story—and uses the immediacy of the retrospective memoir form. Memoirs, diaries, and autobiographical narratives seem to have a historical present-ness almost inherently in them; an example of this is in the immediacy of Cosima Wagner's *Diaries*, which plunge at once into a fine and slightly neurotic day-to-day account of the emotive climate in a composer's household. But no form more naturally *disfavors* the re-creation of a historical present than does the large, scholarly biography of our time.

In *Literaturgeschichte als Provokation* (1970), H. R. Jauss is right to suggest that students of the novel have underestimated the degree to which novel structures and historical narratives have imitated each other. For example, the form and style of *Bleak House* owe much to Carlyle's *French Revolution*. Yet Jauss may make too little of the epistemological difference between a Dickens novel and a Carlyle history. In the one case the novelist's path to reality has been experiential and intuitive; he has gained as much surely from walking around London law courts as he has from studying legal documents, and will draw more deeply on experiences he has half forgotten—dating in part from childhood—than on any document. In the greatest contrast, Carlyle's path to reality for his *French Revolution* has been through his subjective experience of life and then through the rigid, fixed corridors of unalterable documentation. Epistemologically speaking, the Dickensian imagination works without inhibition whereas the historian's or biographer's imagination works through the rigid, twisting corridors of a maze, which places strict and difficult limits on what can be written. Skill as a novelist—in consequence—guarantees one no skill in biography. Moreover the tremendous hypostatic weight of facts tends to push narrative more and more coldly into retrospect, farther and farther from the "historical present-ness" that the novelist seems so much more easily to achieve. This is why good biographies (Boswell's or Bate's) may make more of the narrator than do good realistic novels: the biographer as narrator-commenter becomes a means by which cold retrospective factuality is relieved. In general the English realistic novel has been a poor model for biographical narratives because it makes too little of the narrator; only its reportorial style has seemed imitable. We may note that though its function is complex and important, the narrative "I" in *Doctor Thorne* or *The Bostonians* is less necessary to the illusion of historical present-ness than is the "I" in Boswell's *Life*, or than is that commenting, humane, intruding, generalizing "I" in Bate's *Samuel Johnson*. The realistic novel may or may not have a fairly uniform style. What is noticeable from our viewpoint is that Boswell's or Irvine's apparent playfulness with style, and their varieties of style within a single biography, seem unmatched in the prose style of many a realistic novel. Let me put the case for the narrative presence in another way: *if* Walter Jackson Bate had made no more of his own narrating and commenting presence in *Samuel Johnson* than the narrator does in *Esther Waters,* Bate's book would hardly bring Dr. Johnson before us. *If* George Painter had kept his rather presumptuous Freudian intrusions out of *Proust* and concealed himself to the extent Fitzgerald does in *Tender Is the Night, Marcel Proust* would lack much of the historical present-ness—much of the reality—that in fact it has. The narrator's persona can be a major instrument of present-ness.

Biographers may have made too little use of stylistic variety, even so, because they have thought too little about the properties of narrative. A comparison between long and short biographical forms and long and short fiction forms might reveal something of use. I have no statistics to offer: I only hope the reader may agree that there is an inverse relatedness operating here. Biographical criticism (Sainte-Beuve's or Arnold's essays) and biographical parodies or sketches (*Eminent Victorians* or *New Yorker* profiles) may be highly stylized; lengthy biographies (Froude's or Mrs. Gaskell's or Haight's) tend to be stylistically uniform and less interesting in their use of language. The reverse is often true with respect to prose style and size in fiction: the short form (Joyce's or Lawrence's stories) may reveal *less* stylistic variety and inventiveness than does the fuller form (*Ulysses, Women in Love*). If exceptions occur, it seems true that the shorter biographical form and the longer fictive one offer the most scope to the stylist. We can see that because it is a summary, a generalization, the biographical sketch is freer from the weight of facts than is the full-length Life. The weight of imagined facts in fiction, however, tends to be greater, page by page, the shorter the fictive form is: the short story must establish its world just as the novel, but has less space in which to do it. Short stories tend to be written in uniform styles: they offer less opportunity for stylistic play, we may say, than the novel.

Now, if this inverse relationship in stylistic inventiveness exists, in general, between long and short biographical and fictive forms, then what discourages "style" is naming. It is the hypostatic or naming plane in narrative that inhibits stylistic display, subtlety, and variety, as a rule: but, on the other hand, what encourages "style" is personality. One might rearrange Buffon's formula to say that without the person there *is no* style, without personality there is no variety. Novels with style varieties (*Ulysses, The Sound and the Fury, Bleak House, Tristram Shandy*) may expose to a very striking degree the artistic personality of the novelist as well as the dramatic personalities upon which the novelist focuses. Is there any general rule that we may suggest? The persona of the narrator, as it becomes more fully established, may encourage the legitimate exploitation of style; but the hypostatic plane of naming, as it becomes denser, may discourage the legitimate exploitation of linguistic choice. If historical present-ness depends to some degree on the legitimate exploitation of style, then the biographer who takes great pains in choosing and arranging so as to make the plane of factual naming no larger than it need be, may succeed better in reanimating the past—in getting the living past to reveal itself. That will be to achieve the "life" that the biographer's relationship to the subject truly warrants and supports.

The historical present is important because it helps to give us a better sense of the subject's real experience in life, of the past that was known and lived through with an undetermined future ahead. Good biographical forms will always give us a sense of that "present," if no one has matched Boswell's success with it. But then technically the *Life of Johnson* is instructive in other ways too. (The information it gives is far from being complete, well-balanced, or accurate in every detail—but we have been thinking here of biographical form.) Boswell's glory is to have shown us in 1791 what modern biography requires and to have given us a technical example that no one has ever equaled.

Chapter Four

SOME POLITICS

T IME SORTS all things. It may now appear that Lytton
Strachey's *Eminent Victorians* is the last Victorian classic.
Certainly there is little that is "modern" in it. Strachey's
"Dr Arnold" has much in common with Arthur Penrhyn Stanley's
"School Life at Rugby" in *The Life and Correspondence of Thomas
Arnold, D.D.* (1844), and almost nothing in common with the
Thomas Arnold biographies by Mr. Whitridge (1928), Mr. Wymer
(1953), or Mr. Bamford (1960). Both Strachey and Stanley are chiefly
interested in Dr. Arnold's character; both select certain kinds of details
(and suppress other kinds) to illustrate a definite conception of character; both lack detachment and display emotional attitudes to the subject; both are haphazard in acknowledging sources; both quote
inaccurately; and both achieve considerable vitality and effect.
Strachey's mordant character portrait was made largely out of details
furnished by Stanley's *Life*, and it is not surprising that the heroic and
good schoolmaster (1844) and the tempestuous kidnapper of boys'

souls (1918) look—at this distance—more alike than ever. Strachey approaches the expurgated letters in Stanley's *Life* in an intuitive Victorian manner—much as Dickens approached criminal records, or as Robert Browning used the Normandy newspapers to write *Red Cotton Night-Cap Country*. A truth about a character or situation is intuited, and then the documentary source is scanned again for illustrative details, which the selector colors to fit the intuition. Browning felt he was telling the truth about Mellerio; and Strachey, truncating Dr. Arnold's legs and reducing his twelve continental trips to "one or two," only shocked the bourgeois with unexampled intuitive truthfulness.

The intuitive method has been the mainstay of biographical writing from ancient times to the twentieth century. Boswell's work, which influenced all Victorian biography, is pivotal; he certainly thought that "minute particulars are frequently characteristick" and that evidence was important. Political biographies since the last century have become more and more reliable and hard-headed. We fill our books with "particulars" and, perceiving that myths cling to personalities, we conceive that the biographer's first duty is to peel them away. Let us look at several biographies, marginally in the political category, since 1950; we have become used to them. Robert Blake's *Disraeli* became available in paperback soon after it was published in 1966, Philip Ziegler's *King William IV* appeared in 1971, and the books that I take up by John Prest, Norman Gash, and Georgiana Blakiston appeared in the following year. How well do they hold up?

"Benjamin Disraeli's career was an extraordinary one; but there is no need to make it seem more extraordinary than it really was. His point of departure, though low by the standards of nineteenth-century Prime Ministers, was neither as humble nor as alien as some people have believed." So begins one of the most widely acclaimed biographies (of any Victorian) in recent years. Lord Blake, who understands mid-Victorian politics and writes well, uses a biographical form that is now common. He presents masses of evidence in chronological order, now and again stopping to assess what is problematic, to generalize from the evidence or to look ahead over what is to be contextual background. Thus, several chapters in advance of the one called "The Budget of 1852," there is a surveying one called "The Political Scene 1846–68." The density of factual information here is considerable:

Bentinck was right: the valuation of the timber, estimated at
£8,127 by the vendors and at £7,313 by Disraeli's solicitor, was
fixed by an arbitrator at £7,332, and agreed deductions reduced
it to £7,250, a saving of nearly £900.

The list is impressive: two important Trade Union Acts; the
Public Health Act which consolidated a multitude of earlier
measures; the Artisans Dwellings Act empowering local
authorities to replace slums by adequate houses; an Agricultural
Holdings Act which met, though only partially, some of the
tenants' grievances; an Act to safeguard the funds of Friendly
Societies; a Factory Act to protect women and children against
exploitation—there had already been one in the previous session
to establish the principle of the ten-hour day; and finally the
Sale of Food and Drugs Act which remained the principal
measure on that subject until 1928. No other session was quite
as productive, although the Rivers Pollution, Merchant
Shipping and Education Acts of 1876 were important, and so,
too, was the Factory Act of 1878 based on the report of a Royal
Commission set up two years earlier.

The virtues of *Disraeli* are clarity of style, breadth of background,
thoroughness in the presentation of facts, and moderate commentary.
The intelligence of the biographer often shines through. But the analysis never gives one a sense of what it was that made Disraeli a political novelist; and the slow-moving narrative and exposition only now
and then, for a few pages, give one a sense of political life being lived.
Again and again, one registers the respectful caveat: could not some of
this information be relegated to Notes?

Modern biography cannot return to a tradition that is not respectful
of fact and of evidence. But we can say that not only its research but
its *writing* necessitates painstaking effort, that twenty rewritings of a
single sentence may be needed, and that unless every chapter reflects
an appropriate sense of the subject's presence, the biography at best
has value as an academic reference book. And even so, it may be
poor. Whether a Life illuminates its subject depends upon how well
the biographer relates his information to the problem of character.

Consider Mr. John Prest's *Lord John Russell*. Lord John or "Little

Johnny" was a frail man, five foot four and three-quarter inches tall, and usually in uncertain health. He was said to be proud, capricious, willful, and absentminded. He mislaid papers, lost sheets of statistics, sent envelopes without enclosures or letters to the wrong recipients, filed items under incorrect headings, often missed appointments. His manners were stiff; he was shy; he had a temper; and at one point or another he offended every prominent figure in his party. Between 1830 and 1855, he accomplished more than any British statesman ever had done.

His success is no less puzzling than his foolhardiness and decline. Mr. Prest introduces him in three chapters heavy with dates and other facts, but light in terms of any insight into his character or qualities. We learn that "his small size was a handicap from which he never recovered." Was it always a handicap in successful dealings with vain men? Two quotations are produced to show that he was fond of his mother; another shows that she taught him the months of the year. Somehow, he thought about electoral reform earlier and more precisely than anyone else in parliament; he was the chief architect and pilot of the most contentious reform bill of the century. Having recounted just this in chapter V, Mr. Prest assesses the man in chapter VII. He was proud, but could be "light-hearted"; shy, but indulged in "overeager bonhomie"; and "he was almost totally unpolitical." If unpolitical, what made him realistic about reform? If proud, why so effectively self-effacing in presenting the bill to the Commons? If a blunderer with people, why was he in demand all over the country? Much in chapter VII illuminates complex "Little Johnny." But nothing in the book explains how a man who mislaid papers and offended people could carry out difficult political tasks, rise to be prime minister, and achieve more than anyone else while being "almost totally unpolitical."

It *is* unpolitical not to make a copy of the letter you write to a cabinet minister, and to send the letter not to the minister but to a lady. So there is, perhaps, validity in Mr. Prest's exaggerated phrase. Johnny was complicated. But four-fifths of *Lord John Russell* is unsatisfactory because given the man that Mr. Prest presents, only unbelievable good luck or a contract with Beelzebub would account for his efficiency and success in the House of Commons. Moreover we so rarely see character related to event, or have a coherent sense of Lord John's presence, that we cannot tell which elements in the man's makeup are being brought into play at any crucial turn in his career.

And yet Mr. Prest commands our respect. He assimilates an immense quantity of historical evidence and presents it readably; there are 954 footnotes in three of his chapters together. Not Lord John, but Lord John's political fortunes and the life of the Commons are in focus up to about 1852. And from about the time of the Aberdeen Coalition to Russell's death, or in its last eighty pages, this book really seems to be a biography. Why does it succeed at the end? Mr. Prest, having asked in a mini-introduction why historians have not accorded Russell much honor, seeks to show that temperamental flaws and rash behavior (and not the second Lady Russell) undid the statesman and his reputation. From the "disastrous period" of 1850–1859 Little Johnny never recovered (though he was admired more than ever, perhaps, by intelligent friends). Now this is at least a tenable thesis; to demonstrate it Mr. Prest places an individual at the center of the four last chapters. We have the sense of a person's relation to events. Mr. Prest stops writing about "spontaneous combustion"; he analyzes a man, and lets evidence speak often for itself. In so doing, he follows the method of Johnson, of Boswell, of the Victorian biographers, and even of Strachey at his best; but without Victorian hagiography and without Strachey's fictionalizing. Mr. Prest, a Balliol Fellow, attaches himself at last to a commendable tradition.

Popular reviewers of our biographies are inclined in reverential moods to overpraise them, and in candid moods to complain they are arid and not "vivid." But what good biographical writing has is not vividness; there is not much color in the Socratic dialogues, in Plutarch, or in Boswell. Good or intelligent biography uses language that brings the sense of the evidence about the biographee before the reader. Mr. Norman Gash, in *Sir Robert Peel: The Life of Sir Robert Peel after 1830*, writes in a manner that gives a sense of Peel's personal dignity, a sense of the relative simplicity and clarity of his convictions and emotional life at least in London, and also a sense of his rigidity and the tendency to tighten in a crisis. Indeed, that tendency is often pointed out:

He had not anticipated the abrupt collapse of Grey's
administration. He could not have wanted it unless he felt that it
was possible to form a Conservative government; and this was
still very doubtful. It was true that the steady drift of ministerial
opinion towards a more radical Church policy had stiffened his
own reactions.

Even the discussion of deficits and the income tax in his ninth chapter, "The Great Budget" of 1841, seems to belong to a biography. Peel
is moved, worried, alarmed by events, but not shaken; and a more
dramatic style of narrative, which could convey a suggestion of rage or
nerves, is carefully avoided. At his best, Mr. Gash is Tacitean: "There
was an organised run on the banks; there were public declarations to
withhold taxes; and lower down in the ranks of the radical movement,
talk of pikes and barricades."

But Johnson's complaint about biographers who "have so little regard to the manners or behaviour of their heroes" might apply here.
When Mr. Gash turns from politics to Peel's private life, or to his
wife, family, trips, or shooting, we have Christmas-card analysis—if
not Christmas-card writing:

Julia was now recovering her health and his youngest child,
Eliza, had entered her second year. The eldest of them, Julia
the second, was twelve years old and beginning to grow into a
handsome young lady. Bobby, her junior by one year, was
already experiencing the modified rigours of boarding-school life
at a private establishment at Brighton, and the joys of returning
home for the holidays.

If Mr. Gash won't tell us the truth about Peel's home life, *who will*?
Did the distress of his wife mean nothing to Peel? Why did a tasteful
patron of the arts build a ghastly Victorian pile? That "he enjoyed
good food, fashionable clothes, expensive furnishings," that "women
as well as men enjoyed his conversation," that "not everyone encoun-
tered the lighter side" of his nature, and that it would be "absurd to
doubt the genuineness" of his emotions are valid. But Queen Victoria
says more in a remark about Peel's shyness than do dozens of Mr.

Gash's remarks, which fit Edward Heath just as well. Appropriate political and economic analyses are Mr. Gash's forte. But surely it is a mistake to box character into a paragraph here and there, to try to wrap it up in a final chapter, and to forget it for tens of pages.

Freud and Jung created ordering myths; the biographer may be unwise to trust in myth or to try to psychoanalyze a dead Victorian. But two other ways of proceeding are hardly wiser: first to assume that character will more or less take care of itself if one gets a tenth of one's research material into the Life, and second, to assume that one needs no form whatever and that seventy or eighty years need only be sliced into chapters. Mr. Philip Ziegler's *King William IV* has a semblance of form, and does much justice to the lively and vulgar and then heavy and vulgar pre-Victorian subject, William. "Oh, for England and the pretty girls of Westminster," writes the prince on July 23, 1784, when he is eighteen, "at least to such as would not clap or pox me every time I fucked." Whoremongering, pride, obliviousness to the feelings of others, sulkiness, and a penchant for excessive discipline when he was a naval officer do not turn the young William into an object of sympathy; but they make him colorful; and Mr. Ziegler's achievement has been to let us see through garish externals to the predicament of a king's son. In his youth, nobody believed he would become king. William had much energy, an impercipient father, a rather cold-hearted mother, and no future.

Lightness and fluency in biographical writing are graces, and verbal wit is hard to quarrel with. But wit, and everything else, finds its best use in contributing to the biographical subject. Mr. Ziegler makes us fond of Prince William by explaining his situation, his months at sea, and his futile exile to Hanover. But the style often pulls one away from the real milieu: the king kept his son "like an out-sized yo-yo, whipping up and down in flight from his various mistresses"; "it would come as no surprise" if "William had been bowled over by this languishing beauty"; the King "made soothing noises about his son's future" or "was not prepared to swallow" a one-sided story; and William on the throne is surrounded "by a mafia" of Tories who "organise the brain-washing of the unfortunate King." One breezes through the first half of the biography, only to find by the time William is on the throne that his attitudes are mysterious. Little has prepared us for a man who will play a part in the theater of policy making; not even the areas of William's simplicity and ignorance have been delineated with care. The biographer's political discussions seem stuck on, dutiful, wearisome; indeed, when attitudes are important to know about, we are treated to rather amazing contradictions. We learn that William was concerned with personalities, but also that he was mainly concerned with principles. "He always played fair"—but did he? He was "dogmatic, obstinate, truculent." He "could assess with some shrewdness the needs and wants of his own people" and yet he could not "put himself in the place of other people."

"A series of snapshots is no substitute for detailed analysis," Mr. Ziegler wisely comments. That surely is correct. The analysis of character, based upon historical evidence, is difficult no matter how "simple" one's subject was ever thought to be; and the planning and replanning for an adequate overall biographical form will be no less difficult. The liveliest, vividest writing won't plaster over deficiencies in assessment and form.

There is no biographical plaster in Georgiana Blakiston's *Lord William Russell and His Wife*; but instead alert commentary, an unprecedented form, and a severe enough lesson for biographers. Her book is less easy to read than *John Russell*, *Peel*, or *William IV*. What she offers is a curious and difficult combination of a historical study, a collection of letters, and a collection of biographical sketches and analyses. Mr. Prest says that "Little Johnny's" older brother, Lord William Russell, was "simple, direct, and hot tempered." Very distinguished, he was not. At sixteen, William entered the Army; at nineteen he was the only survivor in his squadron of the 23rd Light Dragoons at Talavera; at twenty-two he entered parliament as the member for Bedford; and five years later he married Elizabeth Anne Rawdon, whose beauty and temperament Byron celebrated in *Don Juan*. The marriage was a difficult one. William begat Hastings Russell, who adored firearms and his mother and committed suicide sixteen years after that lady died; Arthur Russell, who became a lazy *savant* and Liberal M.P.; and Odo Russell, who led a distinguished career as a diplomat in Paris, Constantinople, Washington, the Vatican, and Berlin. It seems possible that only a remarkable diplomat could have survived in close quarters with Elizabeth Anne.

Yet on what scale Lord William could be measured as "simple" is hard to say. (If some people are more like potatoes than onions, a biographer, who is a century removed from the subject, may do well to work *as though* the subject were not like a tuber. How many contradictory assessments of a "simple" soul are given in *King William IV?*) At any rate, Mrs. Blakiston proceeds on what is surely the correct assumption that William's character matters and that the evidence is complex. Interpolating several letters, telling us about the antecedents, the milieux, and the activities of Elizabeth Anne and then of William, she brings us to their marriage and points out interpretative problems ahead. The reader is advised to apprehend errors in their behavior and "assign the blame" for marital failure. Mrs. Blakiston next supplies biographical sketches of family members and friends. Then the book turns into do-it-yourself biography, with four gatherings of letters ("Billikins and Bettina" for the early years of marriage; "Military Years 1824–1832"; "Diplomacy" for the years in Portugal, Wurtemberg, and Prussia; and "Last Years 1841–1846"). Now and then in the middle of a letter gathering, Mrs. Blakiston injects narrative and analytic commentary of her own.

As biography, the book's drawback is that Lord William's achievements and possible failures as a soldier and then as a diplomat are unassessed and unassessable. We haven't enough material here to weigh his professional life. Yet we are given an intimate experience of his character as it relates to his family. His own pathetic diary is seen against a background of letters that concern in-laws, financial matters, military and diplomatic assignments, peregrinations, dinners, health problems, and children's educational problems—and, of course, William and Elizabeth's deteriorating relationship. Sometimes he writes of that with touching brevity: "24 June. Calm. Calm. Calm. Patience. Patience. Patience." The diplomat's see-through cryptology expresses in several ways the state of his nerves, and he records the following in easily deciphered code:

> [Sad scene. Elizabeth says I have a bad heart, no principles,
> selfish, malignant. . . . her dreadful temper. All resolutions
> useless. Hopes I may be absent with my regiment often and
> long. Sad, sad, sad. God help me, God help me].

The crisis came at Baden-Baden in the summer of 1835, and we see it from several viewpoints. Lord William begins an adulterous affair, and everyone from the high-toned Elizabeth to the even higher-toned Princess Lieven, who nourishes herself on everyone else's folly, hears about it. There are three documents for September 3, 1835. First, William's diary, beginning with his favorite phrase:

> 3 Sept. Worse & worse. This world is a mass of vice, hatred and envy. Hypocrites sheltering themselves under their cold, cautious natures to destroy the more open and less prudent. How I hate and despise them, that Meyendorff is a dirty dog, and his wife a dirty bitch.

Next, Princess Lieven writing to her husband Prince Lieven:

> 3 septembre 1835, Baden Baden . . . L'explosion que je crains est arrivée. La pauvre Lady William est dans les larmes. 18 années de confiance et de bonheur sont détruites. C'est un triste spectacle. Le pauvre homme est fou. A 50 ans prendre un amour violent pour une femme perdue, diner avec elle en public, se promener avec elle!

(Dining and sauntering in public with the woman he loves!) Next, Lady William to her brother-in-law, Mr. Prest's friend, Lord John Russell: "It would be most desirable to leave this part of Germany soon, but it is not from avidity to pounce on a new place—I cannot explain—you will trust to my reasons—and give me some dates as soon as you can. The Baden waters did your brother infinite good— douches—vapour baths and waters; we have had enough of it now."

These portions are cold and misleading perhaps when taken out of Mrs. Blakiston's abundant context. One feels the evidence of private diaries and semi-private gossip ought to be subjected to almost continuous appraisal. Mrs. Blakiston may leave a little too much to the reader. But in herself giving, and allowing her two principal subjects to give of themselves, a strong impression of nineteenth-century lives, she fulfills one of the chief obligations of the biographer.

Lord and Lady William Russell are very sensitive to places. Compounding her own frustrations with Weymouth, Lady William during one interval lives in

> a perpetual sirocco—sea fogs as hot as the steam of a tea kettle, and then a monotony quite deadening. One walk, one drive, one view, all the houses looking one way, and instead of a marine smell one of pitch, tar, tallow, sea coal smoke and so forth. Dorchester is 8 miles off, a very melancholy town, surrounded by trees, like boulevards.

"*Figurez-vous* a large rambling scrambling gloomy palace built by an Elector of Hesse 150 years ago in a narrow dark valley in the middle of a large beech forest," Lord William writes earlier, in 1821 from Schlangenbad; and it is when he can no longer write about locale with gaiety that we feel he is disintegrating. Locale, indeed, needs to be treated by the biographer with special care, and the worst deficiency with respect to it is to assume it will take care of itself and need not be researched or understood; in this light Mrs. Blakiston's book on the Russells is instructive. Judging from the other books discussed and from a good many political biographies published since these appeared, I would say that we are still careless with locale. The biographer needs to get maps and Baedekers into his or her room, and needs to get out of the room.

Chapter Five

PROBLEMS OF
LITERARY
BIOGRAPHY

I
T IS a strange, unnerving experience to find one's life the subject of fiction. I discovered this when a novelist, some years ago,
turned my bewilderment in coming to teach in the English Midlands (at Birmingham) into the comic trauma of one of his characters.
David Lodge and I had known each other for some time; we were
to teach in adjacent tutorial rooms at Birmingham University. But
when I reached that university the departmental secretary knew nothing of my appointment; I had nowhere to teach, no room, no students, and then I lost my name. "You must be *Mr. Green*," I was
told, as though the secretary thought I might have lied. I went down a
rather unwelcoming corridor to a door with the sign MR. GREEN on it,
entered a room strewn with fragments of cardboard boxes, and, feeling
miserable and lonely, opened an overhead cabinet. A forlorn, empty
tobacco tin fell out and hit me on the head, and oddly I felt better.
"Then and only then," I told Lodge, "I knew I was in the English
Midlands." David Lodge turned all of that into the deluge of empty

tobacco tins that falls on Morris Zapp's head after he comes to teach at "Rummidge University" in *Changing Places*.

Of course I have wondered what future biographers of Lodge may make of *Changing Places* and of my small, absurd influence on one of its scenes. Everything I told him about my perplexity mixed with Lodge's talent, experience, and feelings to produce the comedy of Zapp. Do biographers have enough delicacy to write of minor "influences"?

Much more delicacy is needed with historical persons—or the "personal" in one's evidence. If it is true that character is always elusive, one may ask if anything reveals the mind of one's subject. If anything does, how is one to convey the complexity of any individual's character in, say, a literary biography? Or point to connections between the intricacies of a mind and the literature which it has produced?

These are major questions, and I propose to respond to them here in a polemical way at first. It seems to me that Bernard Crick (a fine scholar and journalist) has dealt with such questions in theory and in practice. Bernard Crick, as Professor of Politics at Birkbeck College, University of London, published his *George Orwell: A Life* in 1980; I had not seen that book when I wrote *Matthew Arnold: A Life*, published in New York and London in 1981, so my preface to *Arnold* was not intended in any of its details as a reply to his introduction in *Orwell*. Yet the principles announced in the two books (and, in effect, illustrated in their approaches to history and to biography) differ sharply. I have not met Mr. Crick: I respect his work, and I would not allude to his notions—since *Orwell* is a better book than its introduction suggests it will be—if I did not think that Mr. Crick, in 1980, announced principles that are still rather in vogue in the writing of literary biography.

At issue between the principles and methods of *Orwell* and *Arnold* are several questions: Is it true that "human identity" consists only in relationships with other people and not in inwardness, and therefore proper for a biographer to characterize people by guessing about them? And is prose style in the English tradition of biography so false that a modern biography is likely to be more truthful when written in a casual, chatty, retrospective prose; or should one take pains with style so as to give an ongoing sense of historical evidence and of a developing present?

In the preface to *Arnold* I said that one should respect the fact "that an unpredictable future" lay ahead of Arnold, and that his biographer should attend to a "historical present" and bring him as close to us "as the evidence will permit." I believed that a chatty biographical prose would result in distortion. I had newly released journals and diaries with material on Arnold's childhood, letters by Arnold, by his friends and family, many reports about him, and new evidence concerning various aspects of his life. No child in history can have matured in a cultural or intellectual vacuum, and I felt that if I darted back at the past in a casual, backward-looking manner, quoted letters or diaries here and there, and did little to give a sense of Arnold developing in an unfolding environment, I could not show how forces influenced my subject almost simultaneously. I needed a form that would be conducive to a fine clarity and accuracy; such a form would be supplied by enough research into Arnold's family and contemporary society to help me suggest what is knowable about the continuing historical present of the life he lived. I could then show, as accurately as evidence would let me, how persons, events, and his known plans, ideas, and unsolved problems impinged upon him in history. The test of my prose, I thought, should not be whether it was smart or had "pace," but whether it would be delicately accurate enough to do justice to evidence.

Mr. Crick, in the introduction to *Orwell*, recommended a "stress on externality, standing outside Orwell, noting his behaviour" and narrating from a remote viewpoint. Prose style was not important to Mr. Crick. As Orwell the man, in any case, was less "great" than Orwell's works, no particular delicacy would be needed in any biographical prose dealing with him, Mr. Crick implied. Without naming an erring exemplar, Mr. Crick was suspicious of prose style and much else in "the English tradition in biography." Did he mean that George Painter wrote too seductively in *Marcel Proust*, or Mary Moorman in *Wordsworth*, for example? Having cautioned against being "too confident in our judgements of character" in his intoduction, he began to characterize people guessingly. Thus Mr. Crick wrote of Orwell's parents that Mr. Blair "was plainly a tolerant and easy-going man" and Mrs. Blair "appears to have been, in the very nicest sense, a bit of a gadabout" (Penguin edition, 1982, 47, 49). Mr. Crick's theory and practice were not always in accord, and his theory seems to me misleading. The key statement he made to justify his "stress on externality" in biography was this: "Our human identity consists in relationships, not in inwardness."

That reduces life, and gives a biographer leave to neglect all difficult evidence about persons. Surely it is wrong to say that inwardness has nothing to do with identity: what happens, then, to evidence about contemplatives, their writings and lives? Is all inwardness a fiction? Or is it that in an era of scientific positivism, Xeroxes, and footnotes one may become impatient with what one finds hard to judge? If we deny inwardness we may try to reduce any unusual person to a smooth, dull ordinariness. The biographer's treatment then becomes bland; he pleads for a "stress on externality" and comments at a good, safe distance from his human subject, as if he were writing a gigantic obituary made up of this or that, neglectful of historical contexts and even of the subtle influences people have on one another. In her lecture on literary biography in 1980, Dame Helen Gardner pointed out that biographers were already then being reductive, as when they devalued the "creative and shaping spirit of the imagination" of writers they tried to portray. More recently the oversimplifying that occurs with our "stress on externality" has been extreme. Deny "inwardness" and uniqueness in life only more thoroughly, one feels, and the Ministry of Truth may as well write our accounts of historical persons.

Consider a fairly recent biography of Dorothy Wordsworth, given us by two authors who have produced better work in the past. *Dorothy Wordsworth* is written, on principles that seem to be Mr. Crick's, in a chatty, casual, retrospective prose that sketches the most outward details in a writer's life. This book dismisses the problem of Dorothy Wordsworth's sexuality in a few lines. The biographers say little of any force that may have encouraged her talent, virtually nothing of her wider historical environment, little about her reading, and try to account for her early prose with an inaccurate brief discussion of the "vocabulary of sensibility." We sense almost nothing about Dorothy Wordsworth's mental development: she seems to have had almost no inward life at all. The writers say nothing significantly new about her friendship with Coleridge; they seem baffled by Coleridge's relationship with the Wordsworths and complain that it is "difficult to find terms for their friendship." In nearly every respect the book is less convincing and considered than De Selincourt's life, *Dorothy Wordsworth*, of 1933; the new biographers offer additions to her outward history, as they try to make use of facts about her that have emerged since 1933. They liken her to a "sterile" bud clinging to a stem. They betray no knowledge of, or interest in, Coleridge's Transcendentalism, or the complex background of religious thought in the Wordsworths' time, or the European influences on English romanticism, and they neglect even the variety of British ideas that Dorothy Wordsworth was exposed to. She becomes in this biography as average and ordinary as any botany teacher, though it is hard to imagine a botany teacher less interesting.

For all the superficiality of *Dorothy Wordsworth*, its worst fault may be in its impoverished language, and manifest insensitivity to Dorothy Wordsworth's accurate and vigorous use of English. The authors rise, now and then, in an attempt to be vivid about the Lake District, but they never use English to give a delicate sense of anything pertaining to persons in the evidence before them. Mr. Crick's "stress on externality" is in practice very limiting and results in implicit censorship, a fear of trying to find and use language accurate and flexible enough to bring what is personal in documents before us. An external "stress" usually leads to the neglect of the subject's mental life (as in *Dorothy Wordsworth*) and may result in a rubbing smooth of nearly all the edges of character. What is odd about a person is missed or highlighted as eccentricity, but is seldom explained. A chatty, bland, retrospective prose serves for the biographer of "externality"—whose research may be so superficial that no reliable ongoing context for the subject's development is given.

Biography is the most difficult of all long prose forms. Yet superficial "lives" are written quickly. If one takes no trouble to study the development of a mind, avoids research needed to depict accurately the social forces around a life, and adheres to a backward-looking chronicle, one may perhaps produce a book on nearly anyone in six months. Mr. Crick's introduction—that is, his statement of theory—seems to offer a recipe for writing such a book. But adequate modern biographies exist. They give an exact context for the nature of evidence concerning persons, and a sense of an evolving past time so that we can see how a variety of forces impinged on the continuum of a subject's life. And these "lives" implicitly recognize that inwardness is a part of human uniqueness, and is evidenced and can be shown.

Mr. Crick's *Orwell* has unusual value as an assemblage of information and, I think, as a quarry for future students both of George Orwell's life and writings. Mr. Crick is not interested in a person but in a method of avoiding the personal—and that may be just as well since we are too close in time to Orwell to have perspective to understand him. Every advantage accrues for the biographer safely distanced in time from the subject: history, environment, character, thought, feeling, and behavior then appear in contrast with what we think we know of life. One has a chance to care deeply for the subject and to work oneself free from the sentimentality and other confusions of the caring. In my own case, sentimentality has been strong and yet almost the least of my difficulties; I think pride and arrogance, in many subtle shapes, have never helped me to understand anyone, and I doubt if they have been chained and racked in one corner of my mind now. I do know that I was gauche, proud, and mortified when as an undergraduate in 1949 I ran to a library to find "lives" of Jane Austen and of Arnold because I was keen to know about both authors. My standards were vague, but I found that accounts of Arnold's life lacked detail and that those of Jane Austen's were to my mind simply incredible. Many years later—early in 1981 after my work on Arnold—I turned to Jane Austen's life.

Not since the Austen-Leighs' *Life and Letters* in 1913 had any account of Jane Austen been based on her family's manuscript diaries and letters. I set out to find these. Also, since *Jane Austen's Letters* is partly based on faulty transcripts, I wanted to see as many of her holograph letters as I could. Does it make a difference to a biographer that we should have accurate (unchanged) texts of the subject's letters? I am afraid it does. With punctuation and capitals changed and a new word added, Jane Austen's letter of January 29, 1813, for example, was so badly printed in Chapman's *Jane Austen's Letters* that a generation of critics believed she said "ordination" was the subject of *Mansfield Park*. She never did; her holograph letter survives; we can have her accurate text when an adequate edition of her letters appears. Editors sometimes still insist on "house-styling" punctuation, or being cavalier with it because punctuation as well as capitalization and spelling are considered by them (often wrongly, I think) as "accidentals." Chapman had used some bad transcripts.

I wanted to see exactly, then, what Jane Austen wrote, and all that I could of her family's writing about her. Descendants of her brothers let me see the Austen-Leigh collections, and after some four years' work, I had more of the relevant family papers than were available in 1913.

I wanted to present the results of research conservatively, and to give in one book a quite accurate account of what we can know about Jane Austen's life now. The *Memoir* of 1870, the Austen-Leighs in 1913, Elizabeth Jenkins in 1938, and David Cecil in 1978 were useful, and I wanted to relate my work to their precedents. I had letters by Mrs. Austen, by five of Jane Austen's brothers, and letters and diaries by Austen cousins, nephews and nieces, illuminating of the subject. I felt that the accuracy of my narrative would depend partly on a prose manner. My "style" would have to render the sense of what was in the evidence: it would have no other more important mission. And that would mean taking considerable pains. Again, it is surely irrelevant for us to place too much emphasis on whether prose style in a biography is "vivid" or "academic," "lively" or "flat," when what counts most is whether it renders what is personal with a delicate fidelity.

It would be untruthful and bizarre merely to report on Jane Austen's letters or to narrate always from their viewpoint, as valuable as they are. I could, however, be faithful to the evidence by offering a narrative that kept in view many strands of her experience. I would need to shift the camera's eye to members of her family and to give a sense of some of her brothers' experiences, based on good evidence, to suggest the experience *she* had of *them*. And in Jane Austen's life the "family" was particularly important. She extended her knowledge of the world through the affectionate, special closeness of friendship she enjoyed with her elder sister Cassandra and with their clerical, naval, and banking brothers. At the same time, everything in an adequate biography must be pertinent to the subject. I could not allow myself to go off along other roads for their intrinsic interest, or purely for the sake of illuminating any other person. I had only one path to follow— Jane Austen's own. But this path did not lead *only* through tea parties and balls at Ashe or Manydown Park or Bath (though I would give due attention to those); it led, in part, through public events as they related to her. A "Trafalgar" chapter is partly about Frank Austen, but it is so because its whole pertinence is to a Jane Austen who pored over the papers for news of Frank, took steps to outwit enemy courier ships to reach him, reacted to and wrote about his naval life, and plied Frank for data for her novels. I felt, too, that time must not necessarily be uniform in a biography that reflects evidence. The night of December 2, 1802, for example, after she had consented to be Mrs. Harris Bigg-Wither was of no little importance to her. The consequences of a night may be complex and not soon ended, and my narrative here might pause to be fully clear about the issues that disturbed her as well as a family that was related to Sir William Blackstone.

The retrospective method, in Jane Austen's case, would not have been of use in showing relationships between strands of her life that led up to her accepting Harris. Little in her life—or in any life—is easily explained in a sentence. And this is one reason we have biographies. They exist to show the interaction of things as they really were in a person's experience. Anyone's life today and tomorrow might be told in narrative form, but, if so, the narrative would not move like a pair of scissors through cloth. Rather, our lives do advance as waves. Along the front of the wave much is pushed, much comes together and spreads apart, colors intermingle, one thing becomes prominent and then another, as in effect the wave moves through calendar time. A biographer recreates that wave of the historical present not imaginatively but out of the evidence that, bit by bit, provides what we see on the wave's face. This is to say that many aspects of a life have stories, and that only with exacting care for language and form can we reproduce in narrative those separate stories—and show how they are part of one ongoing life.

I also considered that feeling was important to Jane Austen. We still live in an era of scientific positivism in which feelings seem "subjective" matters and, for example, all locales and dates "objective." But what if feeling is factually a part of experience? Again it is not a fault of life, but of our forms, if biographers cannot reproduce evidence of feeling. They can, at least, write of a structure of events in such a way that the events produce, in narrative, an impression of feeling upon our understanding. This cannot be done through emotive writing, but through a proper and accurate ordering of the events. We tend to crush out lives as we write about them, but we need not. It is paradoxical that a biography sensitive to persons runs the risk, in each sentence, of not being just and appropriate in tone. The finer the accuracy, the more scope there is for error. This, I take it, means that an adequate biographer is one who attends to the minutiae of evidence and who consults documents again and again, and recasts and rewrites until the presentation is as appropriate as it can be—and who is still, perhaps, wary and dissatisfied. The rewards for writing quick and superficial biographies are good—publishers are hungry for them, and readers expect them. But adequate biography, at least, has a way of lasting, and may even illuminate our own possibilities.

Seen closely in historical context, Jane Austen is less remote from us than we may have thought.

Chapter Six

ELLMANN AS THE AUTHOR OF *JAMES JOYCE* AND *OSCAR WILDE:* (A PERSONAL INQUIRY)

IN THE MOST unashamed way, I am going to draw on my acquaintance with Richard Ellmann and on several of his comments. My object is not to puff myself or to imply we were close friends (we never were). But since the man is revealed through what he said and the impression he gave, and that man has something to do with Ellmann the biographer of Joyce and Wilde, I find it right to be personal about him—at the risk of seeming too auto-biographical. Ellmann is the best literary biographer to have written in English in our century. No one would call his *Joyce* or *Wilde* "academic"; they lack the stiff, squeezed-dry aspect of other scholarly accounts of lives and do not play false with human experience and feeling. Yet he was an academic professional, leaving a post at Evanston in Illinois to take a chair of English at Oxford. He was a convivial figure at New College, even an early morning jogger. Shortly before he died he was teaching in autumn semesters at Emory in Georgia. I had met him in the 1960s not long after he had published *James Joyce*. We exchanged letters oddly enough about tax laws, and then I asked the publishers Weidenfeld & Nicolson to send him a copy of my *Matthew Arnold* as a matter of course. Neither my editor nor I was seeking a comment from him, and I would not have expected him to send me more than a postcard in acknowledgment, and so I was surprised by his letter from West Germany. "I have just this moment put down your book," Ellmann wrote to me from Höxter about the Arnold biography on September 3, 1981,

> with a great sense of having been successfully ushered through sixty-odd years of the 19th century. Your book succeeds abundantly in changing one's view of father (and mother) and son, but it also re-draws Arnold's character, so he is no longer the somber character "with Matthew Arnold's face" but has ebullience along with irony and intelligence and earnestness. The account of his life as school inspector is fascinating, as with the account of his American tour. Then there is your great coup in identifying Marguerite—a pity that she didn't at least bear him an illegitimate child—one feels for his embarrassment and humiliation, and welcomes the power of poetry to make so much out of their incomplete moments together. His life as a married man is also fascinating instead of (like most married lives) dull. . . . I've much enjoyed my four days in your company!

How typical of his humor and kindness, I thought. Dick Ellmann had no need to praise me—he owed me no favors—and I had no need of his praise. After years of work on a biography one knows its merits and faults well enough oneself. (One may need praise during the writing, or require lavish praise after repairing the plumbing or wallpapering the bedroom.) I had known Dick slightly. At one meeting he seemed relieved to talk apart from other sherry-drinking guests at a reception perhaps only because he knew I would listen. He was an even better listener himself, and I may have chatted idly for five minutes; then he told me that he was not certain that he could adjust to being a professor at Oxford. He disliked committee work, felt that he might be viewed as a shirker, and was anxious about his wife's health. On another occasion he was reluctant to talk about the present at all. He told me about interviewing Carl Jung in Switzerland on the subject of Joyce. I never had any illusion that I had penetrated the veil of Dick Ellmann, and felt that a soft wall of kindness kept us apart: he must have told others as much as he told me. But one tries to peer over walls, and I thought (more than once) that what I detected on the other side was a mild amiable confusion, self-doubt, a sense of feeling outdated and misplaced in a locale, out of touch with the self and everything else—in short, a profound and agonizing humility, the first requirement for a biographer.

A sense of dislocation, confusion, and of being out of touch, with profound humility, I believed I had witnessed before. Bristling with a feeling of rivalry, I had met William Irvine on a luncheon date in London: he was far advanced in a biography of Robert Browning that I had intended to write. (I had a fellowship to help me advance my work.) Irvine, then in his fifties, with a gauzy device worn over one ear to conceal an inexplicable ailment, seemed vulnerable and lost. I took his arm to convey him to our restaurant. He stiffened slightly when I mentioned in passing several of his works, his *Bagehot*, or my feeling for the appropriateness of his prose style with Huxley in *Apes, Angels, and Victorians*. At luncheon, he was receptive, not as if he approved in the slightest way any theory or remark I advanced but as if the kindest imaginable human radar screen—with mild and appropriate comments—were turning this way and that way to receive and sort out anything I said.

Irvine reached the perfection of biography in his chapters on Browning's first fifty years in *The Book, the Ring, and the Poet* (1974), a book that I completed after Irvine died; he had left his twenty-one chapters mainly in beautifully finished form. Richard Ellmann reached his own perfection as a biographer in *James Joyce* (1959), a book which I came to know almost as well as Irvine's work. That is, I had read Ellmann's *Joyce* for about six months along with Joyce's *Ulysses*, the latter of which was the chief text that I would discuss week by week with a dozen young women, late at night, in an informal James Joyce group I ran in the 1960s when teaching at a women's college. (We met in girls' bedrooms, I am glad to say, with most of the group in pajamas, and I have seldom known freer or better discussions.) And so as it seems to me, charmingly but also intimately I had come to know Ellmann's work and a little later Irvine's work.

The first thing to say is that—despite these impressions of Ellmann and Irvine as men, or as acquaintances—their biographical writing is anything but dislocated or tentative. It is painstaking and assured with an effect of flow that conceals the work that has been taken to be exact. Irvine is one of the finest biographical stylists in English; he uses irony, rhythm, diction, and images to give an exact sense of the Browning who appears in letters and other evidence. Strachey in *Eminent Victorians* had brought wit, grace of phrasing, and intelligence to biography but at the expense of delicate accuracy and truth. (It is typical of Strachey to have said that he would alter a fact, if need be, to save the rhythm of a sentence's ending.) Irvine brought the grace and suppleness of English into the service of accuracy and so moved beyond the biographical writing of his time. Ellmann is less various and subtle than Irvine, but warm, confident, at ease, and exact in manner. If Irvine is elegant, Ellmann can be axiomatic almost to the point of a breezy vulgarity— while being perfectly just and controlled:

Joyce is the porcupine of authors. His heroes are grudged heroes—the impossible young man, the passive adult, the whisky-drinking greybeard. It is hard to like them, harder to admire them. Joyce prefers it so. Unequivocal sympathy would be romancing. He denudes man of what we are accustomed to respect, then summons us to sympathize.

And Ellmann, in style and form, brought something new to biography in the long paragraph of unified and concentrated subject matter and accumulating effect. If the bane of biography is its multitude of facts as the bane of an army of invasion might be its two million individuals, the facts (like the men) need not be reduced or pulverized or altered in being but they may and must be marshaled and grouped, subordinated and cunningly organized. In a larger structural way, Ellmann's chapters deal with more than slices of chronological time and the "growth" of his subject. They have prevailing themes of their own, usually signaled or hinted at in each chapter's epigraph and sometimes in an opening sentence. Thus for example chapter 8 in Ellmann's *Joyce* builds up shrewdly to Joyce's early experiences in France, its pleasures, broadening effects, and accompanying stringencies, after the "Paris rawly waking . . ." epigraph from *Ulysses* and Ellmann's first narrative sentence, "Paris was Dublin's antithesis." In good biographies, and certainly in Ellmann's practice, everything *in effect* becomes narrative, and one of his own most effective skills lies in his making literary criticism seem to advance his biographical "story."

"The form of biography," he wrote in *Golden Codgers: Biographical Speculations* in 1973, "is countenancing experiments comparable to those of the novel and poem. It cannot be so mobile as those forms because it is associated with history, and must retain a chronological pattern, though not necessarily a simple one." A lively recognition of this I think led Ellmann to structure his chapters experimentally with careful attention to emotional growth or psychological change in his subject. The Joyce at the end of an Ellmann chapter is usually different from the Joyce at the start of it, and, perhaps more important, our view of Joyce through the chapter has taken on a new dimension. In a long biography Ellmann takes elaborate pains to avoid the effect of repetition; and, in showing us the life of a writer whose art year by year may not be continuously or ceaselessly evolving, a literary biography may all too easily repeat its effects. For example, Leon Edel's life of Henry James is admirably detailed but it is also wearisome; it keeps us for long stretches at the surface of events which, in effect, are telling us what has already been established by Edel in connection with James's habits and character. Edel's literary criticism is far from being feeble, but it is, often, hardly more than a compound of well-written plot summary and speculative psychobiographical theory. Edel traverses the span of his subject's life and works so that we feel little of importance that James did is being left out; but the biographer lacks Ellmann's quick, confident (and confidence-inspiring) penetration. Ellmann avoids the effect of psychological theorizing in both *Joyce* and *Wilde*. Indeed, we are seldom prompted to question the authority of his biographical voice, his critic and presenter; it is not that we feel Ellmann is always right, but that there is a well-planned consistency in the large pattern of his criticism within a book. We feel that what is being said of a work is not adventitious but intrinsic to a much larger, overall interpretation of Oscar Wilde or James Joyce. The intelligent consistency charms and compels; we want to see how the critical re-mark will be borne out in the larger pattern. He is appropriately bold, as he is with the last story in Joyce's *Dubliners:* "The selection of details for 'The Dead' shows Joyce making those choices which, while masterly, suggest the preoccupations that mastered him." That does not point *out* of the biography to Freud but into the biography's pre-sentational structure, and back toward the groundwork of an argument as well as ahead to the promise of confirming evidence about the "preoccupations."

Ellmann could be delicious on Edel's habit of picking up and drop-ping Freudian techniques. In the penultimate volume of *Henry James*, Ellmann writes in *Golden Codgers,*

> Edel seems almost ready to give up Freud, as when he describes
> the turmoil in Henry James's mind: "Two forces contended
> within: his intellect and his emotions. . . . Rational form and
> mind were thus interposed against the chaos of feeling." This is
> the psychology not of Freud but of Alexander Pope. Apparently
> aware that his readers may be getting confused, Edel in the
> preface to this volume explains his biographical method. . . .
> but isn't it peculiar to say, in this generation, that the emotional
> life has nothing to do with sex life or bowel movements?

What Ellmann could not bear was the crass and easy underrating of the complexity of a subject's mind, or the resort to a fashionable idea to save the biographer the task of coming to grips with ambiguous and difficult evidence. There is also something oddly exasperated in Ellmann's comments on Edel, odd just because (as in his dealings with me) he was unshowily generous with other biographers. As a rule no one could be less suited to reviewing a new biography than a biog-rapher; novelists and historians make allowances for each other more readily, I think. In any case Ellmann's comments on Edel are profes-sionally protective, as if he felt Edel had betrayed the guild or the mystery of the craft in slipshod Freudianizing and had failed to realize that a biographer's authority should not be compromised and, further-more, must be earned and demonstrated throughout the narrative of a life. Five hundred scholarly footnotes do not in themselves earn authority, and aridity or mere factuality will never demonstrate one's understanding of the history of a person. But if authority is lost all is lost, and unless it is evident nothing will be evident: nothing one says will then show and convince. Authority depends on the depth, range, and imaginative alertness of one's research; it seems to depend on one's prose style and tone, also on structure within a chapter and the structural sequence of chapters; but most of all, for Ellmann, it depends on an attitude to personal evidence.

On exactly this matter Leon Edel's pronouncements have been colorful but seldom subtle or particularly useful. In his brief *Literary Biography*, Edel stated that "the biographer is called upon to take the base metals that are his disparate facts and turn them into the gold of human personality." Well, I have a room in my house called the Alchemist's Room because a member of my family makes jewelry there, but no more gold is made in it than the medieval alchemists made; gold is gold and nothing else. You have gold, or you don't, but no "base metals" are made into it, alas. Not even fancifully did Ellmann subscribe to a transforming magic, but he did believe in historical evidence about persons. So far as I can judge, he felt that if what Edel calls "human personality" was not evident in the document it was not recoverable. Not every figment of personality or aspect of a mind will be traceable in a letter by Joyce or Wilde, but it is clear Ellmann believed that in this genre one may combine, assimilate, extract, and abstract, but not create; one will fail in trying to turn one thing into something else. He himself is not creative, and his comments on Joyce and Wilde (although too various to be categorized) might perhaps be very generally divided into two main kinds. Ellmann extracts from evidence about his subject at a given time or he abstracts from the whole of evidence he is aware of to make a general remark about a subject's mind, and the generality will be an integral part of his biography's structure. For him many kinds of combining are legitimate, but nothing else can be done in the way of transforming "disparate facts" into some conception of personality. He was not too pleased with Painter's Freudianizing or post-Freudianizing in *Proust* though Painter seemed more "persuasive" in his use of psychology than Edel: Painter let himself be taken away from the judging of personal evidence to an external authority who produced universal truths. Once that happens, Painter, in Ellmann's opinion, loses hold of his materials and, invoking the psychology gods of our time, becomes careless with language, sometimes using "psychological interpretation half-literally, half-figuratively" (see the first chapter of *Golden Codgers*). On the other hand, no particular wish to dispense with psychological insight or even modern psychological theory can be found in Ellmann's essays; his protest is usually against the fashionable biographical method of imposing "a proving frame" upon evidence, rather than facing the task of getting the evidence to yield what information it will. Ellmann most aligns himself with Strachey, oddly, in assuming an intelligent but sceptical reader. Biographical narrative within itself proves its own good sense.

But whereas Strachey found character easy and knowable and would not take it seriously because the Victorians took it too seriously, Ellmann is a disciplined interpreter who knows that character *is* very difficult to estimate. An immense amount of research is undertaken and a complex, dense, but readable structure of history is offered to show a person a portrait of Joyce or Wilde. For Ellmann the Irish are Israelites of our day, greater than their nation, exiled and dispersed, rich in spirit but also torn within, dominated and dominating, forced to fight or to beguile. Ellmann is fond of them. Wilde and Joyce used their Irishness to become heroes of art, of Western culture, in effect. But what are they as men?

To see them steadily at all perhaps is to understand what it is to be modern. "On or about December 1910," wrote Virginia Woolf, "human character changed." Ellmann, in his essay on the epoch of pre-war courtliness and Edwardian literature, "Two Faces of Edward," gravely would put Virginia Woolf's date of the momentous change back ten years: "If a moment must be found for human character to have changed," Ellmann wrote, "I should suggest that 1900 is both more convenient and more accurate than Virginia Woolf's 1910." Wilde to an extent anticipates the change; Joyce, who is eighteen in 1900, participates in it. The modern is not in passionate revolt and is not strictly religious or irreligious, though Edwardians looked "for ways to express their conviction that we can be religious about life itself." The modern writer shares with other Edwardians a belief in a secular miracle, the transformation of the self, or the possibility of its sudden alteration, according to Ellmann. So Joyce appears to agree with Yeats that if we pretend hard enough to be the mask or the self we adopt, we can become that other self; and this takes us back to Oscar Wilde, the peculiarly earnest poseur. For the biographer, the modern writer exhibits an extreme self-consciousness in any case, and a fluid and never easily demonstrable character. For what self is the man who adopts masks, and seems to believe in them, ever expressing? Ellmann the biographer is "modernized" by his subjects, and it is not enough for him simply to record the changing patterns of Joyce's or Wilde's behavior and utterances and being: he must understand a self-conscious subject even to chronicle its behavior accurately.

The idea that character changed in 1910 or 1900 is a useful myth, of course, but a key aspect of the "change" occurs further back in Europe's cultural history, as it seems to me. Goethe and the *Stürmer und Dränger* exhibit a new kind of self-consciousness in the 1770s. Goethe later explains it when he says that the old, innocent, almost somnambulatory poetry of his youth is no longer possible: "Daily criticisms in fifty different places, and gossip caused by them, prevent the appearance of any sound production," says Goethe finally. "He who does not keep aloof from all this, and isolate himself by main force, is lost." Wordsworth, Arnold, and Emerson bewail the new self-consciousness and the introversion needed to stay in touch with *some* self, or to know anything about anyone and write effectively. Isolation preserves individuality but separates one from most of one's material in society. Hence we have anxious Victorian poems about isolation and the double-self, or dramatic monologues in which the poet can hardly be dissected away from the mask; and then Edwardian and Georgian works by Yeats, Joyce, Eliot, and Pound in which the maker is in effect the mask. The biographer can only estimate and penetrate the mask by accepting the subject on the subject's terms, and this, I think, is why humility was so useful to Ellmann the academic intellectual and why he could appear to be mildly confused. His humility was natural; it led him through subjectivity and devotion to a full, confident understanding of two self-conscious writers. He had learned to be passive, hesitant, receptive, or in two or three minds about the subject at hand; but his performance in the two masterly biographies of Joyce and Wilde is cunning and surprisingly confident.

WORKING WITH JANE AUSTEN

Chapter Seven

RICHARDSON'S INFLUENCE

THE ANXIETY OF INFLUENCE

OF ALL matters that have troubled the writing of literary biography "influence" is the most vexing. It is an exceedingly boring subject, deeply a controversial one, and in some ways the most tantalizing of matters. We recall Ph.D. theses, neatly footnoted articles in journals, or now and then books—printed in English at Paris or Poznan because so many *other* "influence studies" were cramming our own presses—with slightly dreary, predictable titles such as "Smollett's Uses for Dickens," "Wordsworth's Influence on Keats," "Reminiscent Victorian Echoes in *The Waste Land*," "The Literary Sources of Donne's Cacophony," and the like. These studies are tidy, useful, and unsatisfactory. They may after all be helpful in ticking off allusions to Smollett in *Bleak House* or in untangling the fabric of *Finnegans Wake* (the bravura style of which suggests that influence is Joyce's subject); but they look inadequate, too, because "influence" seems more important than these studies usually acknowledge. It is part of a subtle, complex, poorly understood process by which any new work of value comes into being; it belongs surely to the heart of darkness, to unknowns of creativity. Mr. Harold Bloom of Yale at least advertises the problem of influence; I find his criticism rather blunt and arbitrary but he ably shows that his subject is an interior matter, and that critics ought to feel anxious about influence as they look into it. In the case of Richardson's influence on Jane Austen we might try to be flexible and tentative at any rate, because the subject involves jokes and dolphinlike maneuvers, and also discovery, memory, satire, rejection, and the formation of a comic talent comparable to Shakespeare's in quality. Let us attempt a few notes on Jane Austen's responses to Richardson and hope, as we have reason to do, that critics in future will approach this topic with new fascination.

THE TAPESTRY OF ALLUSIONS IN
MANSFIELD PARK

Before we glance at her copy of *Sir Charles Grandison* and think of her early life at Steventon's rectory, let us take up a work of Jane Austen's mature art. In her mid-thirties at Chawton she wrote *Mansfield Park*. Her sister Cassandra (who contrary to what is sometimes said wrote *both* of the surviving notes now at the Pierpont Morgan Library on the composition dates of Jane Austen's novels) tells us that this novel was started around February 1811 and finished soon after June 1813. By then she was using Richardson's novels in a mellowed assimilated way, echoing them and weaving into a text her allusions to Shakespeare, Gray, Crabbe, Mme. Cottin, Mme. de Genlis, Hannah More, and others as well. She was a bookish, playful writer (always). Readers of *Mansfield Park* are turned into an elite; they may laugh at or miss the affectionate joke she plays on George Crabbe by using one of his heroine's names, Fanny Price, from *The*

Parish Register and putting Crabbe's *Tales* among her own Fanny's books, or the less kind joke she plays on Mme. Cottin by echoing incidents in *Amélie Mansfield* because of its naive portrayal of sexual relations and its title. Here and earlier Jane Austen is indebted clearly to Richardson's sexual realism. One of her artistic strengths is in creating the tense, amusing, provocative sexual atmosphere of normal social life, from the behavior and talk of Isabella in *Northanger Abbey* or dialogue duels of Darcy and Elizabeth in *Pride and Prejudice*, to the aggressive flirtation of Louisa in *Persuasion* (among many examples). Richardson's sex-saturated novels contributed to her mastery of social sex, parlor sex, or the sexual high jinks we see in the Sotherton episode or in the young Bertrams' and Crawfords' rehearsals of Mrs. Inchbald's *Lovers' Vows* while Sir Thomas Bertram is overseas at Antigua. *Mansfield Park* reaches far back into details of family history known to the Austens; the real James Langford Nibbs—of whose Antigua plantation George Austen was once principal trustee—had taken his own son to the Haddon or Weekes plantation at Antigua to detach him from "undesirable connections" (and later disinherited his son). Sir Thomas Bertram takes *his* spendthrift son to Antigua, but Tom returns home alone. One thinks of an evening at her brother's Godmersham Park in Kent when for Jane Austen the dreary, stupid alternatives had been games with the second Earl of Mansfield's grandsons or Lord Yates's ball; in the novel, while the father and moral guide of the Bertrams is away, a fatuous, crass Hon. John Yates proposes *Lovers' Vows* for amateur dramatics. Kotzebue's politically liberal play was well known in England from Mrs. Inchbald's moralized translation of 1798, which was attacked in the *Anti-Jacobin* and defended in *The Lady's Magazine*; it had reached twelve editions in a year and had six productions at Bath while the Austens lived there; and after seeing Major-General Tilson, later Chowne, a brother of Henry Austen's banking partner, in his early life act the play's young hero Frederick the soldier, Jane Austen was ready to laugh at him again when she met him in March 1814. It is seldom noticed that she responds to Elizabeth Inchbald's "Remarks" (printed with the play in 1808 but missing in the modern edition of *Mansfield Park* which reprints Mrs. Inchbald's play) to the effect that *Lovers' Vows* strikes morally at the crime of sexual seduction and that the "stage," in modern England, may be morally more effective than "the pulpit." "And surely," Mrs. Inchbald had argued, "as the pulpit has not had eloquence to eradicate the crime of seduction, the stage may be allowed an humble endeavour to prevent its most fatal effects." Jane Austen does seem to support *one* idea of Mrs. Inchbald's, the notion of a woman's autonomy in love or of her right to love before the gentleman's love is declared (as Amelia boldly loves, in Kotzebue's play, before Anhalt returns her love), but the author already had twitted Richardson for *his* outmoded views on that very topic in no. 97 of *The Rambler* in chapter 3 of her *Northanger Abbey* (finished in 1803 as *Susan*). Richardson is twitted again in *Mansfield Park*; Fanny Price is made to love Edmund Bertram while Edmund is infatuated with Mary Crawford, and Fanny's jealousy of Mary is endearing. But as for Mrs. Inchbald's claim that stage plays eradicate seduction while the Church dithers, Jane Austen treats it as a fatuous joke. Far from striking at seduction, *Lovers' Vows* is shown to assist it. An evangelical Fanny Price who honors "memory" and religious England is a far more potent force for good at Mansfield in the intensity of her feeling than are those shallow, ill-raised, stage-loving, weak-feeling Londoners Henry and Mary Crawford. Fanny's *feelings*—and the representation of them—are at the heart of Jane Austen's art in this novel; but let us for a moment reflect first on what the use of Shakespeare indicates about her literary allusions in *Mansfield Park* and also—briefly—on the matter of the novel's theme. It is well to note that as a girl when reading and re-reading *Sir Charles Grandison* Jane Austen had had strong political opinions, as her nephew James Edward says, and an equally strong and ardent interest in history—as we see in her partly ironic and merry, partly touchingly thoughtful *jeu d'esprit* "History of England," in which she castigates King Henry VIII. Fanny Price's portrait seems to draw in part on Jane Austen's experience of her own somewhat romantic and immature Tory ardor for Mary Queen of Scots and an older England. She had begun in childhood (as again we know from her early *jeux d'esprit* joke stories) to read and admire Shakespeare. Indeed, Shakespeare enters her novel. In Sotherton's chapel Fanny has evoked an England before the dissolution of the monasteries, and later King Henry VIII's namesake Henry very eloquently recites from Shakespeare's *Henry VIII* and brings the themes of Tudors, Georgians, and modern culture into view. Two plays in *Mansfield Park* catch the reader's conscience, and it is important that Henry Crawford and Edmund Bertram (a clergyman-elect) agree on the cultural importance of Shakespeare. "I once saw Henry the 8th acted," says Henry approvingly, and Edmund agrees that "we all talk Shakespeare, use his similes, and describe with his descriptions"—the point being that Shakespeare is at least a pervading unconscious influence in the nation and that Henry's eloquence and Shakespeare's graces are needed at Mansfield Park.

What is this novel's central theme? Sometimes we have imagined it was meant to be "ordination," because our modern edition of *Jane Austen's Letters* misprints one of the author's remarks this way: "Now I will try to write of something else, & it shall be a complete change of subject—ordination—I am glad to find your enquiries have ended so well." But Jane Austen's holograph survives to show that our standard edition of her *Letters* adds a gratuitous "&" and changes her capitals and punctuation to pervert her meaning. What she wrote to her sister on January 29, 1813 (two years after starting *Mansfield Park* and just after writing three hundred words about *Pride and Prejudice*) was in fact this: "Now I will try to write of something else;—it shall be a complete change of subject—Ordination. I am glad to find your enquiries have ended so well." (She only meant to thank her sister Cassandra for asking about ordination while at their brother James's rectory.) If a real theme of *Mansfield Park* is the training and discipline of the feelings, and if moral training must precede training in eloquence and culture, still the culture of Shakespeare, in this profound and subtle novel, is shown to be needful at the park. But just in pointing to an unconscious influence of culture, Jane Austen calls attention to her tapestry of allusions in her story. As "we all" use Shakespeare's similes and "describe with his descriptions," so we ought to feel another pervading presence, Richardson's, within *this* modern novel; thus the scenes with Fanny at Portsmouth, for one example, evoke *Clarissa*. Fanny is seen to be as spiritually and psychologically isolated as a tragic heroine was. She is under stress, tempted and tested. The adultery of Maria and Henry is reported to Fanny by letter, and Fanny's anguish is reminiscent of Clarissa's—with the difference that it is assimilated in comedy and presented with a gentle, operative irony with which Fanny Price is always brought before us. The gauche Fanny on hearing of adultery wishes "instant annihilation" for Maria Bertram's whole family. (On that standard many of Jane Austen's friends, including the gentleman she rode with at Bath and her own relative Miss Twisleton, would ideally have annihilated their families without delay, and it is difficult to see why even some careful readers miss the irony in Fanny's portrayal. Jane Austen's effects in any novel would collapse if the narrator colluded with a heroine.) In showing the development of Fanny's intense, naive, but right-minded feelings, too, Jane Austen has relied on her predecessor. Richardson's prose had given her examples of direct imitations of feeling, or of the use of language to show accurately what is felt rather than what is premeditated. What Richardson had defied was the cold distance in romances and chronicles; he had moved far beyond Defoe in finding a novel's subject to be the heart's experience and in showing how letters in narrative may duplicate it. This is partly why Jane Austen's apprenticeship was a long one and why she gave up the epistolary form of her early novels with apparent reluctance. Richardson seemed to her not at all sentimental, but realistic in showing that what goes through the mind is chiefly emotive and not so cold, privileged, and settled as retrospective narrative tended to suggest. His merits, for her, were akin to those of the adequate biographer in Dr. Johnson's view. Retrospective accounts of a life may avoid telling trivial lies about dates, places, or outward events, but may still tell gigantic, continual lies unless the biographer somehow conveys an accurate suggestion of the emotional experience of the subject. When Johnson says that most accounts of persons are barren and useless, he implies that biographical detail *ought* to expose the uniqueness of the heart. Fanny in *Mansfield Park* exists after Boswell's *Johnson* had begun to press past the aridity of conventional biography, and indeed Fanny admires poetry and biography—her prescribed readings for her sister Susan at Portsmouth. Richardson, in this respect, had anticipated Boswell; he had given a true history of a servant girl's feelings in *Pamela* or a veritable biography of a servant who might find herself in Pamela's dilemma. Jane Austen was concerned with the truth of reality, and in any individual's history, in her view, the truth must include Richardson's fidelity to the feelings and not fall behind Richardson in suggesting their immediacy.

AN APPRENTICESHIP WITH *SIR CHARLES GRANDISON*

Steventon rectory has now vanished. (Even its stolen pump has been replaced today by another.) But we have one lovely, tangible, frayed, and real survivor of the chocolate-figured carpet room under the white-washed ceiling where she did much of her early reading in that Jane Austen's own set of *Sir Charles Grandison* survives; a private owner at Oxford has it. The edition is dated 1754 (for 1753–54), bound in half calf with gilt spines, and has a bookplate that may be that of Henry the first Marquess Conyngham (1766–1832). The name "Jane Austen" appears on each of its seven title pages in two different styles, neither of which may really be in her autograph. I cannot say how she came by her set of *Grandison*, though she may have received the novel as a gift or bequest from her namesake Jane Austen at Sevenoaks (wife of her great-uncle Francis Austen). She read it repeatedly in early life. A nephew said she knew this novel perfectly down to the Cedar Parlour kiss, and her brother Henry singled out Richardson's novel in his "Biographical Notice" of 1817 in his edition of *Northanger Abbey* and *Persuasion*: "Richardson's power of creating and preserving the consistency of his characters, as particularly exemplified in 'Sir Charles Grandison,' gratified the natural discrimination of her mind," he says, "whilst her taste secured her from errors of his prolix style and tedious narrative." A number of Austen family holograph letters have come to light as well as Fanny Lefroy's "M.S. Family History" (once thought to be lost), so that we know far more about her Oxford brothers James and Henry today than at any time earlier in the twentieth century. They strove for wit in their Oxford stories; they were bookish, though James will have nothing to do with Mme. de Sévigné, and he denounces novels in his poems; and Henry is light-minded, resilient, and such an admirer of the stage that his statement that *Grandison* is "tedious" surely reflects his own view, not his sister's. Certainly Jane Austen tried to please and impress her Oxford brothers, and her liking for the weakest of Richardson's novels suggests she felt it had strong merits to make up for its length. With her niece Anna she later wrote a play for children called *Sir Charles Grandison or The Happy Man*. She alluded to Richardson's *Grandison* in "Jack and Alice" at about twelve and in "Evelyn," written at sixteen, and referred to James Selby in 1804 and twice to Harriet Byron in 1813 when she was thirty-seven. If she had been struck by the "consistency" of Richardson's portrayals, she was also impressed at an early age by *Grandison's* themes and heroine.

Its heroine, Harriet Byron, is provincial but also intelligent and alert, articulate and discerning. She has much in common with the young Jane Austen. Fascinatingly, *both* received an Oxford training. New biographical evidence shows how good Jane Austen's was. Having been trained with a little group of girls at Mrs. Cawley's at Oxford, Jane had been sent with Cassandra to Abbey School at the Forbury in Reading—the sister academy of Dr. Valpy's Grammar School (just across the green Forbury) which had a triennial "visitor" from St. John's College and strong connections with Oxford. Jane Austen had come home to have her reading supervised by a St. John's man (her eldest brother, James), to listen to her father (a tutor as well as a St. John's College–trained clergyman), and to study the moral and satirical stories in *The Loiterer* (edited and written by her brothers James and Henry and other St. John's College men). Appropriately and compellingly, she found that Richardson's novel implicitly pits female Oxford against male Oxford. Harriet Byron of Northamptonshire (the later locale of *Mansfield Park*) has had her mind formed between the ages of seven and fourteen by Grandfather Shirley, who was a scholar of "Christ's, in our University" as Mr. Walden points out. Mr. Walden is an Oxford man (though Richardson makes a mistake in assigning him to a Cambridge college). Having read Milton and Pope and other English classics, Harriet challenges him to a Swiftian debate on Ancients and Moderns when she comes to London and finally tells him, "Every scholar, I presume, is not, necessarily, a man of sense." Her feminism is intellectually resilient and resourceful, and she soon takes on challenges beyond those that Oxford (or Cambridge) can give.

Already in this we discover something about the nature of influence. Far more than in *Pamela* or *Clarissa* there is in *Sir Charles Grandison* a relaxed, natural, realistic, and funny everyday sense of matters as they normally are. No observant girl in a quiet country rectory in Hampshire's chalk hills in the 1780s will for long find herself in Pamela or Clarissa, but she may in Harriet Byron because that heroine's perils and challenges are seldom exceptional. A deep influence depends on identification, and for Jane Austen this rested on likelihood since as she raced through the *Lady's Magazine* and popular novels she was quick to laugh at and get over what was absurd or extreme. She had to meet the standards of Oxford brothers who were assured in their tastes and who wrote under the motto "Speak of Us as We Are" in their own stories. And her brothers would hardly have denied Richardson was a plausible and popular entertainer. An advertisement in the Tory *Hampshire Chronicle* (which circulated at Steventon and once listed Henry Austen's name) gives us an idea of the publisher Snagg's most popular novels for offer in 1776, for example. He includes all three of Richardson's titles, though he seems to have brought them out in condensed versions as "little Books of Entertainment" at "6d. each bound, adorned with three Copper-plates":

1. The comical Adventures of Roderic Random
2. The surprising Adventures of David Simple
3. The pleasing History of Amelia
4. The entertaining History of Joseph Andrews, Friend of Mr. Abraham Adams
5. The Adventures of Peregrine Pickle
6. The Adventures of Gil Blas, Part 1 and 2
7. The entertaining History of the Female Quixote
8. The entertaining History of Pamela
9. The remarkable History of the Fortunate Country Maid
10. The History of Sir Charles Grandison
11. The History of Clarissa Harlow
12. The Adventures of Tom Jones

Possibly a publisher in the 1770s does not need to prefix "comical," "surprising," "pleasing," or "entertaining" when he touts no. 10, "The History of Sir Charles Grandison," or no. 11; and a decade later the tenth novel in Mr. Snagg's list seems to have come more especially into fashion because it suits the new elegance, refinement, prosperity, and the more restrained English manners of the 1780s. But an influence, too, must have a cutting edge, and make some bold advance upon what we are and toward what we would like to be; there must be an acceptable projection of ourselves in what will hold us day after day. What is Grandison's cutting edge for Jane Austen? Harriet Byron's interest is especially in the language of social encounter: she sees that "flattery is the vice of men" and also that "they seek to raise us in order to lower us," or that men are "random-shooters," and that the world in what it favors "is apt to *over*-rate, as much as it will *under*-rate where it disfavours." Men and women together typically collude to distort language. Visiting in London, Harriet perceives that our social education properly ought to focus on our learning to penetrate the screen of talk so that we may perceive character through that screen. She is at war with men in her own exactness and care with language: "O take care, take care, Miss Byron, that you express yourself so cautiously, as if to give no advantage to a poor dog," Mr. Greville tells her. But if her intelligence offends men, she will not yield to the fashion that causes an intelligent young woman to demean herself, to sink to the level of male stupidity. Hence she has an "edge" in two senses: she will penetrate men's talk, but not compromise herself by flattering anyone or blunting her *own* intelligence. "What can a woman do, who is addressed by a man of talents inferior to her own?" Harriet writes to Lucy Selby.

> Must she throw away her talents? Must she hide her light under a bushel, purely to do credit to the man? She cannot pick and choose as men can. . . . If the taste of the age, among the Men, is not Dress, Equipage, and Foppery? Is the cultivation of the mind any part of their study? The men, in short, are sunk, my dear; and the Women but barely swim.

It is nearly incidental that Jane Austen's theme later in *Northanger Abbey* is to be derived from Harriet Byron's perception that our education consists in learning to interpret "character" behind talk—or that Catherine Morland at Bath and at the Tilney's abbey is to learn about language and character (a matter in which she is helped by Henry

Tilney). What impressed Jane Austen at Steventon surely is that *Grandison* credits the value of a woman's perceptive intelligence by putting it in a story of nearly a million words. The novel's chief fault, its feeble outward action, is in one sense its unique strength, for the main "action" is an exposure of persons. Sir Hargrave Pollexfen, whose abduction of Harriet is a surprisingly small incident in the novel's whole structure, is exposed as weak, puerile, self-doubting, and timorous, a pathetic man in need of consolation and understanding. Sir Charles Grandison is exposed as a perfect gentleman in long letters devoted to his extrication from his commitment to Lady Clementina of Italy. "The discretion of a person is most seen in minuteness," writes Richardson, and we may wish it were not so minute, but Sir Charles proves his discretion. He shows that "he never perverts the meaning of words," as Harriet says of him in tribute. The exposure of character at great length is demanded by Harriet Byron herself, and since the structure of Richardson's novel supports the image of Harriet's character seeking, Jane Austen as a young student of character could find every detail fun, instructive, and significant. No novel of hers later is free from allusions and parallels to this one. In *Sense and Sensibility* the Steele sisters, for example, echo the Selby sisters, and are made to have a friend named Richardson.

But the uses she made of *Grandison*—and, too, of *Pamela* and *Clarissa* and of Richardson's extracts from sentiments in his novels with its suggestive index—are only outward signs of an influence that must lie deeper than any manifestation. When we see Richardson very plainly in her work (as in *Northanger Abbey*'s third chapter with its footnote to his *Rambler* essay, or in the sixth, where *Sir Charles Grandison* funnily enters the dialogue), the influence itself is already out of sight. It was in her early reading at Steventon that his works had brought a pause in her light, desultory reading and gutting of popular novels and magazine stories. His *Grandison* had seemed a rich oasis in which she could move; he had proved that a novel can accommodate female intelligence, and that no other topic is potentially more interesting, dramatic, or ripe for artistic working. He confirmed that she need not belittle herself and that she would have the ample companionship of one great portrayer of intelligence and feeling in whatever she chose to write then or in future. He became important enough to be the central thread in her tapestry of allusions, despite what she quickly felt to be his quaintness. Richardson has little to say of the economic constraints upon women and even in *Grandison* very bluntly shows that he shares most of the male views of his time concerning female comportment and appearance. His Harriet Byron believes that women ought to be eager to please, not very studious, and "pretty" despite the facial pits of smallpox. Jane Austen thoroughly rejected Richardson and, paradoxically, she was able to keep him in her heart and to assimilate him, borrow from him, use him allusively, and play over his novels. That which has us in thrall can never be of much use if we wish to make anything new. The really important point about Jane Austen's joke plays and joke stories is that they free the young artist. She raised novel after novel, *Lady's Magazine* stories, the precepts of her Oxford brothers, their stories in the *Loiterer*, Richardson's novels, popular stage plays, and much else jokingly up into the air in her early *jeux d'esprit* so as to view them from all sides—to bring them into her world as things to be got over—and then affectionately was able to return to those works and ideas that had no necessary power over her. It is an extraordinary tribute to Samuel Richardson that she (as the freest of artists) was to return to him so often, particularly to *Sir Charles Grandison*, in the making of every novel she wrote.

Chapter Eight

STERNE AND JANE AUSTEN'S TALENT

T O OBSERVE how Sterne affected Jane Austen is really to see *Tristram Shandy* and *A Sentimental Journey* in fresh light. How shall we do this? To list "echoes" of Sterne—or apparent ones—in her own novels would be a barren exercise, as I fear that it is to list Sternean borrowings in Dickens or Joyce. Rather, let us try to keep in view just what the Austen biographers tells us least about, the concatenation of circumstances and forces that caused Jane Austen's talent to develop in artistically formative years of her life, say from 1789 to 1813, or from the years of James and Henry Austen's St. John's College weekly, *The Loiterer*, and her own "Love and Freindship" when she was thirteen and fourteen, to the year in which *Mansfield Park* was finished and her first three novels were either in print or virtually complete in manuscript, when she was thirty-seven. In these two dozen years, Sterne's novels helped Jane Austen in three ways: as Whiggish foils for her Toryism; as heuristic texts to further her narrative experiments; and as exempla or models of wit, jokes, the comedy of the commonplace, and an attitude to language. Ezra Pound noticed the last point when he claimed that the link between Sterne, Crabbe, and Jane Austen was a shared "value" of "writing words that conform precisely with fact, of free speech without evasions and circumlocutions," and added that they all used direct, fact-oriented styles to record "states of consciousness that their verse-writing contemporaries scamp," and did so with a delicacy we sense now and then in Prévost or Constant.

But there is usually a strong attitude behind a brave new view of prose style. In 1789 or 1790, in between playing a Dibdin air and working on the satin stitch, the younger daughter of a Tory rector in Hampshire surely did not say to herself, "I will write like that nice Mr. Yorick." The Whiggishness of Mr. Yorick made him seem *not nice at all*; "Jane, when a girl, had strong political opinions," as her nephew wrote in his *Memoir*, and her own pro-Stuart, pro-Catholic annotations in Goldsmith's *History of England*, her friendships with Mrs. Lefroy and Mrs. Knight (who admired Mary Queen of Scots), her own juvenile "History of England" (1791) and loving admiration of her father and her brothers James and Henry, all ardent Tories, show us, besides other evidence, that Jane Austen in her youth detested Whiggery. Three early events in her life deepened her Toryism. First, her brothers James and Henry launched in 1789 at St. John's College their weekly periodical, *The Loiterer*, partly to strike at the Whigs of Oxford who had supported the American Revolution and the Whigs of London who were trying to circumscribe the powers of the Austens' beloved King George III. Second, as if to humiliate the Austens themselves, oratorical Whigs such as Sheridan and Burke put the Austens' friend and well-wisher and patron, Warren Hastings, on trial for "high crimes and misdemeanours" and slandered him for seven years (1788–95) before he was cleared of charges fixed to his tenure as Governor-General of Bengal. Third, the Revolution of 1789, about which many Whigs had been soft (or, as we would say in the days of Mrs. Thatcher, "wet"), led to *La Terreur*, which by 1794 had claimed Jane Austen's cousin Eliza's husband, the Comte de Feuillide, as one of its victims. Whiggery, in one form or another, struck savagely at the Austens of Steventon. So it is not surprising that Jane Austen struck back at that Whig, Mr. Yorick of A *Sentimental Journey*, in a key scene in her most profound novel at the end of our period under review. She opposed Laurence Sterne in a very interesting way.

One of her main points in *Mansfield Park* is that Sir Thomas Bertram and his lady have brought up their children so badly that the estate is undermined, and its moral decay is to be seen in Maria Bertram's adultery. What but Mr. Yorick has worked a way into Maria's vain, lightsome consciousness? Maria is engaged to Mr. Rushworth. On the famous visit to Sotherton, Maria and her future seducer Henry Crawford meet at a locked gate in the park. Beyond the gate, their sexual play may begin. "The sun shines and the park looks very cheerful," says Maria to her willing seducer. "But unluckily that iron gate, that ha-ha, give me a feeling of restraint and hardship. I cannot get out, as the starling said."

" 'I can't get out—I can't get out,' said the starling," Sterne's Yorick had reported in *A Sentimental Journey* after fearing that as a passportless man in wartime France he may be locked up in the Bastille:—"And as for the Bastile! the terror is in the word." Indeed, terror *was* in the word. *A Sentimental Journey* was published in 1768. Less than three decades later, "terror" had become a political word associated for the first time with ultimate solutions sought by sane men, and Jane Austen's cousin Eliza lost her husband to the guillotine of *La Terreur* in Paris. Yorick's starling led Yorick to a paean on unbridled "Liberty", and so Jane Austen has Maria Bertram's reckless "I cannot get out, as the starling said" point to the adultery that destroys Maria as a person. Jane Austen damns Sterne even further. Maria is oppressed by a "feeling of restraint and hardship" that suggests necessary ingredients in education that Yorick, a "Liberty"-monger, forgets; and so at the end of *Mansfield Park* Sir Thomas Bertram is redeemed only when he, as father and educator, belatedly knows the values "of early hardship and discipline." Since Maria was overindulged, she is by then ruined and lost.

Yet Jane Austen's political and moral objections to Sterne did not keep her from knowing and liking his work and using him. She thought against her prejudices, which is to think two or three ways about a matter, and let herself be "taken in" by the companionable humor, trivial and time-squandering details, and unrushed reports of moment-by-moment household circumstances in the daily and believable life of Shandy Hall. There is good evidence that she knew *Tristram Shandy* as minutely as the seven volumes of Richardson's *Sir Charles Grandison*, and expected her sister Cassandra to know *Shandy* just as well. "James is the delight of our lives," she writes to Cassandra about a servant at Lyme, on September 14, 1804, "he is quite an uncle Toby's annuity to us.—My Mother's shoes were never so well blacked before, & our plate never looked so clean." That allusion supposes that her sister will recall Uncle Toby's words in the twenty-second chapter of the third volume and the ensuing dialogue:

> —Have I not a hundred and twenty pounds a year, besides my half-pay? cried my uncle *Toby.*—What is that, replied my father, hastily,—to ten pounds for a pair of jack-boots?—twelve guineas for your *pontoons* . . .—these military operations of yours are above your strength . . .—dear *Toby*, they will in the end quite ruin your fortune, and make a beggar of you.—What signifies it if they do, brother, replied my uncle *Toby*, so long as we know 'tis for the good of the nation.

By 1804, Jane Austen's sailor brothers Frank and Charles risked their lives "for the good of the nation"; her brothers James and Henry had risked their reputations at Oxford and her cousin Eliza's godfather Hastings had risked his neck "for the good of the nation." Jane Austen, who read works on the British Empire and debated imperial policy with her brothers, wrote deliberately for the Tory good of the nation. (Despite what we are often told, she was politically well informed, though her novels, in showing the *home* effects of wartime on young women of the gentry class, are more than Tory propaganda.) Why, then, had she absorbed Sterne?

Sterne's *Tristram Shandy* had seemed to her a clearing operation, as well as a storehouse of jokes. It called her attention to each uncritically accepted device of fiction. We have no chapters in our real lives and so instead of mutely accepting the device of chapters, Tristram highlights it. Even Parson Yorick rides "to the very end of the chapter." Jane Austen, as a girl, highlights and plays with the "chapter" device, too, and gets us to laugh at it, as in "The Beautifull Cassandra" written when she was twelve or thirteen:

CHAPTER THE 6TH

Being returned to the same spot of the same Street she had
sate out from, the Coachman demanded his Pay.

CHAPTER THE 7TH

She searched her pockets over again & again; but every
search was unsuccessfull. No money could she find. The
man grew peremptory. She placed her bonnet on his head &
ran away.

CHAPTER THE 8TH

Thro' many a street she then proceeded & met in none the
least Adventure till on turning a Corner of Bloomsbury
Square, she met Maria.

CHAPTER THE 9TH

Cassandra started & Maria seemed surprised; they trembled,
blushed, turned pale & passed each other in mutual silence.

One by one Tristram's devices that call attention to the fictiveness of
fiction are aped. Jane offers a series of meaningless or ironic dedica-
tions in the Shandean vein. One sequence of her mad "Morsels" is
dedicated to a lady six weeks old, "trusting you will in time be older."
Patrons are solicited. "Madam," Jane Austen addresses an aloof, important deity who shared her amusements, her own sister.

> You are a Phoenix. Your taste is refined, your Sentiments are
> noble, & your Virtues innumerable. Your Person is lovely, your
> Figure, elegant, & your Form, magestic. Your Manners are pol-
> ished, your Conversation is rational & your appearance singular.
> If therefore the following Tale will afford one moment's amuse-
> ment to you, every wish will be gratified of
>
> Your most obedient
humble servant
THE AUTHOR

The merriment and flexible, witty tactics of Tristram become touch-
stones of the prose Jane Austen wants; she responds to Yorick, who has
"as much life and whim, and *gaité de coeur* about him, as the kind-

liest climate could have engendered and put together" and indeed she reads (at about the age of thirteen) in Sterne that Yorick carries no ballast, is unpracticed in the world, and knows "just about as well how to steer his course in it, as a romping, unsuspicious girl of thirteen". Almost all of Tristram's comments on his mother are condescending, and Jane Austen at least by the time of "Lesley Castle" (in its seventh letter, written at age sixteen) is a critic of male attitudes; and indeed *Shandy* is valuable to her for its critical, probing catalogue of novelistic devices. By mocking these devices as in *Love and Freindship*, Jane Austen freed herself from slavishly imitating the worst faults of novels. And yet when she began serious comedy of her own in "Catharine or The Bower," she failed.

She failed not so much because "Kitty" is inconsistent as because the author lacked a narrative voice. Here again Sterne was valuable to her because he had found a way of bridging between a cold text and its readers. The point of the "digressions" in *Tristram Shandy*—that word is Tristram's own—is that they interrupt narrative to bring "the reader" into the novel. (*Shandy* makes more of the reader than any other work of the century.) Politically the middle class, in a century of lending libraries, newspapers, journals, and bourgeois revolutions, cried out its importance, and *Shandy* is Whiggish in its digressions, which admit "the reader" into the text. The Shandean narrator is politically alert to his age. Jane Austen's narrator is the last element of her art that she developed. She avoided the problem in cold, uncertain works such as "Lady Susan" and perhaps in epistolary drafts called "Elinor and Marianne," "First Impressions," and "Susan" (all of which are missing). "Susan," later called "Catherine" and still later called *Northanger Abbey*, seems to have been her first lengthy work that reached a third-person narrative form; but we cannot assume that even this was not epistolary in early drafts. What we do know, as Henry Austen tells us, is that his sister's works were "gradual performances," many times revised. One aim of the revisions, certainly, was to achieve in her narrator's voice an intimacy, authority, and likeability close to that of Tristram and Yorick. In other words, she had to reach out to the reader, to bring the reader into her text, in effect, with the amiability of Sterne, and yet without any Whiggish overtones, since the comic Jane Austen wished to accompany her stories—

and in a measure to interpret them—with a winning and morally certain Tory authority in her narrative persona. In the slow development of this personal voice, she was saved from gravity and pomposity partly by Sterne; indeed, she erred on the side of facetiousness, as we see from the opening chapters of *Northanger Abbey*, which we think is the least revised of her three early novels, and in which the narrator is on less comfortable terms with us than the narrators of *Pride and Prejudice* or even *Sense and Sensibility*. We must not overrate Sterne's importance to her: for moral authority she had the examples—and foils—of her brothers' *Loiterer* stories from which she learned lessons. It is hard to imagine that she was indifferent to the *Loiterer* story (we do not know which St. John's College friend of James Austen's wrote it) about the sad Scottish soldier who fought against Washington and was seduced by a democratic ideology, only to return to Scotland and lament that he had forgotten the "pride" and "prejudice" of his nation's monarchical ideals; this story was recited at Steventon rectory not later than 1790. Standing behind James and Henry Austen's *Loiterer* were Addison, Steele, Dr. Johnson, and the rich tradition of the moral periodical essay, which Mary Lascelles correctly assumes to be a mainstay of Jane Austen's art in its formation. But, we recall, she attacks *The Spectator* in *Northanger Abbey*; in that novel it is very clear she carries out a running debate with her most talented brother James, who in his occasional poetry clarifies his (very logical) Tory opposition to novels of all kinds. So, we may say, she worked out her moral positions with the help of her family. She worked out the tone of her narrative voice with the help of Sterne.

But what is the essence of this tone, and how did Sterne's "digressions" help the reviser of "First Impressions" (composed between October 1796 and August 1797) and of "Susan" (written in 1798–99 according to Cassandra Austen's note on the novel she describes as "North-hanger Abbey")? In *Tristram Shandy*, the "digressions" are as functional as they are daring. They give the author special access to the reader; they keep the reader from swallowing a narrative unreflectingly, and they bring variety to *Shandy*'s discourse. But, as they substitute for "story" and displace narrative, they in effect put Sterne out on a very thin high wire over the abyss of artistic failure. They *must* beguile and charm the reader first of all by means of a polished, very clear, seemingly casual, realistic style that has the warmth, wit, and authenticity of Tristram's speaking voice. In no other novels available to her—not in Fielding, not in Defoe and Swift, not even in the finest sections of Burney's third-person *Camilla* (published July 12, 1796, and read before she reached Rowling House that summer by its subscriber Jane Austen, who learned much from this story about a Hampshire clergyman's second daughter named Camilla Tyrold)—is there to be found a narrative voice so spontaneous, precise, and humanly authentic as the voices of Tristram in *Shandy* and Yorick in *Sentimental Journey*. "Digressions, incontestably, are the sunshine," boasts Tristram, "the life, the soul of reading." But most digressors are bores, and Sterne's expert and painstakingly filed digressions hold the reader only because the tone of the prose style is perfect. It is their style that offers the reviser of "First Impressions" her highest mark of style, and gives her an example of the casual, polished perfection of the speaking voice to match; and perhaps among British novelists only Jane Austen in her narrative voice, her most subtle and important achievement, can be ranked with Sterne. She did find models of concinnity and smart polish in Burney, as in this description of Mrs. Mittin, the former milliner, in *Camilla*:

> To be useful she would submit to any drudgery; to become agreeable, devoted herself to any flattery. To please was her incessant desire, and her rage for popularity included every rank and class of society.

But that is lame, compared to this in *Pride and Prejudice*:

> Her mind was less difficult to develope. She was a woman of mean understanding, little information, and uncertain temper. When she was discontented she fancied herself nervous. The business of her life was to get her daughters married; its solace was visiting and news.

We are not looking for *echoes* of Sterne here. Jane Austen's style is her own. What we say is that the authenticity of the rhythm, the casual perfection of the balances, and the unoppressive "speaking" wit in the second example are achieved by a woman who knew *Tristram Shandy* as intimately as her Lyme letter of 1804 shows she did. It is the artistic daring of the Whiggish digressor, in Sterne, that is of value to Jane Austen as she fashions an omniscient voice of Tory moral authority; she could use Fanny Burney because she had studied the casual, accurate felicity of Sterne's prose style in the digressions.

She found in the digressions other lessons, too, only a few of which she could have found in Fielding, Charlotte Lennox, Charlotte Smith, Clara Reeve, Mrs. Inchbald, Jane West, or other novelists or the *Lady's Magazine* (and other periodical) writers she studied. Tristram's digressions help to give life to his portraits of Walter Shandy, his wife, Uncle Toby, Trim, Mrs. Wadman and lesser figures. Tristram animates by changing perspective; he gives the touch of life by a withdrawal, a leaving of the created thing. We imagine, then, that what is sketched has its ongoing life; usually the digression has either a playful relevance to the character sketch that is dropped, or an allusion within it, a digression from the digression to remind us that an action in time waits for Tristram to get back to it. The slight awkwardness of some of the narrator intrusions in *Northanger Abbey* may owe to Jane Austen's underestimation of the complexity of Sterne's digressive tactics. Later, she uses narrative comment, and less often generalization on a theme, with a subtlety that is as effective as Sterne's technique of animating a set of characters by withdrawing his narrator from their presence. By changing her narrative mode, furthermore, Jane Austen appeals to the reader's judgment and feelings alike; she establishes her narrator's intense and sensible moral authority; and, when we have made every allowance for the difference between her own Toryism and Sterne's mild Whiggery, we see, as we should expect to see, beneath the political levels of meaning in their books, a world view that is only slightly dissimilar in Sterne and Austen. Sterne's deepest theme is death or evanescence; Jane Austen's deepest theme is happiness, with death of spirit as its adversary. Sterne would divert us *not* from the thought of final things or Christian teleology, but from gloom or morbidity by appealing comically to the feelings; he is a very unusual, unsaccharine sentimentalist. Jane Austen narrowly saves her Marianne from physical death and saves all of her heroines from a Maria Rushworth-like death of spirit by having them struggle to preserve their full capacity to feel. The test of a heroine's liveliness, life of spirit, is always in her real *sense* and *sensibility*, favorable words for the author as they involve perception, feeling, and intellect. Anne Elliot has "strong" sensibility and Henry Tilney "real" sensibility since they accurately perceive feelings in others; "excessive" or "false" sensibility as long as it lasts, as in Marianne Dashwood's case, prevents just that heightened perception of feeling.

Hence Jane Austen is, like Sterne, another realistic, unsaccharine sentimentalist to the extent that an attitude to *feeling* is at the center of her psychology of perception and her view of human relationships. She could respond deeply to Sterne, the wry, comic, innovating, rule-breaking sentimentalist. His serious delight in lexical games, riddles, wordplay, and word meanings appealed to her after she left off writing *jeux d'esprit* stories and began the hard task of forming her narrative voice. In *Emma,* and elsewhere, Sternean riddles and wordplay are her tools. He had rolled out a comic world for her. He used a subtle, flexible prose style to interpret it. And if not in *Mansfield Park,* at least in writing to her beloved sister, she did in effect forgive Sterne the artist for his Whiggish political folly.

Chapter Nine

REVOLUTION

N O ONE has closely linked Jane Austen's growth as a novelist with the War of American Independence, for after all we do not find Bunker Hill or Yorktown in her novels. But when we reflect that the war began in the year Jane Austen was born, and that memories of it affected the British climate of thought and opinion throughout her life, we may be surprised that we have so far neglected it.

Suppose we were to use good sources we have—about the Revolutionary War and about the Austens—to show how things really were for her family? I shall follow the war for a little before turning to the young Jane Austen herself.

Let us begin with a report of her birth. Her father, the Reverend George Austen, was at forty-four an Oxford-trained rural clergyman of strong but calm Tory views. He believed in the royal prerogative and in the necessity of the Church's prominent role in the national polity. His wife, the former Cassandra Leigh, was a witty and practical woman with aristocratic forebears. Having given birth to two children with literary abilities, James and Henry, and four others, she had expected her seventh child in November 1775—but, as her husband put it, the Austens had become bad reckoners in their "old age." The birth was a month late.

"Last night the time came," wrote Mr. Austen to his half-brother's wife, Mrs. Walter, in Kent on December 17, 1775. "We have now another girl, a present plaything for her sister Cassy and a future companion. She is to be Jenny." And he adds in this report to Mrs. Walter from his own Steventon rectory in Hampshire, "Have you had any fresh news from Jamaica?" Why Jamaica? At least one reason (not the only reason) for Mr. Austen's interest in the West Indies in 1775 is clear: Mr. Austen, as "principal trustee" of a valuable plantation in Antigua, was unlikely to take that charge lightly, partly because the plantation was owned by a man connected with his own Oxford college of St. John's, James Langford Nibbs, whose picture on the rectory wall Jane Austen later called "Mr. Nibbs." London and provincial newspapers told enough to show that *all* British West Indian interests were endangered by December 1775. The immediate cause of danger lay far to the north, for despite the obvious loyalty of most of the colonists and the presence of some thirty-four of the King's batallions in North America, insurrections had begun this year near Boston. We have no reason to think that Mr. Austen knew of General Sir William Howe's opinion, but General Howe—a Whig who was likely to be believed in Parliament—thought that the insurgency could be put down: "The insurgents are very few, in comparison to the whole of the people," he wrote very reasonably in 1775. Though it is not remarked on in newspapers I have seen, Tory loyalty was strong in places along the Atlantic seaboard with the smallest proportion of British settlers, or in the Middle and Southern colonies, but in English-settled Massachusetts civil government had ended when General Gage combined the offices of governor of the colony and commander-in-chief of North American troops. His infantry was rebuffed at Lexington and Concord in April, but on June 17, General Howe's 63rd Foot and 17th Light Dragoons, suffering a little more than a thousand casualties, had attacked in column, not in line, at "Bunker's Hill," won the hill, and bayoneted its last thirty defenders. The bayonet was effective because of the slowness of musketry fire, and rebels were known to fear disciplined troops attacking in column.

But two problems, at least, remained for London, and both seem relevant to the Austens.

First, in 1775, before and after hostilities began, the rebels made a limited demand: they did not ask for independence but rather for the American colonies to be granted the rights of a separate, self-governing empire under the King and with full allegiance to him. This was unacceptable for good reasons in London, where the prevailing attitude to the crisis was that Parliament should have unlimited control over the colonies, that coercion was justified to maintain rule, and that it was just to levy on the colonies taxes that were needed to defend the Empire. Popular support in Britain for the King's policies was strong, but by raising questions about taxation and self-government, the rebels had found some support among Parliamentary Whigs. The disagreement seems to have been primarily British: the rebels' leaders tended to be either English born or of British stock, or men who actually read or knew of John Locke. And the peculiarly fraternal nature of the war may help to explain why Jane Austen's brothers, James and Henry, later published a comment on the American war in their Oxford journal, *The Loiterer*, but did not bother to comment in that journal on the French Revolution. Jane Austen later discussed imperial foreign policy toward America with her brother Henry after informing herself on war, strategy, and policy by reading such a work (on the war with France) as Captain Pasley's *Essay on the Military Policy and Institutions of the British Empire* (1810). Jane Austen's novels avoid war not because she was ignorant or provincial, of course, but because the intention in her comedies was to show what life was like from the female viewpoint at home, or in domestic situations, during a long war with France. In her earliest years, the American war raised questions with which her Tory family was concerned; and Whigs, at least, in the 1770s did not always feel that thirty-four batallions were the proper response to a debate concerning ideas of government. If some of Parliament sympathized with the Americans, it might be that the rebels would not quickly lose heart and fade away.

A second and practical problem of the war touched on Mr. Austen's trusteeship: it was that the need for troops and supplies in the north left West Indian islands more than ever exposed to the French, and indeed King George III and every European maritime power in the late 1770s viewed the seat of the American war as the West Indies. Annually these richly endowed islands sent thousands of tons of cotton, tobacco, some one hundred thousand hogsheads of sugar, and eleven thousand puncheons of rum to England, where the imports were valued (in 1776) at 4.5 million pounds, compared with East India imports of 1.5 million pounds. E. J. Hobsbawm in *Industry and Empire* points to the key importance of this cotton for Lancashire. The subtropical products far better suited the British economy than products from North American farms and fisheries, which were not needed and often banned from England. But rich Jamaica had only four hundred and forty troops to defend itself in 1775, and the scattered Leeward Islands barely more than six hundred, against some six thousand French troops who were believed to be in the Caribbean.

Our details may suggest that Mr. Austen, a responsible, educated man who was "principal trustee" of a West Indian plantation and who asked for news of Jamaica, had some *cause* to be interested in the American war. Even had he been a careless trustee, or hid in his study as Mr. Bennet in *Pride and Prejudice* often does or lived in his very damp cellar, he was obliged by law to observe a fast for the King's North American troops. Furthermore the only local Tory newspaper to circulate at Steventon and to mention the Austens' friends and neighbors (and later Henry Austen's own name), the *Hampshire Chronicle*, reported the war in regular issues as well as in specials or extras under the large banner EXTRAORDINARY.

If so much is true, then the "American war" was one household topic at the rectory as Jane Austen first learned to talk, to read, and to interpret adult opinions, or a part of her early formative experience. Her elder brothers' later response to the war further suggests that the Austen family was aware of America.

Winchester, where the *Hampshire Chronicle* was (and still is) printed, was close enough to the major naval harbor at Portsmouth to be alive with news; roads were improving in the 1770s in Hampshire more rapidly than anywhere else in the kingdom, and war news and war gossip depended on roads and ships. We need not imagine that the Austens or their neighbors read wholly accurate news, although the *Chronicle* reported (often within quotations) army and naval bulletins it received. It said that General Howe was doing well in New York, where "The behaviour of both officers and soldiers, British and Hessians, was highly to their honour. More determined courage and steadiness in troops have never been experienced" (October 14, 1776). Recent studies show that troop morale *was* high, centered on comradeship and the regimental colors; surrendering regiments later at Saratoga and Yorktown burned their regimental colors to prevent their capture. We read in the paper that circulated at Steventon of reports from Brooklyn and Westchester, from Admiral Lord Richard Howe off New York, and we learn that the rebel officer, Washington, had by report, lost "either one hand or an arm" and between "7 and 8,000 men" while some of his troops have an "infectious disease." Just before the King's fast and on Jane Austen's birthday the *Chronicle* reprints from a Philadelphia paper a piece by one "B. Franklin" referring to treason against "the united states of America" and refuses to comment: from a Tory viewpoint, despite the second Continental Congress, the King's colonies were neither states nor united, and "the united states" was mainly a rhetorical term even in Philadelphia. The *Chronicle* gives casualty figures for officers and men on both sides and then after a report that the King's 17th Infantry was attacked in a bitter frost, it falls silent on the war. This does not mean that war reports stopped circulating in Hampshire. Tories who heard of General John Burgoyne's early surrender at Saratoga might have reflected that if "Gentleman Johnny" had put too much faith in artillery, he was at least a witty playwright—and it is pleasant to note that both sides liked plays. In a difficult season at Valley Forge, as we know today, Washington's officers put on a production of Addison's tragedy *Cato*, a play that by coincidence King George III had acted in in his youth. Americans, however, were believed in England to be indelicate or tasteless, and no doubt they often were: Ethan Allen asked a British officer to surrender "in the name of the great Jehovah and the Continental Congress"—and that may amuse us in light of a later piece in James Austen's weekly journal, implying that Americans lacked taste; it was published when the Austens were acting in family theatricals themselves.

We know that the American Department at Whitehall often lost touch with field commanders or took three or four months to reach them. Dispatch ships were few, and winds came from the west, so that Whitehall's orders went out slowly and bad news came back quickly; but if the war was sometimes felt in London to be out of control, it was known in the provinces to be costly. Draining manpower and the treasury, it demanded the largest overseas-supply effort that England would undertake until the Second World War in 1944, and rising prices affected household economies. The strategical position became very grave. By 1782 four wars were being fought against England—by the Americans to gain independence, by France to increase her trade and share of power in Europe, by Spain to recover lost possessions, and the Netherlands to assert trading rights. The strain on the Royal Navy became unbearable as for months it could no longer guarantee the safety of British coasts. Liverpool harbor was raided with impunity, and J. A. Picton's *Memorials of Liverpool* (1875) reminds us of the plight of thousands in the harbor areas, facing either privation or imminent starvation because they had lost jobs in connection with the Atlantic trade. There is in James Austen's Tory defensiveness at Oxford, as later in his sister's Tory and moral severity in *Mansfield Park*, a suggestion that the Austens, in their maritime county, knew times when their political and social values were imperiled along with the nation's survival. At no time in the *next* war (the long war against revolutionary and Napoleonic France) did the navy leave England more exposed. In 1783 the kingdom had to submit to the Peace of Paris, and France it seems tasted revenge: "Pour la France," writes Dominique Dhombres recently, "c'est la revanche de la guerre de Sept Ans et du traité de Paris de 1763, qui consacrait la ruine de l'empire colonial français, en particulier du Canada."

But losers may learn, and two Tory lessons from the war appear to be traceable in Austen writings. The first seems to be the rather Burkean lesson that the navy had been poorly motivated and badly trained to meet their opponents; and Mr. Austen's son Francis or Frank, at naval school in the 1780s, was to take careful notes on American geography and was later to insist on high technical proficiency in the navy. His sister's veneration of the navy and strong belief in the values of early hardship, discipline, and training coincide with his views. Far from being unconcerned with public affairs, Jane Austen at least in writing *Mansfield Park* and *Persuasion* was influenced by Frank and Charles Austen's urgent concern for the well-being of the royal navy.

The second Tory lesson of the war would seem to be that inasmuch as Whigs had weakened the national resolve by sympathizing with American political ideals, those ideals must be countered. In 1789 at St. John's College, young James and Henry Austen launched their weekly, *The Loiterer*, which in sixty issues aimed to satirize many modes of Whiggish and other anti-Royalist behavior and opinions at Oxford, where some students had spoken for the American cause. The Austens and their Tory college friends began with mock diaries of dissolute Oxford men and went on to take in Whiggish country balls, manners, and dress. America was far from being their chief target. Henry Austen's ten pieces are funny enough, and James's twenty-seven so improved in manner that one sees why this journal became one school or training ground for their thirteen-year-old sister Jane Austen, who so far had amused her brothers and conceivably reduced family tensions at Steventon rectory by writing short joke stories and joke playlets. It is clear that some original pieces by the Austen children, and perhaps some by their friends, were recited by Mr. Austen or others at the rectory. James, who was ten years older than his amusing sister, is believed to have had a share in directing Jane Austen's reading, and even by 1789 she had been reading very widely, if only to find laughable exaggerations in *The Lady's Magazine* or in popular novels to burlesque in her jokes. Shy by nature and perhaps (as her brother Frank says) somewhat stiff and defensive with strangers, she was a slender, active, teasing girl in the family, devotedly subservient to her elder sister Cassandra and admired by her intelligent brothers for more than her slightly reddish cheeks and hazel eyes. She wrote very funnily. As "Sophia Sentiment," she may even have sent a letter to James Austen, the editor of the Oxford *Loiterer*, since phrases and cadences in the letter are typical of her early style.

"Sir," wrote "Sophia" to James Austen, "I write to inform you that you are very much out of my good graces, and that, if you do not mend your manners, I shall soon drop your acquaintance. . . . You have never yet dedicated any one number to the amusement of our sex, and have taken no more notice of us, than if you thought, like the Turks, we had no souls. From all which I do conclude, that you are neither more

nor less than some old Fellow of a College, who never saw anything in
the world beyond the limits of the University, and never conversed with
a female except your bed-maker and laundress."

Sophia, in short, wanted stories about girls. James Austen printed
Sophia's letter, and, expanding his scope, soon published his own
two-part story "Cecilia" about the value of children's "sensibility" with
respect to parents.

In November 1789, James printed a rather smartly written story, by
a St. John's College friend, about a Scottish soldier fighting in America. The story satirizes the American ideal of a classless democracy by
investing two moral abstractions, *prejudice* and *pride*, with Tory values
and repeating them. The Scots, as it was then known, had fought well
in the colonies: Lt. Col. Archibald Campbell's 71st Highlanders had
cleared Georgia, so it was said a Scotsman was the first to take "a
stripe and star from the rebel flag of Congress." But here, a Scotsman
is overcome by friendliness in the war. Having met Americans "who
lack all pride of distinction," he returns "with shackles of prejudice
gone" as a democrat to Scotland, where he loses his beloved and horrified Ellen to a good Tory who values the social hierarchy. Then he
marries a symbol of Washington's democracy, a vicious, mean-born
widow. "I sighed for my old prejudices," he weeps too late. "Sacred
prejudices! in tearing you from my bosom what have I substituted?"
He clearly ought to have fostered "pride" rather than renounce it—
Washington's American Revolution ruined him.

I can think of no reason why the words *prejudice* and *pride* would
interest Jane Austen at thirteen and fourteen. Her brother James in
The Loiterer used the phrase "first impressions" prominently, and a
few years later she took that as the title of her Elizabeth Bennet story,
finished when she was twenty-one. But what is striking in 1789 is that
by investing words such as *sensibility*, *prejudice*, and *pride* with Tory
values, *The Loiterer* deepened and unified its stories, and that under
their motto "Speak of Us as We Are" James and Henry laughed at
America sympathizers and other Whigs, while aiming to be realistic in
satirical detail. As Jane Austen turned from her early joke stories and
playlets to writing a realistic comic story such as "Catharine or The
Bower," she lacked a consistent viewpoint. (It may be one thing to
laugh at novel writing as she did in *Love and Freindship*, and another

to make a believable comic world, for which a strong viewpoint, ideas, and moral depth may be needed.) Her manuscript writing reveals her as an ardent Tory, perhaps the most ardent in her household, and we recall her nephew's comment on her "strong political opinions." Those opinions assisted her life of the mind, and partly in reaction to the American Revolution, her brothers now by example were forcing her talent and training her mind.

She did not read *The Loiterer* in complete ignorance of recent history. One of her chief early interests was history. Also, just as James and Henry found ambiguities in words and ideas, and displayed them in their journal, so did she find ambiguities in words and in human character. Without trying to be too positive about her development, we notice that her Catharine (of "The Bower") is an unusual creation, promising and interesting just because she has opposing lifelike traits a little outside the narrator's control. It may follow that what the young Jane Austen struggled to develop was not so much her sense of character, as her narrative voice. For it is this, her finest achievement, that allows her to control and hold complex characters together: the depth and confidence of her narrators allow her to tell increasingly inward stories: and it is her narrative control that is always improving, as we see if we compare her early stories with *Northanger Abbey* and then the rather jumbled mixture of narrative tones in *Northanger Abbey* with the far deeper assurance and authority of her narrators in *Mansfield Park* and *Emma.* Her Toryism, engaged by her brothers' writing and by their responses to war and politics, lost its early simple ardor for Mary Queen of Scots and became one frame for organizing her comic perceptions of life. That Toryism was consistent with her observer's view of an England mainly run by Whigs, and it did not lessen her glee in finding comic absurdity in modern society, or in using ironic modes of comment. The serious Tory lies behind the ethos of *Mansfield Park,* as the laughing Tory does behind *Sanditon.*

Yet she did not write "political novels" (as Charlotte Smith, whom she admired, virtually did) and it is because we can never quite label Jane Austen's ideas that we may profitably examine them in the comparative light of contemporary thought. And here, dropping the question of direct influence, I shall conclude with a remark or two on "happiness." When in 1776 Thomas Jefferson, as one of the youngest at the Continental Congress, dignified a rebellion by implying that a just government promotes "Life, Liberty, and the pursuit of Happiness," he echoed John Locke, who in the *Essay concerning Human Understanding* had said that "the necessity of pursuing true happiness is the foundation of all liberty." Yet there is a difference between a philosopher saying that and delegates taking a similar idea as a basis for a national polity. Jefferson and his fellow delegates were the first to propose that "happiness" is a human right.

Now "happiness" is one of Jane Austen's favored words. An idea about it controls her novel structures, for each novel moves a dramatic character toward a goal of secular happiness—not simply, as in traditional comedy, toward wedlock, but through a heroine's deep readjustment or greater awareness to the certainty of her felicity. A wedding is not the goal at the end of these stories, but rather a sign that a goal has been reached. Each novel, too, offers a plausible alternative to our own world, or sets up what Mary Lascelles has aptly called an "outlaw polity." As happiness is the goal in Jane Austen's outlaw polities, so it is a right and the pursuit of it is seen as essential by the Americans in 1776. To be sure, Hamilton, Washington, and even Thomas Paine doubted before the century's end that Americans had the restraint and discipline to make their polity work; and despite his hope, Paine's doubts suggest that the *terms* of 1776 have darkening results.

There is a curiously darkening evolution in Jane Austen's work, since her later heroines find happiness much harder to win than her earlier ones do. Marianne Dashwood even in illness is never isolated from her watchful sister; Catherine Morland suffers nothing much worse than an abrupt exit from an abbey and delay before bliss, and Elizabeth Bennet is so insouciant that she easily survives her own mistakes and Darcy's pride. But in the later novels, Fanny Price endures hard loneliness and mental pain, Emma is profoundly humiliated, and Anne Elliot almost throughout *Persuasion* suffers in bitter isolation from her own family and from an unperceiving Wentworth. This darkening has been ascribed to the author's disappointments, or spinsterhood, but it would seem that "happiness" in secular uses carries darknesses of its own. In its association with "pleasure" it has been condemned in modern literature as being inimical to spiritual freedom; and the notion that pleasure is a specious good, which Wallace

Fowlie finds in Rimbaud and Lionel Trilling in Dostoevsky, is reinforced even by Henry James in *Portrait of a Lady* when he has Isabel Archer say, "A swift carriage, of a dark night, rattling with four horses over roads that one can't see—that's my idea of happiness." And this assault on happiness as sheer pleasure is reflected by the later American novelist Thomas Rogers, who calls his ironic first work *The Pursuit of Happiness*, and implicitly by those who write on "the American dream" from Fitzgerald in *The Great Gatsby* to Edward Albee and Norman Mailer. When Beckett's protagonist in *Krapp's Last Tape* speaks of the "flagging pursuit of happiness" on "this old muckball," we have come a long way from Jane Austen's work and the eighteenth century out of which it arises.

"Oh Happiness! our being's end and aim!/Good, Pleasure, Ease, Content! whate'er thy name", writes Pope in the *Essay on Man*, and we notice that the eighteenth century, while it is convinced that happiness is our greatest worldly good, and while it is propounding one of its principles of moral and political action, *the greatest happiness of the greatest number*, which passes from Hutcheson in 1725 to Bentham in 1776, is even willing to admit that sensual pleasure belongs to that great good. Trilling in "The Fate of Pleasure" points out that Bishop Berkeley describes the *summum bonum* and reality of Heaven as physical pleasure since he finds that simple men will find *that* intelligible.

In this way, Jane Austen is thoroughly a child of her time: the words "happy" and "happiness" often have sexual connotations in her courtship stories, which contain much sexual energy, so that when Elinor inquires discreetly as to when Edward Ferrars "will be at liberty to be happy," sexual union seems almost explicit. *Happiness* is appropriately a word of the young, and we recall that the author was twenty-one when she finished a draft of *Pride and Prejudice* and began the work that became *Sense and Sensibility*, about twenty-four when she wrote *Northanger Abbey*, and in her thirties when she wrote *Mansfield Park* and *Emma*. Jefferson was thirty-three when he drafted the *Declaration of Independence* and yet what he said of "happiness" quickly convinced older delegates from the thirteen colonies at Philadelphia. They spent two and a half days pruning his intemperate remarks on the king but immediately accepted his contention that happiness is a right. Jefferson could offer no logical demonstration that it is a right, and if people had not accepted his idea as self-evident the syllogistic logic of the *Declaration* would have collapsed for rational readers. He may or may not have supplied the word "self-evident" for the final draft, but in any case it is very likely that he implied it by choosing the word "undeniable": his surviving "original Rough draught," which may include a few changes made by Adams and Franklin, reads, "We hold these truths to be sacred & undeniable, that all men are created equal & independant, that from that equal creation they derive rights inherent & inalienable, among which are the preservation of life, & liberty, & the pursuit of happiness," and the Declaration of Independence as adopted by the second Continental Congress on July 4, 1776 reads, "We hold these truths to be self-evident, that all men are created equal, that they are endowed by their Creator with certain unalienable Rights, that among these are Life, Liberty and the pursuit of Happiness." It is clear that Congress hardly tinkered with his notion that the pursuit of happiness is a "right."

Jane Austen's readers still accept that happiness is a right of her heroines. But in her novels, the controlling concept of happiness is not quite the same as the often mentioned word: to the extent that Jefferson's document suggests an active, outward pursuit of tangible rewards which make us happy, she differs from Jefferson in showing that happiness is most deeply a condition of the mind's outlook, and that the pursuit, therefore, is the pursuit of one's inward and potential character. This is why her narrators are so important, in showing that not events, not even their relations with Willoughby or Wickham or Darcy, are so basic to Marianne's or Elizabeth's happiness as the growth of awareness is. Each story by this author—each of her novels—is filled with false clues for the heroine, and in *Emma* at least, notoriously, for the reader too; these simulacra lead the heroine to be interested in her own outward "story," while being half-aware of something else, just as we, in our lives, are rather Jeffersonian and may be mostly interested in our outward stories though we are half-aware that the one that counts most is the interior one of character and awareness. This duality, this constant presence of "real" and pleasant phantasms or the simulacra of existence, and the narrator's amused acknowledgment of them on the one hand, and on the other the presence of the inward story of character and developing awareness in each novel, may help to explain why Jane Austen's outlook is not easy to describe. For her, and perhaps for us if we are sensible, happiness is having what she called "real sensibility," the power of being accurately aware of others' feelings and with that the generosity, kindness, and restraint to behave well toward others even in adversity. Happiness is an inward and spiritual matter. However, her secular stories do not deny the charms of this world or the worth of obtaining them, though they show the comedy of our attempts to obtain them. Deeply she believed in religious and social institutions as the best guides in the inward pursuit of happiness, and that belief influenced her attitude to America. When Britain and America were again at war, in the so-called War of 1812, and Frank Austen was fighting at sea on the North American Station, or in September 1814, three months before the Treaty of Ghent, she wrote in a letter to her friend Martha Lloyd that Henry her brother believed the Americans "cannot be conquered, and we shall only be teaching them the skill in war which they may now want." Then she quietly stated her own opinion: "If we *are* to be ruined, it cannot be helped—but I place my hope of better things on a claim to the protection of Heaven," on England "as a Religious Nation, a Nation in spite of much Evil improving in Religion, which I cannot believe the Americans to possess." Apparently then, in her view, by overturning the Church's role in a national polity the Americans had created a secular state that left the individual psychologically and spiritually unguided. Or, in the terms of James and Henry Austen's *The Loiterer*, the ideal of a classless democracy helped few people to honor with *prejudice* and *pride* those social and religious traditions that, while they do not guarantee, at least help and protect the vitality of each person's inward life. Jane Austen, however, has much else in common with Jefferson, for instance in her favoring the middle-class gentry (not the aristocracy), or in her belief in the social advancement of individuals, and indeed in her faith in the possibility of worldly felicity. Her novels portray a subtle interaction between the false and the valid in "happiness," and in so doing delight and fortify readers today in just those Western nations that have had their own political and social versions of an American Revolution.

Chapter Ten

GOOD ADVICE

WHY IS Jane Austen concerned with giving and receiving parental advice, and why do we find her theme of "good advice" important and funny? It is funny that Elizabeth Bennet is advised to marry Mr. Collins, and funnier still that the advice of her two parents does not agree, as Mr. Bennet points out:

> "An unhappy alternative is before you, Elizabeth. From this day you must be a stranger to one of your parents. —Your mother will never see you again if you do *not* marry Mr. Collins, and I will never see you again if you *do*."

But advisers such as Sir Thomas Bertram, Mr. Knightley, and Lady Russell seem more grave than funny; Jane Austen herself could be grave or reluctant in advising her nieces Fanny and Anna. She was troubled about the psychological power or persuasive effects of advice. What was she recording?

It would help us to know more about the gentry and the atmosphere in which older people advised the young, especially during Jane Austen's own youth. Fernand Braudel (and other social historians) have taught us to range widely in social, economic, and religious or moral traditions in order to understand the past; the Austens were well aware of the moral tradition, and of habits of mind in the 1780s and 1790s. To evoke that time, let us range widely and have before us a Stoic and a Christian comment on advice before we consider some of the historical factors that were changing Jane Austen's England and leading her to the "comedy of good advice." In a brief survey one dwells lightly on examples and can prove nothing, but I want to suggest that pertinent influences upon this author are to be found in the broad tract of Western cultural history.

In the intertwining Stoic and Judeo-Christian moral tradition, Stoic elements may emerge from time to time prominently as in the work of Vauvenargues in France, or of Dr. Johnson and Jane Austen in England. On the moral quality of advice, Seneca the Stoic (Christ's contemporary) writes gravely in his *Letters to Lucilius:* "Surdum te amantissimis tuis praesta; bono animo mala precantur. . . . Non sunt ista bona, quae in te isti volunt congeri; unum bonum est, quod beatae vitae causa et firmamentum est, sibi fidere." (Be deaf to those who love you most of all; they pray for bad things with good intentions. . . . What they wish to have heaped upon you are not really good things; there is only one good, the cause and support of a happy life,—trust in oneself.) Sibi fidere: Europe and especially France, whose moral philosophy has been influenced by Epictetus, Marcus Aurelius, and Seneca, has never forgotten that message. Rely on yourself: follow your star and resist advice. The New Testament, which I must remark on as one not trained in theology, seems more paradoxical: the writer in *Ephesians* quotes from the Old Testament, "honor thy father and thy mother" and adds, "children, obey your parents," but Jesus of Nazareth as reported in Matthew 10:35 has this surprising (or difficult) thing to say about obeying father or mother: "For I am come to set a man at variance against his father, and the daughter against her mother, and the daughter-in-law against her mother-in-law."

What confronts us at the Christian source is the paradox that one is to obey and to disobey, or to honor the parent and be at variance too. For a thousand years in Catholic England this paradox apparently lies a little quiescent. The trouble seems to begin within about twelve months of or just after November 1558, when the national religion changes for the last time. At the accession of Queen Elizabeth the Marian exiles—those Protestants who had fled the country under Mary Tudor's regime—come flooding back from Zurich, Geneva, and Strasbourg with understandable enthusiasm for Protestantism. Can this well-studied year (1558–1559) help us to understand the Austens' England two centuries later? This is the moment of that famous Elizabethan Compromise that determines the nature of the Church (which George Austen is to serve) or, in many ways, fixes Anglican orthodoxy. Fairly recent studies such as R. L. Greaves's *Society and Religion* (1981) and N. L. Jones's *Faith by Statute* (1982) show, from several viewpoints, that Queen Elizabeth, far from pressing anything on her subjects' heads, had to do battle with her bishops and Parliament in 1559 and accept much of what they wanted. Protestantism from the start is contentious, and requires much of the laity: it turns the eye inward, and makes the individual responsible for his or her own destiny, rather less dependent on external authority or advice. Not only Puritans but an archbishop of Canterbury (Whitgift) are saying in Elizabeth's reign that a wife should obey a husband only if his directives do not contravene Scripture; and, as a wife may disobey at home to save her soul, so a child for spiritual reasons may disobey a parent.

Now, after the Civil War and the Restoration, it is true that such views look too Puritan, or extreme. The Austen parents (born in 1731 and 1739) are raised in an atmosphere of religious moderation in the family, so moderate, so good-natured, that they later allowed their sons James and Henry to put on a saucy play in the family barn at Steventon. James and Henry may have opened little Jane's eyes, then, because their prologue (written by James, spoken by Henry) laughs at Cromwell's Puritans and recommends sexually intimate dancing; and that tolerance is typical of the Austens. Faith may be strong when it is not overt. My point is that just beneath the surface in eighteenth-century Protestantism is the old Elizabethan radicalism and a full awareness that Christ said and meant, "I am come to set a man at

variance against his father, and the daughter against her mother. . . .
He that loveth father or mother more than me is not worthy of me."

The gentry became more worldly and sophisticated by the 1780s,
with new wealth. Imports from East India in two decades rise from an
annual value of 1.1 to 1.9 million pounds; from the West Indies they
rise 1.4 to 2.7 million pounds; and nearly every industry benefits from
unprecedented technological progress. If we think of the collaboration
of Matthew Boulton, at Handsworth near Birmingham, with James
Watt, to produce steam engines, and how it is that one factory in the
1780s is the chief supplier of engines to the Midlands and outrivals
any other such supplier on earth, we must conclude that iron production is especially important in Britain. That must be the case; and it is
not typical of other metallurgical industries, but we may take iron
production at least as symptomatic. The charcoal-fired iron furnace in
Shropshire, on average, earlier in the century, has produced about
200 tons a year. By 1788, the average figure per furnace in that county
is 1,100 tons; and yet at Cyfarthfa, in Wales, the new coke-fired iron
furnaces in this decade yield up to 3,000 tons—a 1,500 percent increase in efficiency within a few years.

And, so far, this is a familiar tale. To speak of a key industrial
process that becomes 1,500 percent more efficient is not to refer to
progress, but to a revolution—or to the Industrial Revolution, which
changed the quality of life in Britain, and attitudes to life, more
sharply than any other series of events in the nation's history. There
has been some debate as to whether Jane Austen's novels refer to this
revolution, beyond Mrs. Elton's disparaging remark on "Birmingham"
in *Emma*. Mrs. Elton, who describes herself as "a great advocate for
timidity," is bold enough to say of a certain family (the Tupmans) in
the neighborhood of Maple Grove: "They came from Birmingham,
which is not a place to promise much, you know, Mr. Weston. One
has not great hopes from Birmingham. I always say there is something
direful in the sound." Surely Matthew Boulton and James Watt's
steam engine assembly room, at least, made a direful sound. We
might say that Mrs. Elton's *nouveau-riche* Maple Grove snobbery is
made possible by something that was happening to Birmingham, and
that Jane Austen's novels are products of the Industrial Revolution in
this sense. Their comic elegance as well as their moral intensity reflect

an atmosphere of feeling that the revolution by the 1780s had helped to produce. The new prosperity affected taste in art—in music, in painting, and in novels, for example. Works such as Defoe's *Moll Flanders* or Fielding's *Joseph Andrews* and *Tom Jones*, or even Richardson's *Pamela* and *Clarissa* begin to seem dated and rather crude, if vigorous and earthy in their way; and Jane Austen's preference for Richardson's *Sir Charles Grandison* seems to have been shared by others in her family. Here the sexual explicitness—an attempted abduction of the heroine Harriet Byron—is reduced to a few pages, and most of the seven volumes are devoted to Harriet's bright remarks and Grandison's gentlemanly behavior.

Something was happening to the Empire, too, as in the case of India, where, at last, British rule penetrates up the Ganges toward the Western Hills, and inland from Bombay and Madras. We know the outward facts, but it is odd how little we know about these far-flung changes in their influence on attitudes of people at home. Influences on Jane Austen herself have a geographical dimension. We may suppose that we must draw the line somewhere; if the moral tradition affected her, we cannot suppose that the globe did; but the fact is that we shall never define the temper of her time unless we see distances. From 1600 when the East India Company was founded, the empire had existed as a series of island outposts. In the 1760s, Cape Colony at the tip of Africa was only a coastal outpost on the route to the Far East and a port of call for ships. Colonizers in America lived along a strip of seaboard or close to the St. Lawrence River. Yet, even in a decade, the empire changed. In 1763, at the peace, England decided to hold on to the great land mass of Canada and to develop that colony. Clive's victories in India opened the way for interior development of British trade there; but to move in India, inland, involved problems of government, law, and understanding. Clive had military gifts; but Warren Hastings, who arrived in Bengal, in 1772 had many more, including a knowledge of Indian languages and Oriental manners. By then, many families of the gentry at home had connections with India. Mr. Austen's sister, Philadelphia, had gone out to Madras, and had married (in 1753) an English surgeon, Tysoe Saul Hancock, who was a friend of Hastings himself. It is possible that Hastings's private life was not impeccable and proper; he may have been the father of

Jane Austen's cousin Eliza, who married a supposed French count before she married Henry Austen; but Hastings's public life was, we may say, at once shrewd and compassionate. From 1772 to 1774 he was governor of Bengal and through the next eleven years "the first titular governor-general of India." Under his regime the East India Company (in return for profits) exported a system of justice in which the law of contracts was enforced, so that Indian land, once the most insecure form of wealth in Bengal, became for Indian landholders by far the most secure form of wealth. Hastings was a superb politician in India because he was devoted to its culture and people, but he never mended his fences at home; he was attacked by Sir Philip Francis (who we believe wrote the *Junius Letters*) and by others in Parliament. He had, however, the good luck to be supported by first-rate Englishmen in the East, including Sir Elijah Impey, chief justice at Bengal, whose family had lived at Basingstoke in Hampshire and were to be connected with descendants of James Austen in marriage. Parliament at last turned upon Hastings, in the struggle for control of the East India Company, and because it did Impey came under fire at home too. Impey's record was so good that it discouraged opponents (though Sheridan tried to get at him), but Hastings was put on trial for seven years at Westminster Hall, until 1795, in Jane Austen's youth. Hastings was cleared of all charges; but the trial advertised the responsibility of empire to the public. The real political issues in the proceedings at Westminster Hall were much less apparent than the rather showy, newsworthy search into the conduct of one man in India, whose defenders cited his moral probity. Hence the trial put the regulation of the empire in a good light, as if the happiness of the Indian people were the sole and entire object of England's interest there. Newspapers reported the trial, many of them week by week, and meanwhile Londoners flocked to the hall to hear Burke or Sheridan speak. They attacked Hastings superbly, in beautiful cadences; they were the best orators alive. Sheridan (the great comic playwright turned Whig M.P.) had pathos. What did it matter that he had no evidence—or very little—against Warren Hastings of India:

> It is he, my Lords, who has degraded our fortunes in the East. It
> is he who has tyrannised with relentless severity over the devoted

natives of those regions. It is he who must atone, as a victim, for
the multiplied calamities he has produced! . . . It is the glory of
the constitution under which we live, that no man can be
punished without guilt, and this guilt must be demonstrated by a
series of clear, legal, manifest evidence, so that nothing dark,
nothing oblique, nothing authoritative, nothing insidious, shall
work to the detriment of the subject.

Well, Sheridan could go on that way for five and a half hours, if need
be. People loved it as if *The School for Scandal* had come to Westminster Hall—with comedy replaced by gravity.

   In the trial's high moral tone, in new wealth, new technology, we
find clues to why the gentry could feel themselves more refined, and
why they now demanded better advice for their daughters. Courtesy
books for young ladies come into fashion; prior to 1774 there had been
few for women. The courtesy book gives advice on the deportment,
interests, skills, and traits required of a gentlewoman, and appears in
James Fordyce's *Sermons to Young Women*, Hester Chapone's *Letters
on the Improvement of the Mind*, John Bennett's *Letters to a Young
Lady*, and many similar works. Jane Austen responds not only to these
books but more deeply to the Empire and Industrial Revolution that
caused them. She herself is lifted by the new national feeling of England's consequence, wealth, and purpose, but she has great fun with
the courtesy books and conduct guides, as we know from *Love and
Freindship*. The Reverend James Fordyce had warned women of the
danger of losing one's virtue in London. Jane, with delight, writes in
her spoof: "Beware of the insipid Vanities and idle Dissipations of the
Metropolis of England; Beware of the unmeaning Luxuries of Bath &
of the Stinking fish of Southampton." Courtesy books insisted on
quiet, modest deportment. Jane offers this advice, which might almost
relieve the worries of psychiatrists at our city hospitals today: "A frenzy
fit is . . . an exercise to the Body & if not too violent, is I dare say
conducive to Health in its consequences—Run mad as often as you
chuse; but do not faint."

   Further, the popular vogue of advice-giving directives is mocked in
her mature novels. Elizabeth in *Pride and Prejudice* does so many
things that advice manuals forbade that one may say she is nearly an

anti-courtesy-book heroine. Girls were asked to be timid and diffident; Elizabeth is bold and outspoken to the point of effrontery; girls were told to conceal their wit, or not to say *"smart* things," as John Bennett advised in *Letters to a Young Lady* (1789); Elizabeth Bennet loves wit, and enjoys being just as *smart* as she likes. Or, whereas the courtesy-book girl never runs, and is not robust but delicate, Elizabeth is seen in that famous chapter 7, "crossing field after field at a quick pace, jumping over stiles and springing over puddles with impatient activity," and bursting into Netherfield, her "face glowing with the warmth of exercise."

It is immediately clear that this author mocks advice, and that for example her Mrs. Allen, Mrs. Morland, Mrs. Dashwood, and Mrs. Jennings as counselors are well meaning but useless; Mrs. Norris's advice is wholly selfish, Sir Thomas Bertram's obtuse and mistaken. The advice of Miss Taylor, Mr. Woodhouse, and Mr. Knightley all together has only spoiled Emma or encouraged her to indulge in her illusions, and so made her way more difficult. What is a good deal less clear, however, is why the topic of advice giving in Jane Austen's novels is almost obsessively present, why advice is made ridiculous by the author, why this motif becomes central in her work. We might say: she mocks courtesy books because most of them are only superficially Christian. That may be so. But Jane Austen herself, though Christian, was troubled by the problem of the unpredictability of the individual's responses: "nobody ever feels or acts, suffers or enjoys as one expects," she wrote. That being the case, how can we advise anyone on an important matter in life, if we do not know how the advice will be received or even what it will mean?

She seems to take up this problem in her last completed work, *Persuasion,* in which she brings the novel of manners fully into the age of opportunity and modern war and democracy. In modern times, with more democracy and freedom, opportunity puts us in a more difficult situation than our ancestors, who were guided and limited by the Church and their rulers and a rigid hierarchical social order; we may easily make wrong choices, and find ourselves in an Anne Elliot-like dilemma, with little hope. The root of much social evil lies in our insensitivity to other persons, this author is always saying; our problems are not far off, but close by. The paradox of the injunction to obey and yet to oppose the parent (or conventional morality or wisdom) is much with us. Anne's adviser has been Lady Russell, a person of "steady age and character" with "an elegance of mind." At first we see Lady Russell advising well, drawing up plans for economy at Kellynch, where Anne's father has been spending himself into ruin. "If we can persuade your father to all this," said Lady Russell, looking over her paper, "much may be done." But then we are carried into the past to see Lady Russell's major act of persuading when she had advised Anne, at nineteen, to give up her indigent naval suitor, Wentworth, when he had been urging her to marry him.

Anne yielded to advice. Now that Wentworth is back, rich with prize money from the sea, and Anne is faded and on the shelf at twenty-seven, the autumnal tone of the novel becomes Anne's tone. Her mistake was to accept advice—or was it? Much of the subtle power of this novel lies in our being led to feel how wrong Lady Russell was, how snobbery and prejudice had affected her advice, and how Anne suffers in consequence, even though we may be led to feel in another way that Anne's moral strength and power of mind (or ability to endure deprivation or suffering) are greater because she has behaved honorably. She is still an effective person, and Wentworth's rediscovery of his love underlines that psychological or inward strength and her effectiveness. Despite appearances, she has been a more powerful and capable (as well as a more intelligent and constant) person all along than he, and, in the light of Wentworth's reformation and the novel's happy and secure ending, one may conclude that she had been right to accept Lady Russell's advice, and that Lady Russell had been right to give it.

Advice (always faulty) can have fair results: if that is so, then there may be a certain historical pessimism in Jane Austen's view. She knew that in comedy most advice *must* seem inappropriate or selfish or ridiculous, and Mrs. Bennet in *Pride and Prejudice* or Mrs. Norris in *Mansfield Park* are all three of these things; neither lady has in mind the well-being of the person she tries to advise. To the extent that she thinks, Mrs. Bennet thinks about money and husbands, and Mrs. Norris thinks about Mrs. Norris. Another kind of adviser thinks of nothing but pleasantry, and may advise by uttering some inappropriate or comic universal truth. Mr. Edwardes, in *The Watsons*, advises by inference as he talks to Emma Watson about her aunt, who (at a certain age) has married for the second time and gone to Ireland:

> "Elderly Ladies should be careful how they make a second choice," observed Mr. Edwardes—"Carefulness—Discretion—should not be confined to Elderly Ladies, or to a second choice," added his wife. "It is quite as necessary to young ladies in their first."—"Rather more so, my dear"—replied he, "because young Ladies are likely to feel the effects of it longer. When an old Lady plays the fool, it is not in the course of nature that she should suffer from it many years." Emma drew her hand across her eyes—& Mrs. Edwardes on perceiving it, changed the subject to one of less anxiety to all."

Advisers, in Jane Austen's novels, are usually no more aware of the feelings of persons whom they advise, than Mr. Edwardes is aware of Emma's. It is peculiar that some of the author's most passive, limp, or trivial talkers—Lady Bertram, Mr. Woodhouse, Miss Bates—seem to record old community truths or attitudes nearly lost at present, as though, in history once, we knew each other better. We recall the talk between Henry and Edmund about the importance of Shakespeare's play *Henry VIII* in *Mansfield Park,* and we may recall Jane Austen's early interest in history, and her half-facetious comment on a Tudor king, as a girl: "Henry the 8th. . . . Why should a Man who was of no Religion himself be at so much trouble to abolish one which had for Ages been established in the Kingdom." Fanny Price, the gravest of heroines though she is naive and not culturally sophisticated, places a high value on "memory," even on history, and seems to allude in Sotherton's chapel to an English religious past before Henry VIII's Dissolution of the Monasteries. But Fanny as a reader of Walter Scott does not recommend doctrines that the Anglican Church does not manifest. Jane Austen in maturity would seem (so far as one can tell) to have retained her earlier respect and sympathy for the Roman Catholic Church and its doctrines, without harboring a merely sentimental nostalgia for Catholicism, such as we find later in nineteenth-century England with the Arnolds, or with Tieck, Novalis, and Richter in Germany. Eighteenth-century Tory families could think of the Roman

Church sympathetically as a part of the past of the Anglican Church. But Jane Austen was formed in part by active historical reading: as a child she had read enough to write a good burlesque of Goldsmith's *History of England*. Further, she had habits of quick and intuitive apprehension; her faith did not exist in a dreamy pocket of hope and imagination, but sorted itself in an applicable way with much of what she read and what she saw.

The new wealth, new elegance, signs of imperial progress, and the plethora of courtesy books (and of novels with courtesy-book elements) might suggest to many people that human understanding in their day was improving. For Jane Austen, history points to no such amelioration: individuals were as mysterious to each other as ever (and beset by illusions). People never suffer, enjoy, or feel as one expects and cannot be deeply advised, and she accepts injunctions relating to parental advice, fathers and sons, mothers and daughters, in the moral tradition. We may interpret that tradition more narrowly than the Austens did, and it is well to remember that she re-read the New Testament and heard exegetic sermons throughout her life. There is a great energy of paradox in the four narrative accounts of Christ's life, and certainly none of these narratives counsels unreflecting, willful disobedience or an indifference to family. Working with Jane Austen, a critic or biographer will find her no victim of pessimistic ideas of human relations, either, despite what she implies about advice giving and advice taking; she is never cynical. The Austen, Austen-Leigh, and Lefroy family diaries or letters that have become available do increase our understanding of family pressures and tensions among Austens at Steventon and later, but they also increase our understanding of the closeness, loyalty, and affection in Jane Austen's family. What her reading and observation told her was modified by the talk of an almost scholarly father, a witty mother, a bright sister, Oxford-educated brothers, and practical naval men; and with them, as her brother Henry says, she was typically "thankful for praise, open to remark, and submissive to criticism." But being "submissive" by no means meant following advice. Jane denied her sister's wish that Fanny should marry Henry Crawford in *Mansfield Park*, and resisted other advice, too, as her letters show. She said that she would not have "generosity" dictated to her, in that she wouldn't submit to being told what to give

away among her belongings, or to whom, when the family was remov-
ing to Bath. There are other more important ways in which she resisted society's tacit advice—especially in her use of language. Her use
of the English language, almost in spite of her merriness, puns, and
ironies, is honest to the point of ferocity; she refused to make the usual
knee-jerk responses in expressing family sentiment or to tailor her language insincerely, or to approve what she could not approve. She is as
scrupulous in her informal letters as she is in every example of her art.
We know that Mr. Austen could give forthright and almost irritatingly
explicit advice, and his son James clearly could, too. Jane's early burlesque *jeux d'esprit* have an effect of making her invulnerable to some
kinds of advice, which she could parry with laughter. In a deeper way,
her art saves her from some of the hard, effective "advice" or dictation
of mere historical circumstance: her novels do not respond exactly to
what *has* happened in anyone's personal history but show what could
and should happen. However, she was impressed by one redeeming
aspect of advice at least, and for this, the affectionate and well-loved if
at times oppressive circle of her family is responsible. She could not
deny that the faulty adviser may have good and loving intentions. And
so in fiction, Lady Russell, for all her faults, is shown to have been
moved by a selfless love in advising Anne Elliot, and for that reason
she is mainly forgiven by the author of *Persuasion*. Human history is
the story of the separateness and mystery of each person; advice that is
given in Lady Russell's manner may not be objectionable; but the
comedy and freedom of life depend on our knowing that advice from
others is inevitably frail, and that, as Jane Austen certainly believed,
we must learn to know ourselves and be instructed from within. Her
late heroines, Fanny Price, Anne Elliot, and even Emma Woodhouse, are shown to be strong partly because they are proof against
advice: they have interior lives. Jane Austen herself had learned their
secret as she reacted to the moral traditions and also to the accelerat-
ing social and economic changes of her England.

PART THREE

VICTORIANS AND MODERNS

Chapter Eleven

BULWER

WE CANNOT know the Victorian mind unless we know something about the career and writings of Edward Bulwer, who became Bulwer-Lytton. The trouble is that a sea of time has washed over him. His works are as strange as sea creatures in exoskeletons, with enormous tails and filaments, living in inky depths. Pull one off a library shelf and stare at its bulgy eyes and you will run away—not in fright, but in anticipation of deep boredom. Or so you and I may expect, for his reputation is low today. What are his plays but bombast? What are his novels from *Pelham* to *Kenelm Chillingly* but turgid mistakes?

In fact he could write superbly well. He charmed Dickens and had an enormous following of Victorian readers. And if Bulwer-Lytton is no longer in fashion his career is extremely significant; it begins ten years after Jane Austen's death, when England and Europe were still bemoaning Byron's loss, and runs on like a bright twisting ribbon. I want to survey that career briefly, and in the light of his first, succinct, unusually skillful and entertaining novel. Bulwer-Lytton's first novel, *Falkland*, was published in 1827 when he was nearly twenty-four and is about a seduction. Its message is simple: a good way to overcome ennui is to seduce a dazzling young woman whose M.P. husband is too busy to notice and whose child is too small to care. Lady Emily Mandeville dies of a "broken blood vessel" in her sexual excitement (presumably some other excitement would have carried her off soon anyway) and Falkland has some horrid dreams, but illicit love cures him of his gloom and sends him romping off to Spain to join a colorful democratic struggle. Yet *Falkland* had a therapeutic value for Bulwer. When he completed it in the gardens of Versailles in 1826 he had composed little else besides poetry and was recovering from a queer epistolary love affair with Lady Caroline Lamb. She had understood him: "You are like me—too fond of Lord Byron." Bulwer had been trying to live up to his own conception of Lord Byron since the age of thirteen.

He was born on May 25, 1803 to wealthy parents of old and impeccable lineage. General Bulwer, bedridden with gout, lived for a time in "hoops that suspended from his body the touch of his clothes" and died when Edward was four. From then on the boy was protected from the cries of the world. He attended four public schools briefly and came home to be pampered by his glittering mother and gently encouraged by a devoted tutor. A Byronesque attempt—*Ismael: an Oriental Tale; with Other Poems*—appeared at his mother's expense when he was seventeen. Two years later he went to Cambridge where he won some reputation for witty skill in debate, his arrogance, and for writing like Byron. Two more poetic volumes and a Chancellor's Medal opus followed. He was also reading quickly and widely, filling up ledgers with notes on English and Irish history, and walking in the long vacations. In 1824, he walked to Brocket Park and met Lady Caroline. For a few days, an affair with the most notorious of Byron's cast-off mistresses fed gossip in London, and at Cambridge, where the arrogant young imitator was suddenly an undergraduates' laughingstock. (Lady Caroline was known for being vain, aging, and a little nutty.) In a highly overwrought frame of mind and with a preliminary draft for *Falkland* in hand, Bulwer left Cambridge in 1825 for Paris.

"I am like one of the leaves I see now before my window," he wrote to Mrs. Cunningham from Versailles, "without an aim. . . ."

Nevertheless, he took aim in *Falkland*. The hero is an ingenious composite of many romantic types (so that the little novel is a literary mosaic) and also a studied version of Bulwer's debilitating view of himself as an arch-seducer of the age. With his soft voice, his "chiselled" lip and light chestnut hair falling "in large *antique* curls," Falkland is Bulwer Byronized; plunged in Byronic ennui, he seeks the infallible Byronic cure—adultery—and then fights Byron's valorous battle, outnumbered, in a purple land. Lovelace and Werther are models for his letter writing. He has Lovelace's intensity in pursuit and Werther's hopelessness in an affair with a married woman. He is indebted to Maturin's devilish Melmoth, Plumer Ward's refined Tremaine, Rousseau of the *Confessions*, Wordsworth of the *Immortality Ode*, and at last, when he cheers his uncle's dispirited troops, to Prince Hal. Bulwer's most audacious stroke is to make him into a precocious Faust, too, a fiend-ridden "Genius" who has mastered astronomy, meteorology, and the rest of human thought and complains, like Jeremy Bentham, of the "inutility" of it all. Slabs of Gothic are lifted from Mrs. Radcliffe's novels. The scene of Lady Emily's entrapment between an unscalable cliff and the rushing tide resembles one in Scott's *The Antiquary*.

All of this ingrafting—partly acknowledged in Falkland's name-dropping—was deliberate for Bulwer. As Sir Joshua Reynolds tells Warner, a young painter in *The Disowned* (1829), "imitation, if noble and general, insures the best hope of originality," and if poor Warner and Godolphin learn it too late, their nervous breakdowns and wild drownings are instructive. (Bulwer complained in public when he thought Balzac had pillaged from *him*.)

Erasmus Falkland is murky in outline, as composites often are, but the prototype of heroes to come. His first transformation is seen in *Pelham* (1828), Bulwer's second novel, whose hero sobers up on Sauterne and soda water and is "never unpleasantly employed." Pelham is Falkland minus gloom and adultery (he resists the seductive Mme. de Perpignan and usefully solves a murder) and is also a social puppy with intellectual properties who is to be seen under other names, dourly in *Godolphin* (1833) and serenely in the late *Kenelm Chillingly* (1873). Falkland's second transformation is into Gothic villains who are intelligent, proud, mad, and murderously amorous, such as Aubrey in *Devereux* (1829) or Arbaces the Egyptian in *The Last Days of Pompeii* (1834). But his third transformation is more complex. The heroes of novels such as *Eugene Aram* (1832) and *Ernest Maltravers* (1837) and its sequel *Alice* (1838) are mental giants—very Faustlike Falklands—who pursue stupendous unknowns while suffering from "chimeras of a horrible hallucination" as Bulwer diagnosed their typical ailment. One of two things happens to them: they die violently, or they become de-Gothicized, de-Romanticized, and properly Victorianized through their experiences into models of simple piety and contentment, of a kind so badly needed by Bulwer's middle-class readers.

Perhaps the worst one can say is that their psychological problems are shallowly explored. It is just this that makes Bulwer's heroines even more easily classifiable: they are all, more or less, Lady Emily Mandevilles, nine-year-old minds in prettily bosomed bodies. Thus the question that interests us about a heroine at the outset of a Bulwer novel is whether he has decided she shall die, go crazy, or survive any ordeal intact. Insanity is the worst fate and comes on with terrible suddenness, Cassandra-like visions, and a good deal of noise:

> Then raising her voice into a wild shriek, "Beware, beware, Percy!—the rush of waters is on my ear—the splash, the gurgle! Beware!—*your* last hour, also, is at hand!"
> From the moment in which she uttered these words, Lucilla lapsed into her former frantic paroxysms. Shriek followed shriek; she appeared to know none around her, not even Godolphin.

Exactly what causes a heroine's death is often obscure: Madeleine in *Eugene Aram* and Viola in *Zanoni* (1842) seem to expire out of sympathy with their lovers who are hanged or guillotined, and in this light Lady Emily's weak artery is a welcome detail. More impressive are the heroines who can get through anything. Alice, in the two Ernest Maltravers novels, is assaulted and pursued by her father, impregnated out of wedlock by the hero, forced to wander penniless, driven to subterfuge, and made to suffer in other ways for eighteen years until—still smiling with "dimpled lips"—she marries Ernest.

However, it is a mistake to weigh these creatures on the iron scale of realism. Particularly so, because Bulwer wished to "resort to a sort of moral or psychological distance" in portraiture, as he says in *Kenelm Chillingly* (1873). "We know that," he continues in the guise of Kenelm, "Werter and Clarissa are . . . as much remote from us in the poetic and idealized side of their natures as if they belonged to the age of Homer; and this it is that invests with charm the very pain which their fate inflicts on us." He is theorizing here half a century later, but it is significant that he alludes to the Goethe and Richardson novels that went into the making of *Falkland*. No doubt Bulwer wished to keep Erasmus and Lady Emily at a psychological distance (although the term hardly would have occurred to him in 1826). They and their literary cousins are poetic and idealized—that is, intendedly unbelievable—and if their minds so often seem stunted or darkly mysterious, their behavior and their fates do hold some charm. In his melodramatic world, even the bloodthirstiest enormities inflict no pain on us since the perpetrators and victims resemble nothing of flesh. And this is why Victorians loved him: what went on in *Lucretia* (1846) or the wilder *Night and Morning* (1841) was even worse than what went on in Birmingham's slums and yet was pleasantly innocuous from start to finish. Melodramatic characters are a godsend if you live near tragic scenery because they invest pain with charm.

Bulwer did more than create a gallery of infantile heroines and crazy heroes, though. His lasting interest owes to his canny ability to mix seemingly incompatible appeals within one book, to his skill at construction, and to his good sense of timing and clever manipulation of nature. *Falkland* combines the Faust theme and the Byron legend, with an adultery story, Gothic terror, and military adventure.

In his next few novels, he surpassed all English predecessors in combining other traditional ingredients with Gothic. *Pelham* mixes it, not too successfully, with silver-fork wit and satire. *The Disowned* and *Devereux* were intended to be best-sellers. (Bulwer was entertaining his wife with fifteen-guinea thimbles by this time.) But they are also coolheaded experiments to see how many different kinds of novel one novel can be, and they surpass *Falkland* in this.

Morton Devereux writes his memoirs of political, philosophic, fashionable, and literary life in eighteenth-century Europe. He meets "grave Mr. Addison," "Dicky Steele," and that "very small, deformed man," Mr. Pope, as well as Dr. Swift, Bolingbroke, Mme. de Maintenon, Louis XIV, and the Czar, and in the Apennines solves a perfectly monstrous Gothic crime when he discovers his wife's slayer in the person of a monk who turns out to be his brother.

After that, Bulwer settled down to combining only two or three kinds of fiction at once. Thus *Paul Clifford* is a *roman à clef* that makes fun of a weekly magazine, the *Asinaeum*, while delivering a serious lecture in penology, and *Eugene Aram* is love idyll plus criminal case history plus terror. *Pompeii* and *Rienzi* (1835) join accurate historical reconstructions to suspense and mayhem. Novels with mythic, occult, bucolic, and Utopian interests, sensational romances and multivolumed domestic tales followed. None is dull except the latter, that is, *The Caxtons* (1849), *My Novel* (1853), and *What Will He Do With It?* (1859) or the Pisistratus Caxton books, which show only that Bulwer was bored by the countryside and was not Trollope.

He turned to the theater for lessons in construction and gave back to it in *The Lady of Lyons* (1838), *Richelieu* (1838), and *Money* (1840), the most stage-worthy of all Victorian imitations of Shakespeare. He also learned "the art of mechanical construction" from Scott's novels, and especially from Goethe's *Wilhelm Meister*, which offers the pattern of the *Bildungsroman* used in tracing so many heroic paths from youth to social conformity or a violent end. But his study of the theater accounts for the more typical structural features in his books—their vast soliloquies, four or five "acts," and catastrophes. Bulwer never tired of writing about catastrophes. In a novel, he said in his essay *On Art in Fiction* (1838), there ought to be a "management and combination of incidents towards the grand end." A "highly artistical" catastrophe must "revive in the consummating effect many slight details—incidents the author had but dimly shadowed out— mysteries you had judged till then he had forgotten to clear up. . . ."

And indeed his catastrophes are large, orgiastic, sweeping, and colorful, and they clear up every mystery. *The Last Days of Pompeii* ends with a stampeding horde of thousands who are trying to toss the villain to a waiting lion in a blood-soaked amphitheater, an earthquake, billows of steam, glimmering lightnings, and a frighteningly lurid and very Gothic Vesuvius:

> Bright and gigantic through the darkness, which closed around it like the walls of hell, the mountain shone—a pile of fire! Its summit seemed riven in two; or rather, above its surface there seemed to rise two monster shapes, each confronting each, as Demons contending for a World. These were of one deep blood-red hue of fire, which lighted up the whole atmosphere far and wide; but, *below*, the nether part of the mountain was still dark and shrouded, save in three places, adown which flowed serpentine and irregular rivers of the molten lava. Darkly red through the profound gloom of their banks, they flowed slowly on, as towards the devoted city. Over the broadest there seemed to spring a cragged and stupendous arch, from which, as from the jaws of hell, gushed the sources of the sudden Phlegethon; and through the stilled air was heard the rattling of the fragments of rock, hurtling one upon another as they were borne down the fiery cataracts, darkening, for one instant, the spot where they fell, and suffused, the next, in the burnished hues of the flood along which they floated!

In this, his most famous novel, history cooperated ideally with Bulwer. Surely in *Falkland* he was already musing about its locale: "We remove the lava, and the world of a gone day is before us!" The eruption continues through four climactic chapters and pictures on a gigantic scale those horrifying gas and phosphorus flames and proscenium-rattling explosions that were entertaining hundreds from Drury Lane's accommodating ninety-foot-deep stage in the 1830s. Other historic catastrophes were comparatively timid but useful: there is the Reign of Terror in *Zanoni* and the "gory ocean" of Tewkesbury in *The Last of the Barons* (1843), for example.

In a very embryonic sense, the catastrophe is present in *Falkland*, which displays the close coordination between nature and mood and the accurate dramatic timing of cataclysms typical of Bulwer's mature work. The situation of an entrapment between a sheer cliff and high tide is used here more pointedly than in Scott: it creates the tension that precedes Emily and Erasmus's first kiss. And the evening of the seduction itself is "breathless" at first, then dark and stormy so that, at a critical moment under the oak when kisses are "like lava" and bosom is throbbing against bosom in abandonment, there is a marvelous "low roll" of thunder.

These effects are *sui generis* even in the canons of melodrama. No Hollywood producer has equaled them, I think, and Charles Dickens (whose Oliver owes to *Paul Clifford* and whose Jingler and Little Nell owe something to *Eugene Aram*) when he is writing scenes of melodramatic content hardly seems to compete. They are partly ludicrous, of course, but never unimpressive, never really failings.

Still there are two cardinal failings that keep many of Bulwer's novels unread and out of print today. The first involves the complicated problem of his style. Oddly enough, his name is symptomatic of a grave deficiency: it lengthened little by little, to his pride, until when he was made a peer in 1866, it rumbled like one of his thunderstorms as Edward George Earle Lytton Bulwer Lytton, Baron Lytton of Knebworth. (One of his biographers reports that he savored the very sounds.) There are bits of redundant rhetoric in *Falkland*, almost none in *Pelham*, but by the time of *Devereux* strident "Bulwerese"— prose that seems to have been written by a theatrical parson brought up on *The Mysteries of Udolpho*—has set in. It is trite, tumid, inexact, archaic, and silly. Large patches of it infect all of his novels after 1829 except for *Paul Clifford* (where Fielding's style is vigorously imitated) and *The Caxtons* and *My Novel* (where Sterne's is) and the very late works.

What complicates the problem is that Bulwer could write with the conciseness of Swift and the epigrammatic smartness of Peacock. There are paragraphs in *Pelham* that glitter with the verbal irony of Oscar Wilde, as Michael Sadleir noticed, and bright epigrams in *Falkland*. Stranger still, he described his own worst faults of style perfectly in 1833 when he condemned young English novelists for writing with "an exaggerated tone and a superfluous and gratuitous assumption of energy and passion." Indeed, one is driven to the conclusion that he cared about style and composed with his own changing precepts well in mind.

In *Pelham*, a bright young friend of the hero named Vincent explains why that novel itself is so crisply written:

For me, if I were to write a novel, I would first make myself an acute, active, and vigilant observer of men and manners. Secondly, I would, after having thus noted effects by action in the world, trace the causes by books, and meditation in my closet. It is then, and not till then, that I would study the lighter graces of style and decoration. . . .

Now, this formula might have sent the author along the trail of the comedy of manners and toward Jane Austen. Style near the outset of Bulwer's career is one of "the lighter graces" that is to subserve the accurate depiction of social behavior. But such a formula is patently unsuitable to the melodramatic novel. The "main essential of style in narrative" of *Eugene Aram's* kind, he declares in a preface to that bloodcurdler, is rather "its harmony with the subject selected and the passions to be moved" and this leads him to write in a very different way.

Since his typical subjects tend to be idealized and unearthly, and since the "passions to be moved" in melodrama are pleasurable fright and simple awe, his language inflates with the showman's hectoring rhetoric, which asks for our delighted attention to unreal freaks and impossible horrors and descends to take in every cliché in the Gothic repertory. Thus *Aram* and *Pompeii* continue in a direction barely noticeable in *Falkland* by depending on key words such as *fierce* and *frenzy*—we read over and over of "fierce and lurid passions," "a thrilling and fierce groan," "a frenzy of jealousy," and on stereotypes such as lips that (reliably) "writhe," eyes that are "feverish," brows that are decorated with "cold drops," teeth that "grind," and so on. With Bulwer, one ought to be able to play the game and accept these, the counters of gas-lit terror, and one usually can: Gothic clichés are at least quick and vivid. His unforgivable fault is in badgering his readers in a style that is also so distended and furry it defeats its purpose, since it neither increases suspense nor prepares for thrills if it puts them into a doze, as it does.

His second cardinal fault is more serious since after all, a reader can learn to skip over swamps of Bulwerese. Philosophic pretentiousness is not so localized. It can hardly be missed in his novels because it is ingrained and pervasive: we are made aware that Bulwer, quite without qualifications, wants to be taken as a Sage. This can be felt in the author's intrusions and letters in *Falkland*; and yet his first novel interestingly points in two directions. On the one hand, it is filled with shopworn notions about nature, perception, and knowledge, but on the other it suggests a very genuine disillusionment with contemporary society. Emily's oafish husband is one of the new "Macadamized achievements," and the lovers can feel godlike because love, "even guilty Love," insulates them from the pettiness and strife of English life. Young Falkland, in fact, has seen enough to suggest that his creator has a social critic's eye and *Pelham, Greville*, and a brilliant treatise on the foibles of his countrymen, *England and the English* (1833), show that Bulwer had Thackeray-like endowments.

But an impulse to analyse society soon gave way to a willingness to placate it. Too often, from 1833 on, the Sage is only mouthing Victorian verities: "If there be anything lovely in the human heart," he writes in that very year, "it is affection!" Fortunately, however, Bulwer was not a prisoner of his deficiencies. The verve and ingenuity of *Falkland* are matched in several novels that followed it and surpassed in two perfect works. One of them is a short story, "The Haunted and the Haunters" (1857), a masterpiece of terror in the occult, and the other is a novel that makes a profound comment on Bulwer's melodramatic world. In *The Coming Race* (1871), an intrepid American lowers himself through a gap in the floor of a mineshaft into a lost civilization of supremely rational beings. In Vril-ya, muscular women seven feet tall study mechanics and abstract thought and woo punier but happy men. Both sexes flit about through perfumed air on detachable wings, direct automata to do the heavy work, and wield rods of such rock-shattering power that dissension and debate have become obsolete. Crime, adultery, passion, ambition, stimulants, doubts, and illusions are all missing—and so is art. Vril-ya is insufferable. The hero yearns (just as we do) for the contention and tumult of real human beings, whose very sign of life is a literature that can include such frenzied adulterers and nefarious villains and long-suffering ladies as Bulwer's.

Falkland would make no sense in Vril-ya. It typifies everything that is lawless, irrational, passionate, gauche, and exaggerated in Bulwer's entertainingly horrific world, since it contains in the bud his astonishing heroes and heroines, his melodramatic catastrophes, his combinations of appeal, even his imitativeness and style and philosophic pretensions, and displays his deep commitment to Romantic traditions and particularly to a Gothicism that his later novels in fact helped to preserve through the whole Victorian age.

Above all, what would mystify in Vril-ya is Bulwer's curious involvement in Byronism, the intensity of which he explained when he described how England reacted in 1824 to news of Byron's death. "We could not believe that the bright race was run," Edward Bulwer wrote later. "It was as if a part of the mechanism of the very world stood still . . . and all our worship of his genius was not half so strongly felt as our love for himself."

Chapter Twelve

THE YOUNG
ARNOLD

URING HIS LIFETIME—in the sixty-five years between his birth in 1822 and his death in 1888—Matthew Arnold was considered by his family and later by the English public to be less important than his schoolmaster father. And understandably, as his father, "Dr. Arnold of Rugby School," was the idol of Arthur Stanley's flattering biography and of several generations of schoolboys and schoolmasters. But in the century after his death Matthew Arnold has seemed more interesting than his father, and there may be two kinds of reasons for this.

First there are his individual achievements. Matthew Arnold is a moving and intelligent lyric poet who reflects the new urban consciousness of industrial Europe. He is a poet of country landscape and city feelings, who is truthful on the topics about which it is easy to tell lies, romantic love and religious faith. In works such as *Essays in*

Criticism or *Culture and Anarchy*, too, he seems to define the modern critical sensibility; he lays the groundwork and proposes the leading attitudes for much of our own criticism of literature and society.

The second reason for Arnold's interest may be more elusive, since it concerns his tone as a writer and the odd fact that there is a consistent unity running through his poetry and prose. He might be called a "strong writer," in Harold Bloom's sense, because Arnold, while retaining a certain urbanity and aplomb, manages to be convincingly sincere. He seems to gloss over no difficulty or regret or doubt that may occur to him, and unifies his intellect and feelings when writing verse or prose.

Much indebted to him, the finest critical minds in England and America have engaged with him, as if to show despite their reservations that Arnold has meanings for a later time: T. S. Eliot, I. A. Richards, Lionel Trilling, and F. R. Leavis carry on running debates with him. More recently, scholarly critics and editors such as the Allotts in England and R. H. Super, David DeLaura and others in the U.S. have produced editions of his works or close commentaries.

In a fascinating recent book called *Arnold and God*, which explores Arnold's debts to such late-eighteenth-century German figures as Eichhorn, Herder, and Goethe, Ruth apRoberts claims that the unifying thread in Arnold's thought and feeling was religious, that the "religious question" was so basic that it moved him to seek in poetry and then in "culture" those values that the religion of his day could no longer supply. There is no doubt that when he was born at Laleham on December 24, 1822, his father Thomas Arnold, a deacon, was wrestling with doubts about the Holy Trinity and the literal interpretation of scripture. But we have to see Thomas—or Dr. Arnold to give him the D.D. he earned in 1828—as an energetic optimist with much secular energy, a curly haired, smooth-chinned, handsome young man with boyish high spirits; athletic, busy, sometimes puzzled by pupils at Laleham who defied his schoolmasterly edicts, and eager to win boys' hearts by being their leader. Dr. Arnold set up what he called a Campus Martius in the garden at Laleham School. His ten or twelve tutorial pupils had a wide trench for leaping, a "peg-pole" for climbing, and a tall gallows for chinning (or pull-ups) and target practice; in his shirtsleeves he often threw javelins, even with his friend

Whately, the Archibishop of Dublin, an expert in boomerang throwing. Or Thomas would practice "Skirmishing," running at high speed over the low Laleham fields in and out of ditches, over hedges and straight through bushes.

If the father at twenty-seven was a boy at heart, his thirty-one-year-old wife, Mary, had the spirit of a girl. Thin and frail, almost fragile, with upswept hair held by a comb in the Louis-Philippe fashion, an aquiline nose, and bright dark eyes, Mary Penrose had been a pest in her father's rectory. She teased her elder sisters, acted in theatricals, and after her marriage to Thomas became addicted to reports of hangings, revolutions, and disasters in the London papers. She would have loved stories headlined SHOCK HORROR in modern tabloids: Thomas Carlyle's *The French Revolution* was so bloody that she simply told her Penrose sisters, "Get it." She was as bored by the plains of northern France as Dr. Arnold would be by Warwickshire and two or three other flat counties. But "when you see the Jura," she told her children, "think of me." The Arnold parents, as younger children in their own families, were in some respects more childish, dramatic, impulsive, and playful than some of their children were to be.

No doubt the so-called Celtic temperament is partly a fiction though Matthew Arnold believed in it; but the former Mary Penrose of Cornwall almost proves the validity of the myth—in her fondness for storms, heavy seas, mountains, vibrant colors, poetry, pathos, and drama; in her French tricolor sewing bag and bright dresses; and in the poignant entries on death in her indefatigably kept notebooks, diaries, and household journals. Death is God's most precious gift, she believed, as it "gives *reality* to what in life is often so Phantom like." She and her husband composed poetry for their household journal, and she responded to her first-born son, Matthew, as if he were a little deity from Olympus. When her husband spoke of the need to "reform" an unequal society, he epitomized an English mood in the years before the first Reform Bill, and Mrs. Arnold expected dazzling achievements of her son. Thus, when in this active and dramatic household at Laleham, Matthew Arnold developed rickets and had to wear heavy iron leg braces, she was full of pity and alarm.

But she had nine children to look after. She continued to praise their physical achievements—from their first fearful tottering steps in

the garden to little Susy's trotting about "in the gaiety" of her heart
and her son Tom's heroic walk in infancy from Chertsey all the way to
Laleham. Meanwhile, in leg irons, Matthew screamed. He gashed his
head on the clawfoot of a table; he cried at night. At the ages of three
and four he was ugly and slow, whereas Jane and Tom were attractive
and agile. The evidence of the household journals is plain that Matthew did not walk properly even after Dr. Arnold became Rugby's
headmaster in 1828, and that while anguishing his mother, Matthew
appealed to her in the only ways left open to him—that is, first by
being "obstinate" and wounding himself, and then by writing little
poems about poignant topics.

When the Arnolds began to summer at Fox How near Ambleside
in 1834, their affectionate friends at Rydal included William Wordsworth, whose green eyeshade, homely nose, and lack of "animation"
at first had disappointed Mrs. Arnold (who preferred Robert Southey
and his active girls), his sister Dorothy Wordsworth, an obese and bald
woman who sat close to the hearth, spoke to her nailbrush, and cried
and shrieked on occasion, and the sensible Mary Wordsworth with her
intelligent squint, who kept the cult of nature appreciation alive at
Rydal Mount. Matthew and his sister Jane, as Dr. Arnold records, are
often "over at the Mount." And again William Wordsworth in his
loose brown frock coat and "trousers of shepherd's plaid" and brown
handkerchief for a necktie would come into the Fox How kitchen to
recite his works or complain about the railways, the "iron tide," that
was an instance of modern "inhumanity" and the way in which city
folk were destroying the countryside.

By then Matthew had learned to walk, leap, and run; he had built
a secret fort on Loughrigg Fell and seen William Wordsworth lean
over its parapet one day. Much or little may be made of his few years
in leg braces, but it is clear that his "bent legs" had given him a little
distance from his family, and taught him that in the competition for
approval from his elders he might have to excel in the wit and beauty
of his writing. Matthew became very affectionate with Dr. Arnold and
Wordsworth, and capable of competing with his brothers for his sister
Jane's and his mother Mary's approval.

By the time he was sixteen Matthew was making good use of
women in his family. As he surprised or slightly shocked his mother

without quite horrifying her, he kept her attention. He absented himself from prayers and stayed out late on fishing expeditions; he once convinced his sister Jane that his boat had capsized on Windermere, since he stayed out all night with his sailing friends in his parents' absence. When he did get in trouble, he chose dramatic means to set himself in the right. When he and his brother Tom attended Winchester for a year and he angered his form by telling the headmaster that class assignments were "too light," the form boys intended to punish him. Matthew obliged by setting his hand on fire with phosphorus. Later he told his mother that he could still see his hand burning after lotion was applied to his wound.

Mrs. Arnold responded to these events very predictably. "Even now," she wrote to him months after he burned his hand, "it is painful to think of that first sight when all alone you had to bear the suffering of so severe a burn—actually seeing the light about your hand from the fire unextinguished by the lotion." And this shrewd boy went through Rugby School effectively shielded by his mother. Instead of living with School House boys, he slept in his parents' apartment: his mother notes him finishing an essay at the last minute, or drinking Champagne in the company of titled ladies, or asking one of the ladies to write out a song, or playing chess with his beautiful relative Miss Ward. Few Rugbeians in the nineteenth century really benefited from the school less painfully than Matthew Arnold. Refreshed by his mother's attentions, he wrote translations for his composition tutor James Prince Lee. Assured of his father's affection, Matthew made faces behind his father's back in history class in the paneled library tower. There is no sign that he was flogged for his misdemeanors, but there are many signs that Mrs. Arnold applauded his successes though he was not a dazzling student. He was only fair at German and French. His mark of ten in Greek Verse (in 1840) is disgraceful when set beside Lushington's twenty-four, Walrond's twenty-one, or Hughes's twenty. He almost broke the school's tardiness record one term when despite his mother's gentle warnings he was late to class thirteen times. Virtually only his quick skill in translating between Latin and English saved him, or kept him just inside the upper quarter of his form in his average marks. True, his Latin is lovely. When given the line *And press her wanton in love's secret bower* in his last school year, Arnold for example, at eighteen, startled the Cambridge examiner by composing this smartly polished verse: *Osculaque in mediis detque feratque rosis.*

What formed his mind, then? What encouraged his talent? Much of his creative strength derived from the steady and continuing emotional support and approval of his mother, and of his elder sister Jane, or "K." By applauding his early lyrics and, in her enthusiasm, demanding better ones, Mrs. Arnold helped his talent to mature. And not only her love but her comforting proximity at Rugby gave him assurance, encouraged his optimism and daring, goaded him, reduced obstacles, and seemed to reward him nearly always. A family may motivate creativity, but may also destroy it. Dr. Arnold, a lovable man of strong will, nearly withered his sons Tom, Willy, and Edward, who were to suffer and struggle under the influence of his memory. Slightly alien in the family ever since his time in leg braces, Matthew was able to view his father critically, while yet showing him a puppyish love. "Matt," wrote Dr. Arnold in 1840, "does not know what it is to work, because he so little knows what it is to think. I am hopeful," adds the father, "and he is so loving to me that it ought to make me not only hopeful but patient and long-suffering." The boy who was "so loving to me" won over Dr. Arnold without being browbeaten by his morally intense precepts.

Also it is clear that Matthew's lifelong attitudes were fostered by parental habits of mind. Dr. Arnold was too impatient to be a good teacher of mediocre pupils, but the exciting cultural comparisons that he drew inspired the best. In history classes the pupils studied two national histories simultaneously—or the teacher illustrated what was said of Periclean Greece or Imperial Rome with reference to Napoleon and modern France, for example. A lazy, bright pupil such as Matthew was seldom bored; his mind was trained to analyze a topic by flying away from it for perspective or illustration, an exercise not unlike that of the poet's work of seizing fresh metaphors from a distance to animate the poem's subject. Within his family Dr. Arnold was emotive, demonstrative, and ready to weep with pleasure, and indeed he feared that his own children might become "hard." He would prefer that they "die," as he once told Matthew and Tom, rather than see them become unfeeling. This seems to us very Victorian—as it was.

A social culture unembarrassed by sentiment and admiring family loyalty, hugging, kissing, and tenderness with tears may give its children
chances to explore the whole range of human feelings within the
home. Its novelists and poets will pay a small price, in sentimental
errors, for the chances they will have to write profoundly of the human condition. This family emphasis on feeling accounts for Matthew
Arnold's later weeping over his children, but also in part for his ability
to combine emotive with intellectual qualities in his essays, to produce works with "felt" structures.

Involved with the question of "feeling" is the religious problem for
many Victorians, since the religious certainty of younger intellectuals
was worn away by waves of the Higher Criticism of the Bible, the
advances of science and new theories relating to biology, geology, and
anthropology, and the schisms within the Anglican Church; no new
viable world outlook seemed profound enough to satisfy the demands
of the heart and head alike. Without religion, we yield our feelings to
anarchy or, indeed, the feelings wither so that we become arid. Arnold was to explore this dilemma in poems such as "Memorial
Verses," *Empedocles on Etna*, and indirectly in his Oxford elegies
"The Scholar-Gipsy" and "Thyrsis." Clearly, his home life and even
his school life in the formative years were, in retrospect, to give him a
fair sense of the life of the feeling intellect—to support which he is to
search in his poetry, and later in his criticism, for an adequate new
philosophical outlook or faith. Certainly, the religious and moral emphasis at Rugby tended to make pupils self-conscious—perhaps un-
healthily so. Debonair and undisturbed in his parents' rooms at
School House, Matthew perhaps inspected his own conscience not
very often, but he absorbed the Rugby ethos. At Oxford, especially
after his father's death and John Henry Newman's conversion to
Rome, he was to confront the difficult problem of the "self," perhaps
the main epistemological problem of the Victorian age. If, as a whole,
romantic writers had asserted the subjective sense of the self, the Victorian tended to question his own identity and even the possibility of
ever knowing his deep identity—a theme of Arnold's poems "The
Buried Life" and "A Summer Night." Romantics typically had felt at
one with nature. Up at the Lakes near Rydal Mount in the summers,
Matthew Arnold in his walks and climbs and trout fishing had many

chances to absorb Wordsworth's semi-pantheistic and almost compla-
cent view of nature, and time later on to find it inadequate, as he does
in his stoical poem "Resignation," for example. He is typically Victorian in being anxious to differentiate man from nature. But he is to
explore the "self" and the new sense of man's apartness in nature with
more subtlety than other poets, since he has had a longer and more
immediate and affecting experience of the earlier romantic outlook
than most Victorians had. That is, he had talked with Wordsworth,
heard that poet's recitals, sounded him out, and sympathized with
him during the Rugby years as well as in the second half of the 1840s.

The later serious attitudes of Arnold, then, have interesting origins
in the apparently carefree life he led in school and with his family.
When he matriculated at Oxford as a Balliol Scholar in 1841, the
university was in the midst of its anguishing controversy over the Anglican "Tracts," in which Newman and Pusey were said to be leading
the Church over to Rome, and Dr. Arnold was praised as a calm
defender of the liberal and Latitudinarian cause. Matthew easily kept
aloof from the religious struggle, as he had learned how to be a cool
fish and much about the value of detachment. After his father died,
he played rather merrily with his friend Clough (his "Horatio") the
role of Prince Hamlet. He plunged to a bad second class degree after
trying to do three years' reading in a few weeks, taught briefly at
Rugby, won an Oriel fellowship, gambled with old friends and ran-
sacked Bodley for books, and then transferred his Oxford life to
Berkeley Square when he became private secretary to the Whig peer
Lord Lansdowne, who usually gave him little to do.

But at Lansdowne House, off an elegant square, in the cool morn-
ings amidst Rembrandts and Gainsboroughs, he not only doodled and
twiddled but wrote portentous notes to himself:

> Meeting a cockney on a Greenwich steamer, instead of
> laughing, say—does this gay unled varmint thing *succeed* with
> his accoutrements better than I do, or worse.
>
> The rich have art as a mere stimulant: it is only for something
> else to do that nous autres pauvres are compelled to regard it
> otherwise.

The artist has not the same power of passive pleasure from sensuous objects as another, else he would enjoy and not *represent*.

Thou thyself, o man, are perhaps to be one of those characters thou hast come across in thy reading, who *fail*: this wilt thou never understand? thou gazest on the successful as so many manifestations of thyself, and on the unsuccessful as on men who have failed to be what thou art: and this, being nothing. Is it that life itself is a present and sensible success, which while thou hast it keeps thee on the level of those who have *wholly existed*, not in like case with those who have failed to exist.

He tried to imitate Carlyle. He tried to aspire to Goethe's mature Weimar wisdom. He tried to be a revolutionary *philosophe*. Luckily, with immense caution he fell in love. His young lady was romantic, with a thin waist and dark blue eyes, and so timid and enticing that Hartley Coleridge—who fondled children and wrote love letters to them—believed she was as beautiful as anyone he had seen. Possibly Hartley was ready to overpraise her simply because her mother (as Mrs. Arnold did) gave him glasses of beer. But others refer to her beauty and to her fittingly romantic and exotic background. The blue-eyed Mary Sophia Claude was baptized in the French Reformed Church at Friedrichstadt and taken to England by her father. The young Claude children had lived a mile away from Fox How, and Matthew in his boyhood had befriended Louis Claude, Mary's pistol-shooting brother who was sometimes a truant from school. (They were to have a chance to talk over early Lake District days when Arnold, then on his first American lecture tour, met Louis Claude—who had immigrated to the United States—at Madison, Wisconsin, in 1884.) "Matt's romantic passion for the Cruel Invisible, Mary Claude" in 1848 must be delayed until our next chapter. We might consider it in a comic light; his relations with Mary Claude from what we gather from Anne Clough's diaries, the Claude letters, and Tom Arnold's help might be the minor stuff from which romantic biography is spun, too. I have given the evidence and told the story in outline in chapter 7 of *Matthew Arnold: A Life* (1981), but in pages just ahead in the present book I want to consider a minor romance in the light of Arnold's early Europeanism and intellectual development. Biographies must present the evidence of outward facts as thoroughly as possible, and what is reported as a "romantic passion" (as Tom Arnold called Matthew's feeling for Mary) obliges us to be factual and circumstantial. But, in looking at the evidence of events, any biographer may give short shrift to what ought to concern us most in the life of any writer: the life of the mind itself.

Mary Claude was by no means the only cause that prompted Arnold to write "To my Friends, who ridiculed a tender Leave-taking" and, after that, an accompanying series of lyrics, which he was to group in various arrangements under the heading *Switzerland*. By the time all these reflective (and very European) love lyrics were published, he had married the daughter of an English judge and become a father—his youth had ended. His lyrics almost neglect his lady's feelings, but they say much about the mood of a son of Dr. Arnold with the weight of a nation on his shoulders, a young man, too, who has meditated on problems of friendship, love, loneliness, and spiritual isolation. Like his honeymoon poem "Dover Beach," the love poems dwell on the present failure of religion and on love as a means of spiritual survival. Arnold advocated marriage—and was happy to marry Fanny Lucy Wightman in 1851. But we hardly live on love alone, and he turned to a search for supporting values and attitudes—even as he collected data on his nation as a school inspector for thirty-five years. His essays develop the ideas of "criticism" and "culture" and "religion" with nerve and energy that remind one of the confidence he had felt as a happy son of Rugby and of the exhilaration he had known in the green Lake District of Southey, Hartley Coleridge, and Wordsworth during his crucial early years.

Chapter Thirteen

MARY CLAUDE'S BLUE EYES

THE IDENTITY of "Marguerite" has been one of the prime mysteries of Victorian literature. She seems to breathe in Matthew Arnold's poetry. All together between October 1848 and June 1863, he wrote some nine lyrics that mention a "Marguerite." She has soft, ash-colored hair, pale features, and unforgettable blue eyes: she is slim and graceful, witty and mocking at one moment, gravely reserved the next. We feel that she must have existed because we have such a vivid impression of her. And, in any case, Arnold's idea of her inspired some of his greatest lyrics, such as "To Marguerite, in returning a volume of the Letters of Ortis" (though, tinkering with his Marguerite poems, he changed the title of this one several times until it became in 1869 "To Marguerite—Continued"). She is even the human object in a splendidly impassioned discourse about our isolation in life:

> Yes! in the sea of life enisled,
> With echoing straits between us thrown,
> Dotting the shoreless watery wild,
> We mortal millions live *alone*.

And if she is squeezed out of some of Arnold's reflective love poems (to be put in a lyric's title, and then dropped from the title), at other times she comes before us tantalizingly as she does in "A Memory Picture":

> Paint that lilac kerchief, bound
> Her soft face, her hair around:
> Tied under the softest chin
> Mockery ever ambushed in.
> Let the fluttering fringes streak
> All her pale, sweet-rounded cheek.

Arnold was to group his Marguerite poems in a sequence he called *Switzerland*, so that they would hint at the story of a broken love affair in the Swiss Alps. He took pains in rearranging the sequence, in several editions of his lyrics, until they settled down into a final order. Marguerite at last acquired the status of being a minor myth in his lifetime. He denied she existed, but, since his death, critics have refused to believe him. Nothing was discovered about her until the 1960s and 1970s except for Arnold's unexplained allusion, in a Swiss letter of September 1848, to a pair of "blue eyes" that he hopes to see the next day at Thun. Then, as late as 1966, a New Zealand letter of Matthew's brother Tom, headed "Nelson June 14th 1849," came to light; it refers to Tom's amusement over a recent letter by one of his sisters in England concerning "Matt's romantic passion for the Cruel Invisible, Mary Claude." Mary Claude, a friend of Anne Clough and of Arnold's close circle of Oxford friends (the "Clougho-Matthean set"), was a beautiful, slender young woman with dark blue eyes. Baptized at the French Reformed Church in Friedrichstadt in 1820, she had been taken as a child from Berlin to Liverpool; she summered with her brother and sisters and her attractive, widowed mother in the Lake District. Sensitive, temperamental, and romantic, Mary Claude learned to dance "in defiance of the godly," and imitated in her own amateur stories European sentimentalists such as Foscolo and Jean Paul. She also went on waterfall scrambles and picnics with Arnold and his friends, and on one occasion (according to Anne Clough's diary) became lost on the fells. In his first poem about Marguerite, "A Memory Picture" (or, as he called it in 1849, "To my Friends, who ridiculed a tender Leave-taking"), Arnold describes no imaginary Marguerite but Mary Claude herself. A French Protestant exile, she had relatives at Geneva, and, in 1848, good reasons for visiting the Swiss German-speaking town of Thun, where Arnold had hoped to see a familiar pair of blue eyes. It does not follow that the fictive Marguerite and the real Mary Claude are identical, though, or that it was part of Arnold's purpose in his lyrics to record literally a love affair of his own.

But let us begin from the beginning. How were Mary Claude and the European sentimental writers involved in the life of a young poet, whose father, Dr. Arnold the headmaster of Rugby School, had in the 1830s built Fox How as a holiday home for the Arnold family in the Lake District?

FOX HOW AND ITS ENVIRONS

When the Arnolds began to summer at Fox How about a mile from the Wordsworths at Rydal Mount in 1834, Matthew was eleven. The house was to be a welcome retreat from headmasterly cares for his father, but it put the boy in touch with the Continent. To Fox How on visits, by the late 1830s, came the Hares and the Bunsens, who knew German philosophy and theology. A visitor on winter holidays was Crabb Robinson, who had interpreted Kant, audited Schelling's lectures, met Jacobi, talked with Goethe, and explained German transcendentalism to Mme. de Staël.

William Wordsworth, who discovered Matthew in his Loughrigg fort in the winter of 1836–37, dropped in from Rydal and reminisced about the Continent; his young admirer was to become skillful in drawing him out on "Italian" topics. Wordsworth had debated with the Italian exile Ugo Foscolo, and Arnold was to meet several other people who were keen on Foscolo's virtues (somewhat keener than

Wordsworth was), namely Lord Lansdowne, who had attended his Italian lectures, and Philarète Chasles, who had been one of Foscolo's confidants. Mary Claude (a girl of fourteen when the Arnolds inhabited Fox How) was to write in imitation of Foscolo. The Claudes wintered in Liverpool and summered at Rothay Bank, less than a mile along the Rotha from Fox How. Rothay Bank stands today; it is a stone house in the Continental style, surrounded by wide lawns, near the bridge leading into Ambleside. Arnold passed it on his way to Lake Windermere and not later than the summer of 1838 he was stopping at its door to see his friend, a boy of about his own age, the hulking, truant, bright, often pugilistic Louis Claude (Mary's brother), with whom he shot and fished.

The Claudes symbolized the mixture of European cultures for Arnold as surely as the tragedienne Rachel would do. The pale, blue-eyed Mary Sophia Claude, with her mixture of romantic longing and mockery, her "wit," "spleen," "power of . . . ridicule" and what Arnold called her "sadness," was to be the model for the woman in "To Meta" and in his first poem about Marguerite. "Matt's romantic passion for the Cruel Invisible, Mary Claude" would help him to see the uses and virtues of the European sentimental school. Connected with Germany, France, Switzerland, and even South America, the Claude girls came into view of the Arnold boys, for Matthew and Tom spent days on Loughrigg Fell behind Fox How. Mary Claude, a child exile with a slender form, seemed to Hartley Coleridge (who knew most of the child population of Ambleside and Grasmere) "as beautiful a creature" as he had seen. She sailed in James Brancker's boat; that Liverpool industrialist functioned as the Claude family guardian (he was a legal executor of Mary's father's will). Brancker's Byzantine turrets at Croft Lodge not far from Fox How, his masks of comedy and tragedy up under his eaves, his black drainpipes embossed with the initials "J.B.," his deific achievement in altering the course of the River Rotha for a mile (scaring away the trout for which Louis Claude and Arnold fished), his almost feminine beseeching of the gifted Hartley Coleridge who talked eloquently in the Fox How drawing room, and his pride in the Friedrichstadt family of Rothay Bank were features of Arnold's life in the 1830s. Mary was too shy to attend a "point de réunion"; but Arnold, at times, must have seen her near at hand. The

Claude girls, as their mother wrote, "love Fairfield and Loughrigg better than anything else in Westmoreland." Arnold's alertness to Continental beauty almost caused him to exhaust the word "beautiful" in the *Journale Gastronomique*, or travel diary, which he kept during ten days in France in August, 1837. In this, he notes everything aesthetic from the outfit of French postillions, to the dresses of ladies, to the affecting legends on tombs in French Catholic churchyards and the architectural glories of Chartres.

Having heard about the Continent, Arnold in 1836 wrote "The First Sight of Italy," and having seen France, he later wrote stylish poems for his family's *Fox How Magazine*. Certain poets who contributed to this twice-yearly publication were less than thirteen years old; and Arnold, imitating Pope, Byron, Scott, and Shelley, did his best to seem worldly in the *Magazine*. It is unlikely that the Continent influenced his notions *about* poetry just now; especially so, because the Arnolds *had* a poetics. We must see, briefly, what it was.

There are two kinds of poetry for the parents. First, there is a kind befitting "the golden opening Prime of Youth," which is descriptive, superficial, charming, and luminous, as Dr. Arnold had written: "Then so should Verse be but a passing Charm / Or sing responsive but to outward Shows." Mrs. Arnold composed this kind of verse with her eyes shut while riding in a coach, and penned it when reposing on the Laleham sofa, in celebration of a panorama exhibit she had seen in London:

> Albania's mountains crown'd with snow
> The purple tint on all below
> The gallant ships that come & go
> What wonder that so fair a sight
> Had power to charm a Lalehamite!

But Mrs. Arnold knew that this mode was inferior. The second variety of poetry is inward, sincere, deeply felt, serious, often religious; it means what it *says*, as Mrs. Arnold put it, and does not strive for effects. If the topic is an inward one, then

> I would not utter idle lays
> Like poets use to those less dear
> In verse which means not what it says.

It is interesting that Mrs. Arnold's inward poems seem rather conventional; but Dr. Arnold achieved much sincerity and energy and even a simple, moving eloquence in this mode:

> Servants of God!—and shall I say
> That ye as blind have gone astray?
>
> Where shall the River end, and who can stem
> The Boundless Sea wherein its Stream is lost?
>
> What boots it though his early years
> Were wreathed with more than Childhoods flowers.
>
> Go my Friends & dig my grave
> For I would from wandering cease.
>
> Dig my Grave, for wherefore stay
> When my course is fully run
> There my Pilgrim staff I lay
> There where earthly toil is done
> There would I myself lie down
> There no Pain nor care are known.

AESTHETIC PROBLEMS

It was after his father's death in 1842 that Arnold's genuine attempt to succeed as a poet began; we must not suppose that he did not exult at the challenge of shaping a world view and a poetics for himself and take pleasure in the romantic malaise caused by his religious uncertainty. We attempt to follow a European thread running through Arnold's problems. After his second-class Oxford degree, he became a Fellow of Oriel College with his friend Arthur Clough and from 1845 to 1847 put himself through a large course of reading in myth and

symbolism, ancient, Western, and Eastern philosophy, history and social studies, literary criticism, and European literature. His gambling
and loose language, and journeys in 1846 to see George Sand and
Rachel, were partly reactions against the circumspect, introspective
atmosphere of Oriel. Arnold, for example, now confronted works by
and about Goethe and Schiller, whom he had begun to take up at
Balliol, and Kant, Herder, Creuzer (of the *Symbolik und Mythologie*),
Schelling, Bunsen, and Humboldt; a few years later he was reading
Jean Paul Richter (whom he perhaps discovered at Balliol), Novalis,
Tieck, Jacobi, Lessing, and Heine. He had many "guides" to the Ger-
mans in the next few years in Coleridge, Saisset, Rémusat, Carlyle,
Cousin, and Mme. de Staël; he also heard about Germany from
scholarly friends: Temple, who lectured on Kant; Stanley and Jowett,
who studied in the summers in Germany (taking up Hegel and Kant);
J. D. Coleridge, who sampled German life; and probably from his
own confidante Jane Arnold, who polished up her German with
lessons from Crabb Robinson. One of the reasons why Arnold took
Goethe as his paramount guide in poetry, criticism, and conduct from
about 1846 was that even the French journals were admitting that
recent movements in German thought were powerful: Goethe was a
titan who had stood over, and influenced, other titans. Through his
long life he had evolved through phases, and had participated in so
many modern movements that there were Goethes to choose from.

Arnold, in writing his first volume of poetry, *The Strayed Reveller*
(1849), clearly had his subtle German mentor in mind. First, one of
Goethe's subjects is manifestly the subject of *The Strayed Reveller*—in
a confused age of false optimism and deep spiritual malaise, how is
the young poet to discipline and preserve himself for creativity, what
should he reject, and what precisely should his attitude be? Often
symbolically and in a manner suggesting Arnold's spiritual autobiography, the first twenty-six poems in *The Strayed Reveller* answer these
questions; and the last poem in the volume, "Resignation," brilliantly
defines the creative attitude. Now, Goethe had addressed himself off
and on in the *Conversations* with Eckermann to the problems and
attitude of the modern poet. He also had done so in his essays "Für
junge Dichter" and "Noch ein Wort für junge Dichter," which Arnold translated in June 1847. A second special reason for Arnold's

interest in Goethe in these years has to do with Goethe's objective poetics. It is a Goethean-Coleridgean theory of the lyric that Arnold voices in his letters to Clough of the 1840s. According to this, a poem is a whole form, with all parts subordinated to the main effect, and designed to give pleasure through its beauty.

But Arnold views that theory of whole forms with increasing anxiety in the *late* 1840s. His anxiety is often directed at Oriel College, the home of spiritual autobiography and of the *Tracts for the Times*. Oriel had fallen off from its earlier days of Hurrell Froude and of Newman even before Arnold reached it in 1845. Clough had described the dons as "silent, grave and almost sleepy" and "grave, silent, and almost bashful," for the aftermath of the *Tracts* had traumatized the College. Arnold exploded less charitably: "I know what hideosities[,] what Solecisms, what Lies, what crudities . . . what Grimaces, what affectations . . . I shall hear and see amongst the born-to-be-tight-laced." Oriel introspectiveness had become cautious, nerveless, and dull, but also infectious. To Arnold's horror Oriel's aridity infected his friend Clough's poems—and even his own. Further, he could see no clear sea between a Scylla and a Charybdis. Concentrating on his own inward, intellectual, and emotional experience of the world and books for subject matter, how could he achieve the beauty of whole forms? And if he abandoned inward subject matter would he not be dawdling with surfaces? In his calmer moods, he took a tendency in Clough's poetry to stand for the Scylla of formless analysis or thinking aloud in the lyric, and a tendency in Keats's and Tennyson's for the Charybdis of dawdling with the world's shell. We see here the residue of his parents' influence; anyone can dawdle with the world's painted shell ("the purple tint on all below"), but that kind of poetry is insignificant. Anyone infected by Oriel can be introspective but that kind of poetry puts one on a level with crudities, affectations, distortions, and Oriel ineffectiveness. When further irritated by his friends who "ridiculed" him over a lovelorn vigil "for the Cruel Invisible, Mary Claude," Arnold let fly at Clough in November 1848. Though exaggerative, his outburst suggests that the "age" is infected by the spirit of Oriel and that restless analysis and introspection are inevitable for the modern English poet: "I have been at Oxford the last two days and hearing Sellar and the rest of that [Oriel] clique who know neither life nor themselves rave about your poem [the *Bothie*] gave me a strong almost bitter feeling with respect to them, the age, the poem, even you," he writes with insulting fury to Clough (who may have been among the friends who had "ridiculed" his romantic behavior with Mary*). We might expect Arnold to damn Clough's poem on a classic basis. Instead, a new emphasis in his poetics is hinted: "something tells me I can, if need be, at last dispense with them all, even with him. . . . More English than European, I said finally . . . and took up Obermann, and refuged myself with him in his forest against your Zeit Geist." Arnold turns to the European sentimentalists, and it is clear that at least at first he sensed no contradiction between the qualities of such a work as Senancour's *Obermann* and the Goethean-Coleridgean theory of whole structures. The latter theory had been voiced with a mild insult to Clough on May 24, 1848: "You might write a speech in Phèdre—Phedra loquitur—but you could not write Phèdre. And when you adopt this or that form you must sacrifice much to the ensemble, and that form in return for admirable effects demands immense sacrifices" (*Letters to Clough*, 81). This statement is still echoed in comments on poetic theory early in 1849, or not long after he says that he is retiring into Obermann's forest of thought, as for example when he writes with a petulant urgency to Clough:

> You succeed best you see, in fact, in the hymn, where man, his
> deepest feelings being in play, finds poetical expression as *man*
> only, not as artist:—but consider whether you attain the
> *beautiful*, and whether your product gives PLEASURE, not
> excites curiosity and reflexion. Forgive me all this: but I am
> always prepared myself to give up the attempt, on conviction:
> and so, I know, are you. (*Letters to Clough*, 99)

---

*Traveling in the Bernese Oberland in September 1848, Arnold certainly had hoped to see a familiar pair of "blue eyes" at Thun in Switzerland. He cooled his heels at the Hôtel Bellevue. Just after this, one of the Arnold sisters wrote a "long letter" about his romantic passion for the girl whom Tom Arnold called the "Cruel Invisible, Mary Claude." Mary Claude had relatives in the Swiss Alps and had been traveling that summer. For discussions of the biographical evidence, see Miriam Allott's lively essay and my reply in the journal *Victorian Poetry*, 23 (1985), 125–43 and 145–59.

But as 1849 advanced his letters to Clough became fewer, and by the time Arnold began to draft his European sentimentalist-style lyrics for *Switzerland*, he was following a wholly new light. His letter from Swiss Thun of September 1849, in which he discusses spiritual rebirth and refers to his need to "get into prayer," is written in the mode of the European sentimental school's reflective passion, the *passion réfléchissante*, which is at once moral and inward looking and wide seeking. It seems clear that Arnold, who at twenty-five and twenty-six tried to be more chic, worldly, and cool than his friends, had reacted rather badly to being laughed at as the man who had traveled to the Alps to see a "neighbouring" girl who had not appeared. He had made himself look lovelorn and ridiculous. Mary Claude was an intimate of Anne Clough, and a friend of Tom Walrond and Arthur Clough: the news of Arnold's waiting for her at the Hôtel Bellevue, beside a turquoise lake, apparently had become current in the "Clougho-Matthean set." But his friendship with Mary Claude, a very committed sentimentalist, had unusual consequences for his poetry.

LA PASSION RÉFLÉCHISSANTE

In Germany, Goethe's *The Sorrows of the Young Werther* and subjective lyrics had been one fountainhead of a literary movement that was consistent with romantic values but took an extreme stand against the value of rational thought. Jean Paul Richter, struggling between the pietism of his upbringing and the rationalism of the *Aufklärung*, became an exponent of it, as did Jacobi, Tieck, and Novalis. This movement appealed to one of the Claude girls, in the 1840s in the Lake District, because it was German and because it exalted the value of feeling. After the death of her sister Anne Lucrèce, Mary Claude had written a little prose tract called *Consideration* (1847), citing Dr. Arnold with approval but pointing to the "impotency of the human mind," the "littleness of the human understanding," and to that in nature which is "far beyond the comprehension of human reason"; after that she championed the writings of German sentimentalists and adopted Richter as her key author. Since the mercantile Claudes taught their children languages (Mary's cousin Jeannette knew Italian,

German, French, Spanish, and English at twelve), Mary was something of a linguist. She read the sentimental Germans enough to be
called "a good German," and in her writings, such as "The Sea" and
"The Moon," imitated Andersen and Foscolo. Like Richter she
sought a release from thought in high feeling and in the emotional
world of children.

In the summer of 1847 Anne Clough, staying at the Claudes'
Broadlands and sometimes with her mother and brother nearby, led
Mary Claude into the "Clougho-Matthean" circle. Clough, Walrond,
and Tom Arnold went on pony rides, waterfall scrambles, and romantic walks with these women and Mary came to Fox How. By the end
of the year the pattern of her intimacy with the Arnolds was established; and it was on January 2, 1848 that Matthew Arnold wrote an
anguished statement about the "tie" of passion. He did not wish to fall
in love; but "Matt's romantic passion for . . . Mary Claude" certainly
had a basis in fact later in this year.

The woman who attracted him had (from the evidence of her own
writing) a mind that was sharp and eager enough to condemn habits of
modern thought on principle. For Mary Claude the mind in its arrogance has reduced and discredited what it can learn from feeling. To
illustrate her scorn for that arrogance, she exaggerated her pose; she
was witty and scornful at home with her mother, and emotive and
intense usually with her friends, as Anne Clough shows in a diary of
1847 written in the Lake District:

In the evening Mary & I staid at home while the others went to
church. We talked about various things. Mary spoke of her great
love of Natural History. . . . There is in Mary Claude such an
intense love of the beautiful & such an intense degree of feeling
for suffering. . . . We spoke too of devotional feelings & agreed
that church going in a general way did not tend to excite, at
least not in our own case. . . . Then we talked of the doctrine of
the Eternity of punishment which seemed to disturb Mary very
much. She could not bear to think of it even in the case of the
most indifferent people. She spoke too of the weariness and
painfulness of thought and what a relief any employment was
which could make one think less.

The staying home from church, the criticism of the doctrine of punishment, and such phrases as "she could not bear to think of it," "the
weariness and painfulness of thought," and "any employment . . .
which could make one think less" illuminate Mary's amateur poem "The
Sea" of 1847, which suggests a divorce between Christianity and the
power and beauty of the "dreadful sea." For Mary, the sea is divided from
the observer on land, feeling is separate from thought, the modern
church cannot satisfy the soul. Thus thinking itself is oppressive. Yet
Mary is a "good German." The "soul" of the "Denmark of Hans
Christian Andersen" could be found in her work, as Arnold wrote long
after he composed "The Forsaken Merman," and after references to
"Matt's romantic passion for the Cruel Invisible, Mary Claude" had been
suppressed to protect Mary, who continued to live at Ambleside, unmar-
ried, until she died in 1912. It is important that Mary connected him not
only to the "soul of Northern Europe" but to his own freer youth. The
stories she wrote of symbolic daisies and anemones carried him back, he
confessed less than two years before he died, to "long-past days," to her
"youth," to the time when she was a "vision," to "Westmoreland . . .
when Westmoreland was the Westmoreland of Wordsworth and Hartley
Coleridge," in short, to a time before Arnold himself, as a young man,
was choked with ratiocination. This is why she becomes the symbolic
"Marguerite" in poems which are *Obermann*-like in using reflective
passion to assess problems such as isolation, friendship, and love itself;
Mary Claude is like a time machine in helping to transport the poet's
mind over a large area of his experience and reminds him of Obermann's
alpine flowers, the *marguerites des prés*, which have the power of evoking
the past vividly ("les souvenirs qu'elles suscitent ramènent fortement au
passé"). In "Parting," Arnold traverses a span of time from the analysis-
ridden present to his Lake District past with its simpler nature worship
and its Fox How family prayer bells; in those days he had first encoun-
tered Shelley, and there are Shelley-echoes in his verse:

> Forgive me! forgive me!
>   Ah, Marguerite, fain
> Would these arms reach to clasp thee!
>   But see! 'tis in vain.

    In the void air, towards thee,
      My stretched arms are cast;

    Far, far from each other
      Our spirits have grown;
    And what heart knows another?
      Ah! who knows his own?

    Blow, ye winds! lift me with you!
      I come to the wild.
    Fold closely, O Nature!
      Thine arms round thy child.

    To thee only God granted
      A heart ever new—
    To all always open,
      To all always true.

    Ah! calm me, restore me;
      And dry up my tears.

Mary Claude helps to account for what is often thought to be an adolescent quality in the *Switzerland* lyrics (notably "Parting"); in fact the feeling, at times, is not that of adolescence but of childhood. A poem such as "To Marguerite, in returning a volume of the Letters of Ortis" replies to Foscolo's *Ortis* and gestures toward Mary Claude's own "Letter Addressed to a Friend in Returning a Book"—and reflects the isolation theme of her stories—but this poem also echoes some of Arnold's earliest reading, beginning with Keble's *Christian Year* (which he knew when in leg braces at Laleham). The first value of Mary and the sentimentalists to him as a poet was that they helped him to concentrate large spans of his emotional life in brief lyrics. The intensity of "To Marguerite" is not surpassed in his other lyrics.

    European sentimentalists also helped him to rid himself of English literary influences. By the end of the 1840s he is far more acerbic about English Romantics than before, and his new detachment helps him to appraise Wordsworth effectively in the Obermann "Stanzas" and implicitly in "Resignation," for which "Tintern Abbey" is a foil. In "Memorial Verses," Wordsworth is refashioned as an English sentimentalist or accorded the highest praise, at his death, which the poet can accord in the perspective of European sentimentalism. One may add that we cannot accurately treat the topic of Arnold's romanticism until we take both England and Europe as the *context* for the problem; in Germany romanticism from the middle of the eighteenth century until the death of Goethe has a longer span and a more pervasive influence on philosophy, history, and all of the arts than in any other country; and Arnold as a young man plays England and Germany off against each other, freeing himself from English Romantics by adopting German guides, and criticizing the German guides ("lumbering old cart-horses," he tells his mother before going to Thun in 1848) in the light of English literary graces. France, Italy, and Germany together influence his lyric poetry in 1849.

Further, the sentimentalists encouraged a confident inwardness of viewpoint, missing in his earlier poems such as "Mycerinus" and the "Fragment of an 'Antigone'"; they helped to free Arnold from the poetry of statement, exhibited in "Wellington" or even in his Schelling-influenced "Cruikshank" (which becomes more interesting in the light of Schelling's "Plastic Arts" lecture). The sentimentalists' mode of twofold vision is practiced in Arnold's 1849 letter from Thun, in the Obermann "Stanzas," and in *Switzerland*. The epistemological premise of the double, or inward-outward vision, is "I feel." "Nature is dark everywhere," writes Senancour in *Obermann*. "'I feel' is the sole affirmation for him who would have truth only" ("Je sens est le seul mot de l'homme qui ne veut que des verités") (Senancour's *Obermann*, 1804, Lettre LXIII). The premise "I feel" implies a detachment from the society of one's friends and especially from the immediate object of one's emotions. As Mme. de Staël implies when she finds in *Werther* the "passion réfléchissante, la passion qui se juge elle-même," reflective passion is conditional upon the failure of romantic love. But guilt (as in Chateaubriand's *René*) or dissatisfaction with society and an obsessive longing for truth (as in Senancour's *Obermann*) or longing for the medieval world view (as in Novalis and even in Mary Claude) may isolate the one who feels. It is at the farthest remove from society, or from a milieu with social norms, that the sentimentalist's passion becomes the reflective kind that produces insights into the self and the world. Chateaubriand's hero René tells the savages of Natchez how his incestuous feeling for his sister Amelie and guilt drove him to the edge of Mt. Etna's crater, where at one glance he perceived the panoramic world maplike and ordered, and at another looked "dans le cratère de l'Etna" to find a symbol of the inner self. René impressed Arnold, but Senancour's *Obermann* did so even more, because "of all writers" Senancour "is the most perfectly isolated" and because deep insight into the self and unsparing broad sight over the dilemmas of modern society suffuse the latter book.

In one sense, then, the "sentimental school" solved Arnold's problems by suggesting a way ahead for his art, beyond analytic introspection to a deeper and felt inwardness and a stronger symbolism. He remained for some years under the philosophical and aesthetic influence of German and French sentimentalists; that infuence is shadowily operative as late as "Thyrsis." On the other hand, the European mode has a difficult epistemology, and Arnold must have wondered as early as 1849 whether he could live with it. It left him, emotionally, on Mt. Etna's crater with René, or brooding in the Alps over an "abyss" with Obermann, who cries, "But on what shall disillusioned thought repose?" If the reflective passion requires that the poet shall impugn analytic thought and, in an inward sense, utterly detach himself from society, then from what source is joy needed for creativity to come? Arnold approaches this problem in *Empedocles on Etna* and gives it flesh in the alternative figures of Empedocles and Callicles. He certainly knew in 1849 and 1850 that he was struggling for his survival as an artist; and yet he could feel that Goethe, who helped to provide him with a theory of the lyric, and who had dramatized the mode of the reflective passion in *Werther*, might see him through deeper difficulties after his rather embarrassing love affair with a blue-eyed exile from the Continent had ended. His efforts to succeed as as a poet were to continue for years after he married Fanny Lucy Wightman in 1851, and he was to write—with acknowledged difficulty—of the beautiful exile from Friedrichstadt's French Protestant community, Mary Claude, as late as 1886 or two years before he died.

Chapter Fourteen

BROWNING AND THE LYRIC TEST

R OBERT BROWNING'S LIFE is entertaining and yet respectable, almost a moral version of Lord Byron's life. One feels that no other prominent Victorian lived a better "story" within the bounds of propriety. There are not more than a few scandals or cupboarded skeletons here—such as Robert's feeling for Shelley's atheism. But in his early twenties he gave up the atheism to please his mother, just as he had given up his University College studies after a few months to return to her home. (Gower Street was so far from Camberwell—a good two-hours ride—that he had been forced to live in London, far from her good-night kiss; the solution had been for him to withdraw from University College.) Daringly, he at last eloped to Italy, but not before marrying Elizabeth Barrett, with whom he had offered to live as a brother. Now, all of this might be dull as ditchwater had he not written intelligent, fraught love letters, and had not Elizabeth Barrett been a keen and talented letter writer herself. The Brownings' correct existence in Italy is fascinating because Elizabeth in her correspondence brings its minor traumas to life. After she died, Browning's frustrations and bafflement with his son Pen have some remarkable interest of their own.

But if the life is a success, what is the poetry? It is often marvelous; Browning influenced Eliot, Pound, and other "modern" poets, and his blank-verse dramatic monologues have some following today. But I shall put them aside. For this poet, let us propose a severe *lyric* test and ask what is unique about his lyric art? We begin with Oscar Wilde, who states the main objection to Robert Browning.

Wilde writes in "The Critic as Artist":

> There are moments when he [Browning] wounds us by
> monstrous music. Nay, if he can only get his music by breaking
> the strings of his lute, he breaks them, and they snap in discord,
> and no Athenian tettix, making melody from tremulous wings,
> lights on the ivory horn to make the movement perfect, or the
> interval less harsh. . . . If Shakespeare could sing with myriad
> lips, Browning could stammer through a thousand mouths. . . .
> The only man who can touch the hem of his garment is George
> Meredith. Meredith is a prose Browning, and so is Browning.
> He used poetry as a medium for writing in prose.

The tettix (or cicada) witticism is the critically important one.

Even very good English lyres, from time to time, seem to snap strings and emit harsh chords. But when they do, there is a compensating cicada's "melody" or euphony in the movement to make the "interval less harsh." Yet when Browning deliberately breaks his lyre's seventh string, and is harsh, there is no compensating euphony whatever.

No cicada sings for him.

Of course the passage amuses us because it seems damning and at least half true. Wilde locates a feature in Browning's versification that is new, even revolutionary, and yet he fails to suggest a principle that would lead us to search for aesthetic functions of tonal harshness. We are left with the scandalous image of a bad poet who forgot that prose is prose, verse verse. Wilde's Browning neither sings nor speaks—only stammers.

But Wilde, a pleasant lyricist himself, is in a bad position to appreciate stylistic experiments. In the eighties and nineties, a very deep reaction against early Victorian innovations in style has set in, so that one finds "smooth" traditional lyricists like Tennyson esteemed and "rough" experimental prosodists like Browning mainly admired despite their styles. The few scraps of Hopkins that get into print in Wilde's time cause no stir, and Hopkins and Browning alike influence prosody later. Significantly, Donne waits to be "rediscovered."

Even so, the principle that governs Browning's lyric versification and that Wilde misses does not come suddenly into being and then go quickly out of fashion. It exists, rather subversively, in the sixteenth century. It can be felt behind some metaphysical lyrics and with other "anti-Ciceronian" styles. While it does not impress itself very strongly on neoclassical poetry it does influence prose style in the rising genre of Pope and Johnson's age, the novel. Later on it is implicit in the Wordsworthian revolution, and Coleridge, as we shall see, supports it in theory. After his *Paracelsus,* and indeed with his *Strafford,* a play that is at once crude, defective, and boldly new in style, Browning is consistently within limits its advocate.

This is the principle that is directly opposed to the elaborate decorum whereby each literary genre and subgenre has its more or less fixed range of appropriate styles. The opposing principle insists that style should be determined primarily by the requirements of the literary subject. And Browning proceeds further under its special influence, with lyric versification, than Donne, Wordsworth, or other successful English lyricists had gone before.

What is chiefly new with his prosody, so far as the style-subject principle is concerned, is the method of compensation for irregular rhythm and phonetic dissonance.

The English lyricist from Wyatt to Tennyson has been at liberty to achieve some degree of vigor and contrast in sound, and some degree of imitation or sound symbolism, by exploiting to various degrees the three potentials of cacophony:

(A) metrical variation from an expected norm;

(B) phonetic difficulty (including harsh clusters, harsh or discordant verses, sequences of phonemes, and no assonance);

(C) syntactic breaks or punctuation pauses within the line.

While each of these is properly a lyrical device, in its extreme each one is strongly disruptive or anti-lyrical. Traditionally, the English lyric genre has not tolerated noticeable degrees of (A), (B), and (C) in one verse—and among good lyricists before Browning, chiefly Donne, (and most of all in his "Holy Sonnets") will raise the question as to the exception:

Th'hydroptique drunkard, and night-scouting thiefe,	9
The itchy Lecher, and selfe tickling proud	10
Have the remembrance of past joyes, for reliefe	11
Of comming ills. To (poore) me is allow'd	12
No ease. . . .	

But even in such a case, though Donne seems to veer as far from Spenserian smoothness and toward cacophony as he ever does in a short lyric, each verse effectively compensates for its own harsh or disruptive features.

While in lines 9 and 10, there is definitely (B), there is little of (A)—only single inversions—or little of (C) since the effects of the comma pauses are weak. And while (C) is prominent in line 12, (A) is not, nor is (B): "comming ills" and "me . . . allow'd" have a pleasant, transverse pattern of sound repetition—(m)(1): (m)(1)—that saves this line from phonetic difficulty.

As a good student of the metaphysical lyric—Arnold Stein—aptly observes, Donne's "harshness and discords are an absolute artistic necessity, reflecting the state of his soul and the world", but lyrically he pursues *asperitas* only so far. Euphonic features compensate for dissonant or disruptive ones in each of his verses: very typically, (A)'s absence or presence in a line sets off (B)'s presence or absence, and though Donne sometimes strains against the limits of an established style-genre decorum, he does not violate it.

His famous "controversial" openings, as in

> For Godsake hold your tongue and let me love

or

> Now thou hast lov'd me one whole day

are metrically but not *phonetically* audacious. They have (A), but not (B). Assonance, resonant sequences of vowel sounds, iterated and sometimes alliterated consonants—all compensate for daring stress sequences. If the style-subject principle is nearly at odds with the style-genre one in such cases, and can be felt, Donne's concern for "reflecting the state of his soul" does not lead him to a new prosody, nor does he ever veer so far towards unrelieved jolting in a line as the Jacobean dramatist may:

> Up—so. How is't? Feel you your legs? You stand.

Lear's genre tolerates that extreme in sound, but "The Canonization's" does not.

We spend some time with Donne for our purposes not merely because we have Browning's repeated word of high esteem for him—esteem that does itself, perhaps, lead students of their lyrics to conclude that their prosodies are alike and that Browning is only trying (ineptly) to do what Donne did (superbly)—but because Browning's prosody begins where Donne's leaves off.

Their methods are not the same. Neither of the two style principles disappears with Browning but their precedence is inverted. Requirements of the lyric subject have priority in determining what his style will be like, rather than do the traditional and implicit requirements of the lyric genre. Prosodically what this means is that the verse need not compensate for its own irregular rhythm or phonetic difficulty if its tonal extremes contribute to expressive effects in the stanza or larger lyric structure. Aesthetically his practice seeks its justification in this: euphony or resonance is temporarily suspended not merely for the sake of surprise or variety, but always, when Browning is successful, for expressive intensity. Cacophony increases the relevance of rhythm and phonetic features to the lyric's manifest subject: the particular thoughts and feelings or vision of life that it presents.

Browning's lyric prosody, we should note too, accords with Coleridgean rather than Wordsworthian theory—and it is Coleridge, rather than Wordsworth, who suggests a critical standard to employ when we imagine that Robert Browning had a bad ear. Browning's poetic diction is partly to be explained biographically. His own energy, zest, and restless impatience led him to extend the range of poetic diction, and follow in the path of Wordsworth's precepts. But, having taken that path, the young Browning became an elaborately careful and painstaking artist, and one far more Coleridgean than Wordsworthian in theory and practice. Wordsworth regards meter in all poetry as something pleasingly attendant or superadded to natural language, "a supernumerary charm," as M. H. Abrams puts it, whereas Coleridge sees meter and sound as structural devices, integral parts of poems, and finds poetic value to lie "in the balance or reconciliation of opposite or discordant qualities." Thus Coleridge anticipates Browning's use of metrically irregular, harsh verses with more resonant ones as components of expressive structure. For Coleridge antithetic features in a poem are not only permissible but highly desirable, providing always that they are synthesized, and their imaginative synthesis is for him a prime criterion of poetic excellence.

Correspondingly, in Browning, the synthesis that should arise from the use of verses with extremely different meanings or styles is the test—and properly the only test—of the lyric's success. We cannot reasonably excerpt "beauties" (or even aesthetic "horrors") from a Browning lyric by holding up this or that verse for inspection. None of his verses in isolation absolutely reveals itself to be good or bad. And when prosody is governed by the style-subject principle, only the stanza's and in some cases only the whole poem's expressive structure will indicate the *tonal* felicity or failure of a verse.

Now let us turn to his shorter poems.

He writes primarily three kinds of lyrics. Since the road through Browning criticism is dotted with gorgeously schematic classificatory wrecks, one should be warned against attempting to classify much more finely. Distinctions between his three kinds—the character lyric, the musical lyric, and the lyric of dramatized thought and feeling— are not invariably firm and fast.

In Browning's typical character lyric, the subject is either a particularized dramatic speaker or an entity particularized through details or emblematic images so that it seems to have a limited essence or a character of its own. "The Laboratory" and "Soliloquy of the Spanish Cloister" are typical character lyrics. So are the two "Earth's Immortalities," with their ironic emblematic images for the characteristics of Fame and Love. Or "Sibrandus Schafnaburgensis"—with its details that offer a vision of nature's essence, or character, as it contrasts with human pedantry.

Let us see how rhythmic and phonetic elements figure in "Sibrandus." For obvious reasons this poem is unlike any of Wordsworth's nature lyrics. Its effervescence, the fascination for the insect world that it attests to, and the jaunty ridiculing of pedantry are all Browningesque—and yet no aspect of it is more typical than its versification. Take the rollicking stanza:

> How did he like it when the live creatures
>   Tickled and toused and browsed him all over,
> And worm, slug, eft, with serious features,
>   Came in, each one, for his right of trover?
> —When the water-beetle with great blind deaf face
>   Made of her eggs the stately deposit,
> And the newt borrowed just so much of the preface
>   As tiled in the top of his black wife's closet?

That is humorous and lively, apparently casual, but it is not lax. For one thing, the stanza's indented or even-numbered lines have features that are not paralleled in its odd-numbered four. The indented verses are fairly regular metrically with two and three-syllable feet. Primary stresses are arranged so as not to fall in juxtaposition (the spondee effect is mainly avoided) so that with their regularity and some assonance and alliteration, these lines seem of a traditionally lyrical variety. For example,

> Tíckled and tóused and brówsed him âll óver
> As tíled in the tóp of his bláck wífe's clóset?

But the odd-numbered verses have juxtaposed primary stresses that break up the duple-triple rhythm. These four verses are not phonetically smooth enough to compensate in a traditional manner for their own queer rhythm. They seem relatively harsh, distinctly and peculiarly Browningesque:

> And wórm, slúg, éft, with sérious féatures
> —When the wáter-béetle with gréat blínd déaf fáce

What accounts for their style? Bunched stresses and some harshness very closely support the stanza's expressive structure. Nature is multitudinous, quickly scurrying and jumbled to the casual eye; but deliberate, methodical, purposeful to the selective eye that watches the individual detail. So through images that are increasingly particularized and alternate verse movements that seem on the one hand quick, easy, and expected, and on the other, curious and slow, nature takes on a doubleness—or two appearances of overall disorder and intricate order—that it has to the human eye. Verse style does not impose on the subject more harmony or unity than it should have, and the whole effect is subtle: even as the point of view narrows, the alternating quick and slow lines preserve an impression of nature's two aspects. Style-genre limitations would not permit this effect, but the style-subject principle does since it allows for a method that synthesizes in stanzas relatively harsh, metrically irregular verses.

In character lyrics, all effects of tonal components depend on the vividness, force, pertinence, and particularity of the *characterizing* that is going on in stanzas. For example:

> At the meal we sit together:
>   *Salve tibi!* I must hear   10
> Wise talk of the kind of weather
>   Sort of season, time of year: 12
> *Not a plenteous cork-crop: scarcely*
>   *Dare we hope oak-galls, I doubt:*   14
> *What's the Latin name for "parsley"?*
>   What's the Greek name for Swine's Snout?   16

These verses characterize by contrasting a dramatized speaker with his gentle-mannered foil (Brother Lawrence). As always in a good Browning lyric, rhythms and sounds sharpen the pertinence of details to the stanza's expressed subject. The most pertinent verse, the last, seems even more abrupt and grating than it would if the trochaic movement of lines 9 to 15 were not so regular. Its harshness, indeed its coarse prosiness, emphasizes a bitter, richly perverse, comically bursting hatred suggested in its meaning (surely with an intensity that equals that of other verses expressive of strong feeling in English dramatic lyrics). Yet in reading "Soliloquy of the Spanish Cloister" we are not troubled by the harshness but rather delight in what line 16 so pungently reveals. Its tonal anti-lyricism is perfectly synthesized in the stanza.

Contrast a notoriously cacophonous verse that fails because it is not synthesized:

> Poor vaunt of life indeed,   18
> Were man but formed to feed
> On joy, to solely seek and find and feast: 20
> Such feasting ended, then
> As sure an end to men;   22
> *Irks care the crop-full bird? Frets doubt the*
> *maw-crammed beast?*

Verse 23 is not synthesized because the stanza's structure does not particularize a character, only an anti-FitzGeraldian idea, and a character is all that the cacophony in style relates to. Anti-FitzGeraldian *ideas* have no relation to the harsh texture. We may agree that "Rabbi Ben Ezra's" style is an appropriate one for a prophet whose tough old heart is afire and who shouts as he sings, but in this structure the prophet is only a shadowy entity since the imagery and sense of the six lines particularize no one. That is why the cacophony and abrupt break in the parisonic syntax of 23 will only jolt and glare no matter how often we are reminded by the well-intended critic that the style happens to suit Ben Ezra. The subject that governs the style must be vividly and forcefully depicted if anti-lyrical elements in the style are to become synthesized—that is, if they are to become *lyrical*.

Here is an even bolder prosodic experiment in a character lyric— the sonnet "Rawdon Brown" (1884), which Browning did not collect. I quote lines 2 to 11:

> I needs must, just this once before I die,
> Revisit England: *Anglus* Brown am I,
> Although my heart's Venetian. Yes, old crony—
> Venice and London—London's "Death the Bony"
>   Compared with Life—that's Venice! What a sky,
>   A sea, this morning! One last look! Good-by,
> Cà Pesaro! No lion—I'm a coney
> To weep! I'm dazzled: 't is that sun I view
>   Rippling the . . . the . . . *Cospetto*, Toni! Down
>   With carpet-bag, and off with valise-straps!

No one can say of this that the subject has not realistically determined the style. Furthermore, metrical disorder, syntactic disjointedness, and phonetic discords in these extremes are not out of place in style-subject poems. Browning's principle allows for this texture, and in some verse-paragraphs of "Mr. Sludge, 'The Medium',", one might show that a similar style is effectively used. The trouble here is that the subject is not depicted forcefully enough to justify the tonal harshness: style relates to chatter—not to character. All we are told about Brown, really, is that he loves Venice and will not leave.

But we always have strong impressions of the subject when character lyrics are successful. We do, for a final, brilliant example, in "The Laboratory," where rhythms and sounds and literal and symbolic sense together lay bare the heart of a grotesque daughter of the *ancien régime*—whether in her ghoulish chanting, in her impulsive energy felt through driving rhythms in stanzas expressing wonder and delight in all that is lethal, or in her anti-lyrical opening lines where the deliberate indefiniteness of the meter supports finely imaged symbols of her treachery and duplicity:

> Now that I, tying thy glass mask tightly,
> May gaze thro' these faint smokes curling whitely,
> As thou pliest thy trade in this devil's-smithy—
> Which is the poison to poison her, prithee?

These instances of artistic success and failure remind one that Browning's prosodic principle is rigorously demanding. While it allows for immense range and sharp contrasts in the style of verses, it demands that the lyric structure depict its subject with the utmost relevance and intensity. When the structure fails to do this, we become aware of a failure in his tonal style.

There are fewer sheer failures among his musical lyrics. Browning *depicts* music with ingenuity and finds it everywhere—not only in the fugue or toccata or march or orchestrion's improvisation, but in the mind's reveries, in chanting, in the hoarsely shouted toasts of soldiers, or in the thud of hooves. Since in the musical lyric rhythms and sounds represent music, they are intended to be noticed, "heard" for themselves. Style is intrusive, patent, always bravura, forcing itself into the foreground. As Turner's pictures are visibly made out of paint and do not conceal their technique (the "visibility" of the paint is the mainstay of their technique), so Browning's musical lyrics are audibly made out of sounds.

Their subjects are music's occasions. When the occasion is insufficiently developed in an expressive structure, rhythms and sounds will seem monotonous no matter how ingeniously they are used. "Through the Metidja" is a flat failure:

> As I ride, as I ride,
> With a full heart for my guide,
> So its tide rocks my side,
> As I ride, as I ride,
> That, as I were double-eyed,
> He, in whom our Tribes confide,
> Is descried, ways untried
> As I ride, as I ride.

But "How They Brought the Good News" is successful because its subject—a ride that is no more complex in its essential circumstances than the "Metidja's"—is developed in stanzas that express through their particularity a sense of immense urgency under disciplined control so that one attends through the imagery to the prosodic music of the gallop:

> Not a word to each other; we kept the great pace
> Neck by neck, stride by stride, never changing our place;
> I turned in my saddle and made its girths tight,
> Then shortened each stirrup, and set the pique right,
> Rebuckled the cheek-strap, chained slacker the bit,
> Nor galloped less steadily Roland a whit.

There is nothing anti-lyrical to be synthesized in "Good News" since nothing obstructs the powerful movement of its anapests. Punctuation pauses and heavy syllables (with vowels of considerable quantity and consonantal clusters of some difficulty) before the primary stresses, as in the first of these two feet,

—strap, chained sláck | er the bít,

only impart energy to the rhythm.

But while the hoof music of the gallop is appropriately rendered in even rhythms, man's sophisticated instrumental music really is not. "It is more likely to be the harsh, rugged, dissonant poem," as Northrop Frye observes, "that will show in poetry the tension and the driving accented impetus of music," and several of Browning's musical lyrics use anti-lyrical verses to imitate and depict that more complex, formal music. In this respect his prosodic principle gives him another advantage in realistic representation that the style-genre lyricist lacks.

His imitation of the fugue in "Master Hugues of Saxe-Gotha" is essentially humorous. "Hugues" parodies music. The occasion of the fugue playing—a rather gaily ironic encounter between an organist and a defunct composer heard only through his fugue—is just sufficiently developed to sustain interest and synthesize dissonances through twenty-nine stanzas in which bravura verse style performs imitative tricks:

> *Est fuga, volvitur rota!*
>   On we drift: where looms the dim port?
> One, Two, Three, Four, Five, contribute their quota;
>   Something is gained, if one caught but the import—
> Show it us, Hugues of Saxe-Gotha!

The bravura quality of style is heightened in "A Toccata of Galuppi's" in the same way: the illusion that a dead composer is speaking in and through his music focuses attention on verse sound as well as on verse sense. But in the "Toccata," with great poignancy, the sense deepens. Galuppi's music has superficial qualities that are apparent, at first, even to the unaccustomed ear. So at first, rhythm is almost monotonously even in time and regular in stress:

> Oh Galúppi, Bâldassáro, thîs is véry sâd to fínd!
> I can hardly misconceive you; it would prove me
>   deaf and blind;
> But although I take your meaning, 'tis with such
>   a heavy mind!

The rhythm is regular for six stanzas, which conjure up a conventional sense of aimless hedonism in a midnight Venetian ball with Galuppi "stately at the clavichord." But this composer has something unconventional to say as well: it is heard by the well-attuned ear that can pick out qualities in conventional "sevenths" and "suspensions"— or by the ear that has become aware of variation and subtlety. In stanzas 7 and 8, we hear the music with this ear, alert to the message music gives through imitating and answering lovers' talk:

> What? Those lesser thirds so plaintive, sixths
>   diminished, sigh on sigh,
> Told them something? Those suspensions, those
>   solutions—"Must we die?"
> Those commiserating sevenths—"Life might last! we
>   can but try!"
>
> "Were you happy?"—"Yes."—"And are you still
>   as happy?"—"Yes. And you?"
> —"Then, more kisses!"—"Did *I* stop them, when
>   a million seemed so few?"
> Hark, the dominant's persistence till it must be
>   answered to!"

Bravura style renders both the conventionality and subtlety of Galuppian music here. We attend at once to a prevailing "toccata" rhythm (established earlier) as well as to the magnified toccata-variations that contain the heart of the composer's message for Venice. Typically, the tonal style is effective not in being traditionally smooth but in being functional—intricately synthesized—in the expressive structure.

A fuller study of Browning's bravura styles would take into account lyrics as different as "Cavalier Tunes," "The Pied Piper," "Thamuris Marching," "Up at a Villa—Down in the City," "Holy-Cross Day," "The Heretic's Tragedy," and "A Grammarian's Funeral"—and several dramatic idyls such as "Echetlos" (which, it is no surprise to learn

from Colvin, Browning read with "his foot stamping vigorously in
time") and "Pheidippides." All of these are musical even in their occasional harshness: sound supports sense in them, while sense heightens
the bravura appeal of sound's imitativeness.

Yet very disrupted and very smooth verses alike tend to be missing in Browning lyrics that dramatize thought and feeling not
musically, and not to depict whole characters, but to emphasize
psychological processes in their own right or for their own dramatic
appeal. "In a Year," typically of these, uses a middle style—or
one that avoids both cacophony and lyrical melodiousness—to depict
the process of a woman's reflecting on a love affair that is virtually
over:

> Never any more,
>   While I live,
> Need I hope to see his face
>   As before.
> Once his love grown chill,
>   Mine may strive:
> Bitterly we re-embrace,
>   Single still.
> Was it something said,
>   Something done,
> Vexed him? was it touch of hand,
>   Turn of head?
> Strange! that very way
>   Love begun:
> I as little understand
>   Love's decay.
>
> That was all I meant,
>   —To be just,
> And the passion I had raised,
>   To content.
> Since he chose to change
>   Gold for dust,
> If I gave him what he praised
>   Was it strange?

These structures depict a mind of delicacy and sensibility in the act of searching through its store of memory. Imagery is bare since feeling is quiescent. Short lines emphasize the lambency and rapidity of thought's process, and verse rhythms are varied temporally to support the illusion of a mind conversing with itself. Although each stanza is made up of foreshortened double "quatrains" of 3, 2, 4, and 2 trochees, catalectic, correct to the syllable, phonetic contrasts constantly alter the tempo from verse to verse:

> Never any more (is quick)
> Once his love grown chill (is slow)
> While I live
> Mine may strive (are relatively slow)
> As before
> Single still (are quicker)

Assonance and consonance are present, but rather limitedly, since very much sound repetition (the basis of melodiousness) would defeat the illusion of the mind in colloquy with itself; and it is just this "conversational" illusion that focuses attention on the mind's introspective, recollecting process—which is, indeed, suggestively given in the spare stanzas of "In a Year."

The *process* of the mind's reviewing emotional experience is really the subject of a great many if not all of Browning's lyrics that are concerned with love. When the subject is not such a process, but is dramatized romantic feeling itself, style can be extremely smooth and can even approximate the lyrical melodiousness of a Herrick. This is the case, for example, with the simple and atypically resonant "One Way of Love":

> All June I bound the rose in sheaves.
> Now, rose by rose, I strip the leaves
> And strew them where Pauline may pass.
> She will not turn aside? Alas!
> Let them lie. Suppose they die?
> The chance was they might take her eye.

Certainly not very much more than the name of the disdainful young lady would indicate that Browning wrote that stanza. Thought is not important in it. Mildly (and conventionally) despairing feeling is.

But contrast tonal style in the more typically Browningesque "Two in the Campagna"—the first four verses of whose stanzas are in "One Way of Love's" meter:

> No. I yearn upward, touch you close,
>   Then stand away. I kiss your cheek,
> Catch your soul's warmth,—I pluck the rose
>   And love it more than tongue can speak—
>   Then the good minute goes.

The subject of this stanza is not a feeling, but is the process of a speaker's reflecting on his emotional experience. Thus slightly broken rhythms with somewhat reduced sound-repetition place emphasis on the act of observing what is felt, rather than on feeling itself:

> No ‖ I yearn upward ‖ touch you close
> Then stand away ‖ I kiss your cheek

A similar style is achieved in the iambic pentameter—the "speech" meter of dramas and dramatic monologues alike—of "Any Wife to Any Husband," which closes with these two conversational stanzas:

> And yet thou art the nobler of us two:
> What dare I dream of, that thou canst not do,
>   Outstripping my ten small steps with one stride?
> I'll say then, here's a trial and a task—
> Is it to bear?—if easy, I'll not ask:
>   Though love fail, I can trust on in thy pride.
>
> Pride?—when those eyes forestall the life behind
> The death I have to go through!—when I find,
>   Now that I want thy help most, all of thee!
> What did I fear? Thy love shall hold me fast
> Until the little minute's sleep is past
>   And I wake saved.—And yet it will not be!

Of course there is a "dissociation of sensibility" in both of the last poems, but the dissociation is exactly what Browning's "love lyrics" are so often about. What they frequently express or depict is thought that is slightly removed from feeling and in the act of contemplating it, and it is just for this reason that their lyricism is deliberately restrained. Their subjects dictate tonal styles that help to suggest either the silent conversation of the mind in contemplation of feeling, or overheard talk that reveals contemplated feeling. These lyrics dramatize psychological processes with a new realism that extends to their sounds, and their methods have influenced the development of modern English versification.

In fact Browning's vigorously experimental lyric styles are only one indication—but an important one—of the general shift in the nineteenth century from a closed decorum of style and genre to an open decorum of style and subject. This shift is already under way in 1798, and it may be seen not only in the poetry of Wordsworth, Coleridge, Browning, Arnold, and Hopkins, but in the genre-crossing prose styles of Carlyle, Disraeli, Dickens, Ruskin, or Meredith, and even though the last quarter of the century witnesses more "purism" in poetic and prose styles than had prevailed in earlier decades, the open decorum becomes the norm very soon in our own century—the century of *Ulysses* and *The Waves*, of free verse and Hopkins's fame, and of radical stylistic experimentation. The genres still mean something to us, but they no longer rigidly limit literary styles, or even sharply divide verse from prose.

Browning's lyric prosody contributes vitally to this shift. He enlarges the tonal range of the English lyric by showing that lyrical effects are not intrinsically dependent on the harmony or isolated beauty of the individual line of verse but may arise from verses in which resonance is restrained to enhance illusions of conversation, or even from seemingly unpleasant, joltingly harsh, "prosy" verses if they are expressively synthesized. His modern aim is to suggest the particularity and complexity of actual experience, or (in "Pisgah-Sights'" terms) to bring

> Life there, outlying!
> Roughness and smoothness,
> Shine and defilement,

into the lyric by representing "life" as closely and realistically as technique will permit. His lyrics imitate life's sounds, and in so doing they prepare the way for bolder, later experiments in free verse and open rhythms, and for the end of the absolute dominance of versification based on a syllable-stress metric. For traditional harmony, Browning substitutes a difficult harmony that blends tonal extremes in the lyric, and that can contribute with unusual intensity to lyrical effects—as Ezra Pound of the *Cantos* and T. S. Eliot of the *Four Quartets* have recognized.

Chapter Fifteen

POINTS

I N CERTAIN rare cases, the best biography of an individual will
be totally impersonal. Hardly anything in the way of details
about a person's birth, marriage, or locale will seem relevant.
The man or woman will emerge well enough as a figure in a large
context—sometimes, as in the present case, a context of time stretch-
ing over two centuries. Every modern writer of English owes a debt to
John Wilson the printer, and to a text he published at Manchester in
1844. Wilson was the finest field-captain in a long, chaotic war of
immense importance, but he did not win the war all by himself. It is
easy to overpraise him (and I shall come to his achievement in due
course). His "biography" has to do with the war.

Its chief issue was this. How shall we punctuate? Punctuation is not
a mere "accidental" in most modern poems, plays, and novels, but an
artful element of style. We may ignore any element of style we wish,
and write more lamely or less accurately and artfully as a result. Anyone who cares about style however, willy nilly, does owe much to the

Manchester printer—and may find my chronicle instructive. In the first place, we have taken a too-simple view of the history of sentence punctuation or pointing. We have had the notion that eighteenth- (and even nineteenth-) century pointing, ideally and practically, was based on a "desire to reveal the precise grammatical structure of every sentence," as Reginald Skelton wrote in *Modern English Punctuation* (2nd ed., London, 1949, 162). Another student, examining a number of grammars dated from 1589 to 1900, has found that "the structural basis of placing the points of punctuation appears without exception."

It is time to look at the facts about the war over points, or at the historical context which involved John Wilson. I shall try to evaluate the notion of a strict, syntactically based punctuation between 1700 and 1900 by taking into account a fair number of grammars, spellers, rhetoric, and pointing treatises, and other miscellaneous sources of the period. What emerges is, I think, a surprisingly complex and lively picture of pointing theory. Theory here, the going ideas of the day, may not tell us all that we desire to know about punctuation in use, of course. But theory surely illuminates usage—and has something to tell every poet, novelist, playwright, or other user of our language who believes, in his or her heart of hearts, that English punctuation matters.

I

For commonly accepted notions of pointing in the early eighteenth century one is led to the grammar of Brightland (1711); it is one of the first "popular" grammars of the century, appearing in eight editions by 1759, and it contains a punctuation section never appreciably altered. Speaking of the common marks, Brightland says:

> The use of these Points, Pauses or Stops, is not only to give a
> proper Time for Breathing; but to avoid Obscurity, and
> confusion of the Sence in the joining Words together in a
> Sentence.

Then he states a single comma rule:

> After a Comma always follows something else which depends
> upon that which is separated from it by a Comma; as
>
>> If Pulse of Verse a Nation's Temper shows,
>> In Keen Iambics English meter flows.

The treatment is worth careful note. What is arresting is not perhaps
the evidence of a grammarian's lingering infatuation with elocutionary
pointing, or a system that would designate "Time for Breathing," because this basis can be traced through the last century in treatises like
those of Daines (1640) and Cooper (1687). Nor is it surprising to find
a crude but clear syntactical element present; Fries and others have
indicated we would find that. What is striking is to find these two
contrasting theories of punctuation voiced at the same time. In view of
what we have thought was a "desire to reveal the precise grammatical
structure of every sentence" in the eighteenth century, we might, at
any rate, expect the elocutionary element quickly to die out after
Brightland. But this is not so. The grammars of Isaac Watts (1721),
Barker (1733), Lowth (1762), Buchanan (1762), Burn (1766), Perry
(1774), Sheridan (1780), Coote (1788), and Lindley Murray (1795), to
name a representative few, all refer to such a basis. As we find in
Harrison:

> Points are used in writing for a double purpose, and have respect
> both to *grammar* and to *elocution*.

In fact, the elocutionary basis, far from dying out, receives what may
be its most elaborate explanation as late as 1771 in James Burrow's *De
Usu et Ratione Interpungendi*:

> THE GENERAL IDEA of *Pointing* seems to include nothing
> more than MARKING *down upon Paper*, by different Signs or
> Notations, the *respective* PAUSES which actually were or ought
> to be made in *pronouncing* the Words written or printed;
> together with like *Hints* for a *different Modulation of Voice*,
> where a just Pronunciation would require it. . . . Some people

indeed speak rapidly; some slowly; some make many Pauses;
some, fewer; some, longer; some, shorter: But this makes no
Difference with regard to the *Facility of Pointing*; because the
PROPORTION between the Pauses will not be thereby altered;
and the whole affair of Pointing is to *mark those Proportions*
upon *Paper*, conformably to the Pauses really made and the
Proportion really observed between them in actual
Pronunciation.

It is even true that a few writers, such as Thomas Dyche (1710), the
author of *Some Rules for Speaking and Action* (1716), Burrow (1771),
Brittain (1788) and Burr (1797), seem to recognize no foundation for
punctuation *but* the elocutionary one; yet these are exceptions. In the
majority of cases the breath-pause theory appears side by side, often in
the same sentence, with the syntactical. Johnson's *Dictionary* tells us
that a comma is the "point which notes the distinction of clauses, and
order of construction in the sentence," but that a colon is a "point [:]
used to mark a pause greater than that of a comma, and less than that
of a period. Its use is not very exactly fixed. . . ." Likewise Sheridan,
another lexicographer and a grammarian more interested in punctuation than Dr. Johnson was, permits the syntactical comma definition
and the elocutionary colon one to stand in the same volume of his
own dictionary (1780). Well into the next century punctuation rules
applying to oral expression on the one hand and sentence structure on
the other appear on the same pages of instructional tracts:

Rules for Punctuation &c.

2. The voice must almost always be elevated at a
    comma.

4. The *Semicolon* is used to distinguish the different
    members or parts of a sentence. . . .

5. In general a *semicolon* demands a depression or ca-
    dence of the voice.

17. The *Parenthesis* requires a pause equal in duration of
    a semicolon; and the words contained therein, must
    be pronounced in a lower tone than the foregoing
    part of the sentence; at the end of which, the voice

should be elevated as at a comma, and the following part of the sentence begun in the same tone as the former.

That there could be two such differing sets of guides to pointing usage without the utmost confusion is not observed in a significant treatise until about 1780. Confusion itself was widely recognized. Printers, whose task it was to commit manuscripts to the press with one sort of punctuation or another, had little time for the niceties of paradoxical theory and simply recognized anarchy. Luckombe in *The History and Art of Printing* (1771) knows that for all the commotion over pointing, "no rules of a prevailing authority have been . . . established," and punctuation is one more all too human endeavor "that has nothing but fancy and humour for its authority and foundation." Chambers can make no sense of the common definition of the comma for his *Cyclopaedia* and finds deceptive "difficulty in *pointing*. . . . In effect, there is scarce any thing in the province of the grammarians so little fixed and ascertained as this. The rules usually laid down are impertinent, dark and deficient; and the practice, at present, perfectly capricious, authors varying not only from one another, but from themselves too." Bishop Lowth will propose few rules in his authoritative treatise: "the doctrine of Punctuation must needs be very imperfect." Buchanan of *The British Grammar* warns that "pointing a Discourse is a Province beyond the Capacities of mere Youth," and Noah Webster vouches in 1785 that the "characters we use as stops are extremely arbitrary," and in 1807:

I have never examined any author, whose use of the points is either accurate or uniform. . . .

Only late in the century was the true nature of the difficulty brought into some focus. Sheridan had deplored the fact that pointing seemed to be regulated by grammatical principles and not by the more fitting "art of speaking" in his essay of 1780, and John Walker took up the thesis much more grandly in his *Elements of Elocution* (1781) and *A Rhetorical Grammar* (1785). Speech requirements extend beyond those of syntax:

> In order . . . to have as clear an idea of punctuation as possible,
> it will be necessary to consider it as related to grammar and
> rhetoric distinctly. A system of punctuation may be sufficient for
> the purposes of grammar; or, in other words, it may be sufficient
> to clear and preserve the sense of an author, and at the same
> time be but a very imperfect guide to the pronunciation of it.
> The art of speaking, though founded on grammar, has
> principles . . . that arise from the nature of the living voice,
> from the perception of harmony in the ear, and from a certain
> superaddition to the sense of language, of which grammar takes
> no account.

He finds the incongruity only apparent, however, and offers a new
pointing system calculated to meet the needs of syntax and elocution
alike. Despite its occurrence in the frequently quoted 1781 and 1785
volumes it appears to have had small influence. But Robertson's *An
Essay on Punctuation* (1785) has a strange indebtedness to Walker.
The *Essay*, printed anonymously, is a rather important one; it pro-
pounds no less than forty rules for the comma, an unprecedented
number, almost every one of which is strongly rooted in syntax; Robertson's whole approach seems syntactical; and yet at the end of his
painstaking comma chapter, he bows, citing Walker, to the cardinal
principle of "the wants of respiration." It is this "and the laws of
taste," we learn, that has fostered some three dozen syntactical precepts.

In his *Elements of Punctuation* published the next year, David
Steel senses the paradox. He compliments the author of the 1785
Essay, to which his own work is essentially a reply, for making more
progress "in elucidating the doctrine of points" than anyone has attempted, "by producing . . . systematical rules," even though some
ten of these are found to be defective. But the chief failure of previous
writers has not been their paucity of rules; it is rather that

> Grammar, which ought to be the basis of punctuation, has
> seldom been considered as adequate to the purpose: too much
> accommodation to the reader, and too little attention to
> grammatical construction have usually been the sources whence
> the doctrine of points has been deduced.

Pointing is acquired only "by a kind of internal conviction, that the rules of grammar are never to be violated." Moreover:

> Punctuation should lead to the sense; the sense will guide to modulation and emphasis. When punctuation performs its office thus, it will point out likewise the grammatical construction; for the sense of a passage and its grammatical construction are inseparable. It follows that a knowledge of grammar is necessary . . . and I speak with perfect conviction, that any rules, militating against grammar, may be made specious, but they will ultimately be found defective.

According to Steel, one cannot enunciate forty "grammatical" rules as Robertson has and still invoke the elocutionary Muse to insure correctness in pointing. Elocution will militate against grammar; one guide or the other must be followed; and nothing but the grammatical construction of a passage, indicating its sense, can logically be that guide.

It is the nearest the eighteenth century ever comes to destroying the classical concept of punctuation as a guide to oral expression. The *Elements* is read for the next fifty years; and it marks the nadir of elocutionary pointing theory before 1800, but it hardly marks the end of it. Indeed, the idea surges on through treatises and textbooks of the 1790s and positively swells, amid mounting weariness and confusion over what the "correct" use of stops may be, through the first four decades of the nineteenth century. One nods almost sympathetically at Byron's refusal to do his own final punctuating, or the report of a learned ms. "larded with Greek and Latin quotations" that was sent to the printer's without a single stop from beginning to end. "High" or dense marking comes into fashion. Steel had asserted in 1786, "Whenever I am doubtful if a sentence will admit a comma, I generally end my hesitation by inserting it, provided it do not militate against grammar," and by 1800 points were sprinkling the written and printed page with feverish and often very fanciful liberality. Whatever stylistic effects it had, such punctuation tended to obscure theory and burden the printer. Complaints over the condition of pointing abound. Almost every serious treatment published between 1800 and

1850 has its standard lament for the absence of principle and the wildness of practice; Justin Brenan (1829) is indignant:

> But after an experience of above a thousand years, and after all the laws that have been solemnly laid down, no two authors of eminence punctuate alike, or even according to the same plan throughout! Nay, they are, always, at variance with themselves, for where can the work of any length be found, in which an undeviating system of pointing, is steadily and invariably maintained? Can punctuation, therefore, be an art? Or, if it be an art, why has not something been done to establish the fact?

Francillon finds no department in all literature "of which so little knowledge is to be acquired from books, ancient or modern, as Punctuation." At the same time definitive tracts on the "art" or the "science" multiply; a movement gathers to abandon some of the stops altogether and thus purge the air. Cobbett (1819) would drop or restrict the dash; J. Johnson (1824) "confidently" expects "the total exclusion of the colon, a point long since considered unnecessary"; Brenan would discard colon and semicolon: "I have come to this conclusion as a general principle—that the punctuation of the parts or members of sentences, can be accomplished, with propriety and effect, by the comma and dash only."

It is the confusion of the eighteenth century with perhaps an added note of insistence. Grammarians who had read Walker, Robertson, and Steel, the significant theorists of the 1780s, and were convinced that a pointing based on syntactical criteria alone would put an end to perplexity, made little headway against the mass. If writers like Stackhouse, Francillon, or Day denied the elocutionary concept, there were many others left to employ it. Doherty in 1841, for instance, could give as the first function of the comma, "a very short pause merely to afford time for respiration . . ."—and be reasonably sure that he was voicing not only a "universal principle," as he contended, but majority opinion.

II

The most influential name in nineteenth-century punctuation history is almost certainly John Wilson. "As a printer he had ideals; as a theologian he was a keen progressive . . . and all the days of his long life he studied punctuation," as C. H. Ward has eulogized. For Summey, Wilson's *Treatise* is "the great nineteenth century authority," and a more recent writer refers to Wilson as "the able codifier of reputable customs of punctuation." Whatever the extent of Wilson's prestige, it would be inaccurate to credit the *Treatise* alone for shifts that took place in pointing after 1844. The central shift—the virtual abandoning of elocutionary for syntactical theory—was a massive one, a change that centuries of punctuation development and scores of grammars and pointing treatises had so far failed to bring about. Until more evidence is in from French and German it will be difficult to say precisely what bearing foreign languages have had on the problem; but nineteenth-century German punctuation sources are plentiful, and at least one direct line of influence is traceable from the French.

By 1825 the issue between a system of stops which would mark breathing pauses and one which would "distinguish phrases" or clarify construction is clear in France; Lemare had opened his attack upon the disciples of pause.

> Nous verrons que la ponctuation est l'art, non pas de marquer
> *les pauses qu'on doit faire en lisant,* mais de distinguer les
> phrases entre elles, et les sens partiels de chaque phrase.

Breathing requirements are strictly denied: "il est évident que la respiration n'a rien, absolument rien à démêler avec la ponctuation." A few years later the matter was put before the French Academy for debate and a decision, and by 1835 that distinguished linguistic jury had rendered its verdict. The marks of punctuation are defined in the sixth edition of the Dictionary in plain syntactical terms:

> *Deux points* (:), *Point et Virgule* (;), Signes qu'on met à la fin
> d'une proposition dont le sens grammatical est complet, mais

qui a une liaison logique et nécessaire avec la suivante. Les deux
points s'emploient surtout à la fin des phrases qui sont
immédiatement suivies de ce qui sert à les éclaircir.

By the end of the next decade the significance of these findings was
made plain in England through J. B. Huntington's translation of a
treatise by Chauvier in 1849. The translation includes a brief account
of punctuation history, a discussion of the French Academy's definitions and an application of the Academy's syntactical view of the stops
to English sentences. It seems to have had some certain effect on
English pointing theory; with its aggressive emphasis on syntax and its
appearance a few years after Wilson's *Treatise* of 1844, Huntington's
work at least augmented the theoretical trend away from elocution.

In addition, the trend was certainly aided by a situation in England
that accounted, in part, for the success of Wilson's book itself. Printers
had come increasingly to feel the need, as Johnson points out in
Typographia, for either a radical simplification of the pointing system
or some generally acknowledged guide to it. Neither was forthcoming.
Compositors, C. J. Addison tells us in 1826,

> are confessedly in the dark as to the principles upon which this
> science [of stops] ought to be founded; and one of the most
> scientific in the line acknowledged to the writer, that he was
> ignorant of the existence of any work that might be called an
> authority; that their knowledge was chiefly gathered from hints
> in different publications or Grammars, and though improved by
> experience, yet still influenced by doubt or uncertainty, the
> same reader . . . varying in his opinions within the day or even
> the hour.

George Smallfield's attempt after twenty years as a printer to produce
an adequate punctuation guide may have alleviated the condition
somewhat, but Smallfield was not a "codifier of reputable customs,"
as Wilson was to be; he admits a strong leaning toward C. Hartley, a
follower of David Steel. In the 1840s there was a need for one complete, systematic, ready-reference handbook of known punctuation
usage; it would have to be *acceptable*—a book with a minimum of

derivative or original theory and a maximum of faithfully recorded and codified practice. It could not very well advocate dropping some marks for convenience, as the *Typographia* had, or adopting others, as Chauvier was to suggest; it would be conservative; primarily it would be a manual for printers.

A *Treatise on Grammatical Punctuation* (1844) is based on a much shorter work of 1826, which had taken its pointing rules largely from Lindley Murray's grammar. But the *Treatise*, John Wilson is careful to explain, is "so different . . . so much augmented, as to entitle it to be regarded as, to a great extent, new." Its sources are fresh and varied: the author has used many other tracts, drawn on his own observation and experience, and "inserted much, that, though existing in practical operation, he could not find anywhere in books." In one hundred and twenty pages, Wilson includes twenty-five headlined rules for the comma, four for the semicolon, seven for the colon, six for the period, and nineteen for the "Minor Points" (all with exceptions, examples, and exercises), as well as lists of compounded words, definitions of the lesser typographical marks, medical, astronomical and arithmetical signs, abbreviations, and fifteen rules for capitals and italics. It is all stated with great care; qualifications are frequent and meticulous; he has (as he says) "devoted pages to the elucidation of some of the points, which by most grammarians are despatched in a few lines." On the surface it is the useful, impartial toil of a scholarly printer. Only when one searches for theory in Wilson's *Treatise* does a rather striking partiality appear. In the Introduction, after an eloquent plea for system, Wilson notes a "false light" in which punctuation is commonly regarded:

> Many persons seem to consider points as being only the representatives of rhetorical pauses,—as showing merely those places in the utterance of a composition, in which time for breathing is required. . . . But, though it is not denied that the points are, to a very great extent, serviceable to a reader in knowing when he should pause, occasion will frequently be taken, in the course of this work, to prove that the art of punctuation is founded more on a grammatical than a rhetorical basis.

And the theme, as promised, runs strongly through the fine print of pages devoted to rules:

> We again venture to repeat, that the sense and the grammatical form of the construction of a passage, and not the rhetorical mode of its delivery, is the fundamental law by which the art of punctuation should be regulated.

> That the notes of interrogation and exclamation, as they are termed, have much less to do with the inflections of the voice than is commonly imagined, will be fully apparent.

The *Treatise* was justly popular, even though the cause of elocutionary pointing did not collapse all at once. By 1856, in his work's sixth edition, Wilson had condensed his comma precepts to nineteen but added an appendix on proofreading, an index, more exposition, and exercises and nearly trebled the bulk of his pages to 334. The *Treatise* was under steady revision until his death in 1868; after the twentieth edition in 1871, "the great storehouse which every succeeding text-maker has pillaged without acknowledgement," as it has been called, succeeding editions were simply reprints.

It is a bit paradoxical that a text so important in theory should have been accepted by a writing world and by printers manifestly sick of theory, eager for a standard guide to usage. But Wilson's syntactical motif in a short but methodically thorough work served to clear the field. Its rules were the common ones, even if rhetorically tinted precepts had been omitted or qualified. *The Treatise* was logical; it accounted for all cases at hand. It was not inventive, but fair, exacting, inclusive. Significantly, it ushered in a conservative but rational age in punctuation that was to outlast the century.

Treatments of pointing after 1845 display a lingering uncertainty as to how far rules should be applied, but few texts hold for the old elocutionary view. W. Mills (1848), MacIntosh (1852), Bedford (1858), and the author of A *Manual of Punctuation* (1859) all set the syntactical pattern for coming decades; W. C. Fowler in 1850 carefully cites both bases, adding that "current practice is generally more in accordance with the grammatical than the rhetorical." At least in pointing theory, one does not sense what was called in 1905 a "revolt

from strict constructional punctuation . . . noticeable in the latter part
of the nineteenth century." It is true that less rigidity developed in the
very statement of rule; Allardyce (1884) for instance speaks of a
comma that *may* be used, or is *often* used, or which *usually* separates,
but this would seem, rather, to exemplify a new dimension in the
theoretical sources of the time. As Allardyce elaborates, the stops are

> intimately connected with style. As forms of thought are infinite
> in number, so are the modes of expression; and punctuation,
> adapting itself to these, is an instrument capable of
> manipulation in a thousand ways.

Given some generally recognized norm of use, the points may be
adapted artistically; but there must be the norm. Punctuation flour-
ishes exactly when we are willing to concede it a logical ground and a
standard practice. Genung (1900) and later writers heed this, exploring
what Genung calls that "skillful employment of punctuation as a flexible, living, artistic thing which makes it so truly a cardinal factor in
the organism of the sentence." No such dynamic view of the stops is
evident in the hundred-and-fifty-year period after 1700. Struggling
under twin concepts that made rational rule impossible, pointing appears to attract little interest and even less skill beyond limited circles
of theoreticians and printers. Only when punctuation theory becomes
relatively stabilized—after the 1840s—do the common marks assume
more than a conventional value. John Wilson's *Treatise* in effect freed
the points for the artist's full use. From Browning's dramatic monologues to James Joyce's amusing symbolic punctuating in *Ulysses*
(1922), and after, we find artists who truly understand the point.

Chapter Sixteen

TROLLOPE'S LIFE AND TROLLOPE'S NOVELS

R. H. SUPER, who brought a great deal of fresh illumination to Anthony Trollope's dogged administrative career in a book called *Trollope in the Post Office*, gave us, back in 1988, the first adequate biography of Trollope. Most literary biographies are inadequately researched and deficient in style. Super's *The Chronicler of Barsetshire: A Life of Anthony Trollope*—published by the University of Michigan Press—is exhaustively and lovingly researched and written in a prose style that is at once robust and delicately accurate in conveying a sense of historical evidence.

Here is a comic example of Super's very effective biographical manner. Trollope in the mid-1850s is uncertain that his friend John Merivale has chosen a good tavern in South London for meetings of a dining club to be called "The Goose and Glee." Trollope is a heavy man, and at the club he will have to unbutton his trousers in safety from time to time:

> The tavern had recently become modern to the extent of
> constructing a second-floor room that projected out from the
> walls of the building, for use as a toilet, but though that
> construction made obsolete a by-law prohibiting members from
> urinating into a chamber pot in the banqueting hall, Trollope
> was afraid the supporting props were not strong enough for his
> bulk and that if he used the new room he might be plunged to
> the street in an undignified disarray.

That style would not do for Dickens, or Thackeray, or Reade, or Gissing, or Hardy—but it is perfect for the information it has to convey about Trollope.

The Chronicler of Barsetshire is especially excellent with outward details. It is a little deficient in not giving us a sense of pressure in human relationships, in avoiding almost any analysis of persons, and in saying a minimal amount about the women in Trollope's life—not that we know much more about his wife, Rose, than that she died at ninety-six, in 1917, and that her wavy hair "turned to ivory-cream" when she was young.

But my purpose is not to review Super's biography here—I did find it a pleasure to review for the learned pages of *Journal of English and Germanic Philology*, while sitting in a sunny French garage a summer or two ago—but rather, I want to inquire into the relationship between Trollope's art and Trollope's life. These remarks were occasioned by my thinking about him from a biographical viewpoint not long after his centenary.

What is exceptional in him is, first of all, self-confidence. He is the least self-conscious novelist among readable Victorians. He is immune to a virus of labored artistry that infects his contemporaries and develops into an epidemic among our moderns such as Joyce, Woolf, and even Conrad. There is an earlier exception in Walter Scott— prolific, certain, relaxed—but even near the outset of the century we find in Jane Austen a novelist who had to struggle with her "gradual performances" to polish the labor out of her writing.

Yet Trollope seems to be immune. Considered with Dickens, Charlotte Brontë, George Eliot, and Meredith, he is the least fussily inclined to oblige readers with new aesthetic structures, or to play and fret with complex meanings, symbols, myths, or poetic flights. The Flaubertian precedents in diction and style affected him not at all. They were late in coming to England and by the time Henry James codified Flaubert's notion of the artistic novel in "The Art of Fiction" (1884) Trollope's gloriously homely career was over. He had been dead two years, and his disarming apology for not being an "artist"— the posthumous *An Autobiography* (1883)—was then being read by the clergymen, politicians, and their wives who had seen their neighbors (if not themselves) pictured with good sense, fun, some satire, and a mainly redeeming intelligible straightforwardness in Trollope's novels.

An Autobiography made James uneasy. Yet Trollope's claim that he had written by the clock, or that he wrote an "allotted number of pages" daily in a ship cabin between Marseilles and Alexandria to produce *Doctor Thorne* could not have upset James, who had a rational view of inspiration. (James often wrote or dictated a predetermined amount of work in a day.) What irritated Henry James was Trollope's reduction of the novelist to a clothmaker whose notion of *quality* was that it might be as good, or as low and humdrum, as the trade would bear.

"I was moved now," Trollope had written frankly, "by a decision to excel, if not in quality, at any rate in quantity. An ignoble ambition for an author, my readers will no doubt say. But not, I think, altogether ignoble if an author can bring himself to look at his work as does any other workman. . . . It is not my conscience that I have scamped. . . . Had I taken three months of idleness between each they would have been no better. Feeling convinced of that, I finished *Doctor Thorne* on one day, and began *The Bertrams* on the next." No, not ignoble to regard one's work "as does any other workman"—but then one's novels, in James's view, may have no more significance than so many fitted floorboards, servants' frocks, or tricycles. "Art," wrote James a year after *An Autobiography*, "lives upon discussion, upon experiment, upon curiosity, upon variety of attempt, upon the exchange of views and the comparison of standpoints." If art does, then surely Trollope, who, despite his friendship with novelists, exchanged "views" mainly with postal employees (since Trollope worked daily as a postal inspector), *must* have produced very flawed novels.

James looked for the flaws. There are signs in his cavils that he came up against the problem of Trollope's artistic (or craftsmanly) self-confidence. Either Trollope was sublimely confident, or perverse.

> He took a suicidal satisfaction in reminding the reader that the story he was telling was only, after all, a make-believe [wrote James]. These little slips at credulity are very discouraging, but they are even more inexplicable. [And] when Trollope suddenly winks at us and reminds us that he is telling us an arbitrary thing, we are startled and shocked in quite the same way as if Macaulay or Motley were to drop the historical mask and intimate that William of Orange was a myth or the Duke of Alba an invention.

It is surprising how often James's complaints about flaws, and especially about Trollope's authorial intrusions, still turn up. "There are a good many examples of such 'suicidal satisfaction'" in Trollope's novels, wrote James Pope-Hennessy in his life of Trollope, "examples in which he seems to treat both the reader and himself with scorn." The conviction that novel writing is a craft and not an art "presumably, inspired these exasperating asides. Had he ever discovered that posterity would consider him as a great artist he would have turned in his grave at Kensal Green" (*Anthony Trollope*, Panther Books ed., 1973, 160). Since Pope-Hennessy—although apologies for Trollope's intrusions and for his art began before his book—we have been told often enough that Trollope was a great artist. But I remember when reading Robert Polhemus's tactful, suggestive *The Changing World of Anthony Trollope* how often Trollopians ask us to take the "artistry" on good faith: "One really has to read this part of *Can You Forgive Her?* to see the delicate mastery," wrote Mr. Polhemus.

This leaves us with the problem as to how he is seen, or what his reputation is, more than a century after his death and several years after Super's biography, *The Chronicler of Barsetshire*. A Trollope Society meets in England; but he has always had enthusiasts. In the more general view, he is powerful but loquacious, less artful than Dickens or Flaubert or James. We still see Trollope as a natural, self-confident genius, downgrading his art so that his affinity for places and people and his inventiveness may burble up in . . . words, words, words. Was James partly right? Had he seen novels as artful, and exchanged more "views" with artists, wouldn't his work be better?

But if *Candide* was written in three days, and *Rasselas* in seven, rapid or steady composing isn't harmful. If Arnold talked far more often to schoolchildren than to artists, James's "discussion" and "exchange of views" may not need to precede the writing of good prose. (List the artists Jane Austen knew.) Art surely thrives on inwardness and pressure, on a desire to give permanence and stability to a world whose values are unnoticed by others or in danger of being obscured by evanescence, neglect, or untoward forces. Always fixed against change and conservative in this sense, art—whether in a Picasso girl or *Barchester Towers*—constantly re-creates for us the exact time of its composition. The Victorian pressure for reform, change, and improvement was incessant. Super's research has revealed Trollope in a Post Office bureaucracy where his superior, Sir Rowland Hill, sometimes met the pressure for reform by proposing an unlikely scheme and taking credit for a modified scheme put forward by drudging subordinates. One could hardly oppose reform in the Post Office. It is interesting and paralleled in Arnold's experience with the education committee that Sir Rowland's reforms might look well on paper at the expense of morale. Sir Rowland, for example, "breathed fresh life into every branch of the service"—to quote his nephew's article in the *Dictionary of National Biography*—by setting up "promotion by merit." That sounded well, but Trollope in vain opposed it as "injurious" in May 1863, since it meant promotion would go to "the best man, let the merits of those who are to be superseded be what they may." Even if a man has given his best services, or married on the assured belief he will be promoted, he will lose promotion if someone better qualified comes along at the last hour. "No amount of excellence is safe," wrote Trollope in the Post Office, "because a greater amount of excellence must always be possible.

To know whether a man be absolutely fit or unfit for certain
duties is . . . beyond the capacity of any officer however
intelligent and observant to say who is most fit. Zeal
recommends itself to one man, intelligence to a second, alacrity
to a third, punctuality to a fourth, and superficial pretense to a
fifth. There can be no standard by which the excellence of men
can be judged as is the weight of gold.

His words in the bureaucracy are supported by his novels. His opposition to inhumane change underlies George Eliot's affectionate
remark about Trollope as a man "clinging to whatever is." Trollope
certainly tried to understand the changing world under his feet. Having in childhood feared change and wondered what his mother would
do next, and hoped for it, as his miseries were endless and cruel, he
needed to get the blurred flux on paper to understand it. His act of
sometimes writing 250 reassuring words every fifteen minutes—
though he varied from that, and was less regular than he himself suggests—relieved him enough to permit him to see the forces of change
as comic, personal, ironic, pseudo-romantic, partly absurd, even
partly benevolent. Trollope does well when he turns these forces into a
fine circus of freaks—as Slope, Mrs. Proudie, Bertie, and Signora
Madeline Vesey Neroni in *Barchester Towers*—where, with light and
comic Homeric overtones, the Trojan horses among the Towers dart
and squirm into the nerve center of his world. But when Trollope
views the forces of change as impersonal, or implies that an unlocated
source of evil predooms society, he is less successful. Rich and filled
as it is, *The Way We Live Now* (1875) is not a satisfying whole as the
Barsetshire novels are. He personified forces of change to his own
satisfaction and ours, at his best, and showed that the conservative,
stabilizing characters are at last fortified by the changers who have
threatened them. Who would deny that Madeline or Mr. Slope, Lady
Arabella Gresham, and her sister-in-law Lady de Courcy ultimately
strengthen the forces of stability in *Barchester Towers* and *Doctor
Thorne*?

He knew that nothing is more stable than landscape—and few novelists have anything like his fine sense of landscape and place. With
Dickens, we may be with a guide who knows London blindfold—as

Browning said—but also with a guide who is unsatisfied by a real city, and who pitches his words at a poetic level above the place he knows. With Trollope, we feel no such thing. Rather we sense a loving geographical particularity. And it is worth reading his place descriptions closely, to find the author *in* them.

Here, in *Doctor Thorne*, is Greshambury House (are we to think of Gilbert White's Selborne?):

> Greshambury consisted of one long, straggling street, a mile in length, which in the centre turned sharp round, so that one half of the street lay directly at right angles to the other. In this angle stood Greshambury House, and the gardens and grounds around it filled up the space so made. There was an entrance with large gates at each end of the village, and each gate was guarded by the effigies of two hugh pagans with clubs, such being the crest worn by the family; from each entrance a broad road, running quite straight, running through to a majestic avenue of limes, led up to the house. This was built in the richest, perhaps we should rather say in the purest, style of Tudor architecture; so much so that . . . it may in some measure be said to be the finest specimen of Tudor architecture of which the country can boast.
>
> It stands amid a multitude of trim gardens and stone-built terraces, divided one from another: these to our eyes are not so attractive as that broad expanse of lawn by which our country houses are generally surrounded; but the gardens of Greshambury have been celebrated for two centuries. . . . Greshambury Park—properly so called—spread far away on the other side of the village. Opposite to the two great gates leading up to the mansion were two smaller gates, the one opening on to the stables, kennels, and farm-yard, and the other to the deer-park. The latter was the principal entrance to the demesne, and a grand picturesque entrance it was. The avenue of limes which on one side stretched up to the house, was on the other extended for a quarter of a mile . . . and what with the massive iron gates . . . the spot was sufficiently significant of old family greatness.

Trollope is intrusively here, to give the highest praise to the house ("the finest specimen of Tudor architecture of which the country can boast" and "significant of old family greatness"), but there is no hint of that "suicidal satisfaction" James found in his reminding the reader that the story is only make believe. Greshambury House seems to exist. One would like to visit it, or view it from the lime avenue. But just after it is so set in our minds, Trollope in chapter 2 begins in one of those pernicious and "discouraging" little "slips at credulity" to mumble, as James would say, about whether Dr. Thorne or Frank Gresham is to be "our hero" and whether it isn't boring to have a chapter full of locale and another, to come, of character description:

> I quite feel that an apology is due for beginning a novel with two long chapters full of description. . . . It can hardly be expected that any one will consent to go through with a fiction that offers so little of allurement in its first pages; but twist it as I will I cannot do otherwise. . . . This is inartistic on my part, and shows want of imagination as well of skill. Whether or not I can atone . . . is very doubtful.

Here is James's "inexplicable" Trollope, not just wasting words (advancing his story in no way) but giving his game away. A good Trollopian might reply that after reading two chapters of *Doctor Thorne*, James's own openings seem a little febrile in being taut, selective, and self-consciously artistic. And James had a mainly aesthetic devotion to locale: his settings subserve his portraits of a Lady, of Mrs. Gereth and Mona Brigstock, of Strether. Trollope is English, in giving even his sketch of a house a moral pressure. He stands, I think, between Jane Austen's *Mansfield Park* and Forster's *Howard's End* (with Waugh's *Handful of Dust* and *Brideshead Revisited* as whimsical and sentimental aftermaths), since his first concern in a novel is to establish, firmly, the worth of an area of combat, or the value of the place that is fought over. A cathedral town is worth something. Or he supposes that Greshambury House from the Tudors and guarded by "two hugh pagans" is worth an outside protector such as Dr. Thorne, and an inside inheritor such as Frank Gresham, who struggle (through Mary) for its proper continuance. Trollope's authorial intrusions and apologies bring his discussions of such a house into our real world. "This is inartistic on my part." Most of the intrusions are deliberately artless, outside of art, to remind us with matter-of-fact urgency that English locales matter more than stories about them, life matters more than art. They say that something (Greshambury House) is outside the novel, and almost too difficult to bring into it, slightly outside and beyond Trollope's deft control. Mary Thorne, for example, is so important in his story—"my heroine"—that poor Trollope has to confess:

> Of her personal appearance it certainly is my business as an author to say something. She is my heroine, and, as such, must necessarily be very beautiful; but, in truth, her mind and inner qualities are more clearly distinct in my brain than her outward form and features. I know that she was far from being tall. . . .

He can be sure about only some notion of Mary's quality, which his novel must illustrate. As in *Mansfield Park*, in which Fanny Price is the standard of value and we wait for Edmund's eyes to open to his pearl of price, so in *Doctor Thorne* the question is when Frank, who is "lackadaisically sentimental" and "certainly an arrogant puppy, and an egregious ass into the bargain" will be worthy of his Mary—and Greshambury and England.

And what is likely to change an arrogant puppy and egregious ass into a man, after all, sooner than a battle with agents of social change? Trollope's slow, patient battles in the Post Office bureaucracy are related to the pace and direction of his novels.

Still, we cannot say that he always succeeds. Only the ardent Trollopian will deny some of his work is slack and deplorably written. And though, I know, the ardent will fret over any ranking of his novels, it seems to me that Michael Sadleir's *Trollope: A Commentary*—first printed in 1927—does what the ardent neglect, and displays critical brass of a kind Trollope might approve in its classifying of his fiction. I suppose that nobody will defend all of Sadleir's "classes." Even if it is convenient to speak of six "Chronicles of Barsetshire" and four "Irish novels" which, from *The Macdermots of Ballycloran* of 1847 to *Castle Richmond* of 1860, at least, are critically neglected, Sadleir's discriminations among them are rather too cut and dried. It is impossible to speak of some novels as those of "Manners" and others as "Social

Satires," when these features are mixed in his novels including the "Irish" and "Political." But Sadleir's egregious asterisk-ranking, though debatable and prejudiced, is a good feature: when we no longer find *The Claverings* (three stars) better than *Orley Farm* (one star), or this worth arguing over, we won't read Trollope. The ranking system is only bad in failing to account for freshness of tone, and local appeals, in indifferent structures: for example, *The Warden* (1855) and *La Vendée* (1850) are unstarred by Sadleir, as I would not star them in his system, though the first is fresh as the dew and the second of unusual historical interest.

The Political Novels need to be acclaimed for their females (Lady Glencora or Lady Dumbello), and Trollope's women remind us that he had immense sentimental energy. (But he wept mainly over *The Three Clerks*.) He invests his women with a romantic intensity that seems realistic. If he did not, we would not feel the sexual power of a cripple (Madeline) or the worth of struggling towards—and for—a heroine such as Clara Amedroz in *The Belton Estate* (1866). "In no other novel is the essence of Trollope so concentrated" as in *Belton Estate*, wrote Sadleir, a long novel with a simple plot, and that is because Clara's matrimonial dilemma becomes as vital to us and to Will Belton as the world's riches. Trollope's women are glittering prizes or strong threateners, or both, as his mother was both to him. They are complex and unknown enough to surprise us in a long story, and they suggest, too, that the seemingly "inartistic" in Trollope and his tendency to regard moral worth in his changing England and in the bureaucracy in which he worked to be of more consequence than "art," are two of the prime factors that give him great power and very high artistic stature.

Chapter Seventeen

ARNOLD, ELIOT, TRILLING

I N THIS CENTURY we have had no dire shortage of critics, but
so far literary biographers have not been notably successful in
helping to explain how the critical sensibility is formed, or in
telling us which experiences or processes the good critic must pass
through in his or her apprenticeship. Perhaps there are no applicable
rules to draw. But the refreshing general critic of society and culture is
rare, and if there is a certain tradition in criticism to which we can
never admit more than a few names, it is worth seeing if the lives
and careers of our best critics really do seem to share anything in
common.

It will not harm us to think of excellence, or of what Arnold means
when he says (in the Homer lectures in 1861) that a critic is one who
has been baptized seven times in the fire. It would seem that Arnold,

at just that time, was preoccupied with the teasing or blinding effect—
as he rather self-consciously considered the matter—of his own
emotions. We know that he hoped in the early 1860s for a calm self-
control, an inner ease and freedom that would help him to write
adequate verse. The relation between poetry and the poet's emotions is
a topic of debate from Wordsworth's prefaces to T. S. Eliot's *The Sacred Wood*. Arnold and Eliot agree that you cannot make a good poem
unless you have a significant personality (Arnold's cited *bedeutendes
Individuum*) and some emotions to escape from. "Poetry," wrote T. S.
Eliot, is "an escape from emotion; it is not an expression of personality, but an escape from personality. But, of course, only those who
have personality and emotions know what it means to want to escape
from those things." Arnold knew what it was to indulge emotions: he
was immobilized by his father's early death. Despite the play actor in
him and the half-serious and yet still indubitably ludicrous (in his own
eyes) posings as Hamlet in his letters to Clough, he did at least in the
early 1840s avoid new friends at Oxford and meet regularly with a
small "Clougho-Matthean set" of Rugbeians whose grief for Dr. Arnold he shared. At Oxford he read little that he was supposed to read
as an undergraduate, but as an Oriel Fellow he assaulted the Bodleian
and read books until weary. At last he became a disciple of European
sentimentalists (as we have seen), men such as Foscolo, Novalis, Jean
Paul, and Senancour who believed that feeling is, after all, a guide to
truth about the self, society and nature. In "Memorial Verses", he
praised Wordsworth as the poet who made us feel. "He found us," he
wrote of a friend and neighbor at Rydal Mount whom he had known
for seventeen years,

> when the age had bound
> Our souls in its benumbing round;
> He spoke, and loosed our hearts in tears.
> He laid us as we lay at birth
> On the cool flowery lap of earth. . . .
> Others will teach us how to dare,
> And against fear our breast to steel;
> Others will strengthen us to bear—
> But who, ah! who, will make us feel?

But paradoxically in other poems he rejects the subjective emotiveness of Wordsworth and Senancour. His critical career begins in poetry; he sorts writers useful to him, rejects most of them, and uses poetry to explore a dividedness between thought and feeling in the modern mind, and then at last explores the bane of contemporary feeling. In "The Strayed Reveller" Arnold's painterly Olympian gods are childish spirits of feeling with no penetrating insight into human life. In *Empedocles on Etna*, modern thought has overwhelmed the hero's capacity to feel anything but a self-pitying despair. In "The Scholar-Gipsy," controlled feeling is only possible for a timeless figure who lives outside the modern era with its debilitating nostalgia, complaint, and sentimentality, and the speaker is infected by that typical nostalgic complaint. "O born," he tells the Gipsy-Scholar self-pityingly,

> in days when wits were fresh and clear,
> And life ran gaily as the sparkling Thames;
> Before this strange disease of modern life,
> With its sick hurry, its divided aims,
> Its heads o'ertaxed, its palsied hearts, was rife—
> Fly hence, our contact fear!

A difficult period for Arnold had begun after this poem appeared in 1853; it was not so much that his first child Thomas was born unhealthy, or that in time he knew that three of his boys would die, but that having renounced subjective feeling in the preface of 1853, he wrote poorly and became demoralized with himself. When we think of Samuel Johnson's walking between Lichfield and Birmingham to stave off suicide, we may conclude that suffering helps a critic. And it is when Arnold, who has failed to write well in verse for four or five years, at last succeeds as a critic in *On Translating Homer*, that he refers to his need to be "purged seven times in the fire." The critic must be purged of emotion, he believed, since the critic's primary task is perceptual; he must *see* the object. To see "the object as in itself it really is," is to come to it without prior emotions of any kind, not even with the emotion of respect, which Shakespeare's reputation seductively incites. It is even a small matter that the critic of literature happens to be ignorant. "Mr. Newman," Arnold says of a Homer translator, Professor Francis Newman the Latinist of University College in London, and to the delight of Oxford students who heard this lecture in the Sheldonian Theatre,

> ends by saying that my ignorance is great. Alas! that is very true. Much as Mr. Newman was mistaken when he talked of my rancour, he is entirely right when he talks of my ignorance. And yet, perverse as it seems to say so, I sometimes find myself wishing, when dealing with these matters of poetical criticism, that my ignorance were even greater than it is. To handle these matters properly there is needed a poise so perfect that the least overweight in any direction tends to destroy the balance. Temper destroys it, a crotchet destroys it, even erudition may destroy it. To press to the sense of the thing itself with which one is dealing, not to go off on some collateral issue about the thing, is the hardest matter in the world. The 'thing itself' with which one is here dealing,—the critical perception of poetic truth,—is of all things the most volatile, elusive, and evanescent; by even pressing too impetuously after it, one runs the risk of losing it. The critic of poetry should have the finest tact, the nicest moderation, the most free, flexible, and elastic spirit imaginable.

Although in this lover of Oxford there is nothing really anti-academic, one finds in that reply to a University College professor a warning against academic literalism. More than anything else that Arnold wrote, the passage explains why two adequate critics, T. S. Eliot and Lionel Trilling, later were able to make themselves over with his aid. For Arnold the watchwords of good criticism are those such as *poise, balance, perception, flexible, free,* and even *ignorance.* Their harmful opposites are terms of emotion and of learning: *erudition, crotchet, temper.* Yet erudition harms in making the mind less flexible, not when it brings fresh light to keep one from intellectually hardening. Trilling, in 1950, was to comment in an Arnoldian vein on critics who simply believed anything whatever "can be discovered through hard intellectual work and concentration," and Trilling's complaint about the academic critic is that he or she treats influences too simply and imagines that ideas "have a life independent of the thinker and the situation."

When in 1920 Eliot tried to improve taste by countering the effects of Edwardian dilletantism and impressionism, he produced, in *The Sacred Wood*, one of the most delightful volumes of criticism in our century. Eliot's essays illustrate the Arnoldian message that style, tact, and beauty of expression are critical tools. He uses Arnold as a foil almost throughout *The Sacred Wood*, and offers essays in the Arnoldian way as being specimens or examples of the critical act. He comments on emotion: "A literary critic should have no emotions except those immediately provoked by the work of art." Thus Eliot begins a strategic attack on emotive critics, and, as we might expect, on Shakespeare's failures as an artist. For again the eminence of Shakespeare corrupts seeing, so that if we see or read a tragedy with prior respect or reverence, we neither see nor read the play as it is. We should bring no emotions *to* Shakespeare, and keep his faults in mind; his worst fault is a "vice of style," which is "a tortured perverse ingenuity of images which dissipates instead of concentrating the imagination, and which may be due in part to influences by which Marlowe was untouched." That interesting complaint was inspired by Eliot's reading of Johnson's "Life of Cowley," but later he is more original. The tragedy of *Hamlet* is "most certainly an artistic failure" since Shakespeare lacked the art to delineate Hamlet's "emotion," and Eliot supports that comment with his famous idea of the "objective correlative." He introduces it in an offhand manner when he says that the only way the artist can express emotion is by finding "a set of objects, a situation, a chain of events which shall be the formula of that *particular* emotion," so that when the sensory facts or events are given the desired emotion is evoked.

Arnold and Eliot do not think emotion is foreign to art. What I have been saying is that they agree on a severe dietetics for the critic, who is adequate when purged of emotion. Arnold as a poet learned to purge or control his emotions, the last and most subtle of which was the emotion of respect he felt for writers he most admired. Today a criticism of Arnold that intends to account for his development must take his emotional history, his dalliance with the sentimentalists, and his entire commentary on "feeling" into account.

Lionel Trilling in the 1930s and 1940s made himself over by react-
ing to Arnold and Eliot, and indeed as a critic he shares with Arnold a
perceptual emphasis, a concern with the critic's needful beauty of
style, a sense of the unparaphrasable nature of art, a belief that the
critic exists to hand on the instrument of criticism, a sense of foreign
literature as a part of English and American, a desire to bring in light
from other fields (such as Freudian psychoanalysis), and a conviction
that a literary comment impinges on politics, religion, philosophy,
and other aspects of a contemporary society. Since Trilling excels in
four essay collections we need to know his essay "The Sense of the
Past" and the rest of *The Liberal Imagination* (1950), all of his *Beyond
Culture* (1965), at least the essays on Flaubert, Dickens, and Jane
Austen in *The Opposing Self* (1955), and the pieces on American topics—on Edmund Wilson, David Riesman, the academic vice of a
lack of manners in the essay "On Not Talking," and the fine
revelatory comments on America in the essay on Santayana at Har-
vard—in the collection called *A Gathering of Fugitives* (1956); these
are the minimum but I would add his last book, *Sincerity and Authenticity*, and even his unfinished report of a Jane Austen seminar at
Columbia (first printed in the *Times Literary Supplement*). To know
these and Arnold's *On Translating Homer*, two volumes of *Essays in
Criticism*, and the *Discourses in America*, as well as Eliot's *The Sacred
Wood* and *Collected Essays* and a handful of Eliot's later pieces such
as "The Music of Poetry" and "The Frontiers of Criticism," is to know
the best criticism in English from the 1850s to the 1970s, and therefore to have a sense of how the Victorian sensibility relates to ours.
Trilling's first book, *Matthew Arnold* (1939), is the venue through
which he comes to terms with his chief mentor. As a "biography of a
mind," it is weak on Arnold's poetry and religion, based on a poor
edition of his letters, and filled with inaccuracies (such as that Arnold
died when leaping over a low fence). Even so it is valuable, since this
is the book in which Trilling purged his debilitating emotions about
Arnold himself.

Why, one asks, do Trilling and Eliot cite Arnold so often, when his
reputation after the First World War and on into the 1930s and 1940s
was in general not very high—though I. A. Richards was virtually his
disciple and F. R. Leavis devoted a perceptive essay to him in *Scrutiny*

in 1938? Eliot's tireless concern with Arnold reminds one of the behavior of articulate lovers when they are apart; in its verbal phases love
is a kind of pleasurable exercise in epistemology, it seems, in which
John can never find the best images or phrases he needs in order to say
what he feels about Mary, and, clearly, neither John nor Mary wants
to *get over* the process of knowing the Self and the Other. What is it in
Arnold's writing that Eliot and Trilling do not wish to get over learning about? Part of his lasting value to them is that he does not assume
that either art or criticism matters; hence he must implicitly justify art
and the act of criticism in each essay, and in no other respect does he
better merit his place in the company of Sidney, Dryden, Johnson,
and Coleridge, the major critics before him who can still refresh us.
Since he does not take it for granted that Heine, Keats, or Wordsworth
matter, he must show in each essay why the artist is relevant to life,
and how art is involved in society. His implicit topic is the relation
between art and society, and this is essentially Eliot's and Trilling's
topic.

Understandably Eliot, to define his position and to challenge the
view that poetry can substitute for religion (though that is not quite
Arnold's view), is often severe with his mentor. The most interesting
of his attacks on Arnold are in the two early essays "The Perfect
Critic" and "Imperfect Critics" (1920), then in "The Function of Criticism" (1923), the essay on F. H. Bradley (1927), "Arnold and Pater"
(1930), the essay concerning Matthew Arnold in *The Use of Poetry
and The Use of Criticism* (1933), and in the two books *After Strange
Gods* (1933) and *Notes Toward a Definition of Culture* (1944), all of
which show a useful Arnold. The test of a critic's worth is not that he
or she cannot be refuted since critics thrive on being damned, but
whether he or she can be usefully cited and re-read. Though Eliot can
lower Arnold to the status of a "propagandist" and quarrel with his use
of words, he views him as a master critic who kept a delicate balance
between the rival claims of society and aesthetics; and, indeed, Arnold's essays helped Eliot to correct his own initially restricted aesthet-
icism. Trilling from the start was almost too distracted by society's
needs and likely to forget art's claims; he is far less censorious of the
socially minded Arnold and more able to adapt Arnold's positions

profitably than Eliot can. Trilling is also a more concealed and subtle adapter since the most Arnoldian of his essays do not casually reveal their Victorian sources.

Eliot's praise of Arnold tends to be stylized, smart, and vaguely evasive. "Matthew Arnold was intelligent," Eliot stated in *The Sacred Wood*, "and by so much difference as the presence of one intelligent man makes, our age is inferior of Arnold's." This is reasonable, if it is rather unfair to the intelligent Eliot himself; but it is vague. What Eliot implies is that Arnold wrote without the vices of sentiment or impressionism, and that in the general imprecision of feeling and during an explosion of new information from science, he brought a cleared sensibility to the essay—that was his intelligence. As Eliot recognized, at historical times when science tells us too much, the mind resists a surfeit of facts so that most of the "thinking" we do is only to consult our emotions. Scientists themselves are too frequently sentimentalists. Recoiling from emotion, the sentimentalist may insist on rigid and over-refined definitions of "culture," "criticism," or of anything else that is necessarily ambiguous in human life. Arnold resisted that oddly sentimental and academic temptation to be hard and literal with terms, and could be valuable to Eliot and Trilling because he had cleared himself of the emotionality of his own temperament, family, and sentimental era and thus could write with a clarity they really found in no other critic since Coleridge's time.

No other word Arnold used has had a deeper influence on twentieth-century English and American thought than the word "culture." Arnold's propagation of his concept of culture, or of the attitude of seeking the best that has been thought and said so as to turn "a stream of fresh and free thought upon our stock notions and habits," is usually involved in Eliot's and Trilling's responses. In 1920, Eliot could accuse Arnold of having wasted his time by writing *Culture and Anarchy* and of misdirected efforts in social criticism. Art, for Eliot, makes demands of its own; Arnold should have saved his critical strength for poetry. But by 1928 Eliot can admit that poetry has "something" to do with morals, religion, and politics; and in editing his journal *Criterion* between 1922 and 1939, Eliot gradually undertakes a more and more

Arnoldian program. His aim was to reform English provincialism by bringing to bear the mind of Europe on current thinking about literature, and Eliot published essays on history, politics, and a large number of social topics as well as on literature. By 1930, in "Arnold and Pater," however, he makes clear his chief objection to his mentor when he says, "The total effect of Arnold's philosophy is to set up Culture in the place of Religion, and to leave Religion to be laid waste by the anarchy of feeling." Unfortunately by then the objection hardened him too often against Arnold, and Eliot, whose classicism was out of key with the political issues of the 1930s, became less effective as an essayist.

In contrast, Lionel Trilling, maturing in a politically conscious decade, felt more comfortable with Arnold's social essays. He studies them well in his book on Arnold in 1939. Starting with *The Liberal Imagination* (1950), he is subtle and capable in adapting Arnold's social insights. It is true that the preface to *The Liberal Imagination* is naive and dated, as when Trilling equates the liberal tradition with "ideas" and the American conservative tradition with "irritable mental gestures which seek to resemble ideas." (In its political enthusiasm that remark neglects the Hamiltonian tradition of intellectual conservatism.) But Trilling elsewhere is humane and balanced; to take one delightful example of his use of Arnoldian tactics against literalism and mere quantification, in his essay "The Kinsey Report" he criticizes Professors A. C. Kinsey, W. B. Pomeroy, and C. E. Martin for taking an absurd quantitative view of sex in their book *Sexual Behavior in the Human Male*. Kinsey in his interviews had found a man, "clearly the hero of the Report," says Trilling, who had "an orgasmic frequency of thirty times a week." (Some other men had about half an orgasm per week, to the alarm of Kinsey, who believed that good robust sex means nothing but frequent orgasms.) "Masturbation in children," Trilling mildly comments, "often is the expression not of sexuality only but of anxiety; its frequency may not be so much robust as compulsive." Trilling thus exploded a minor instance of the modern faith in quantity and helped us to see that by confusing love and sex with ejaculation, forgetting anxiety, and taking Americans as the only "human males," *Sexual Be-*

havior in the Human Male is nearly as naive as a Salem discourse on witchcraft.

A biographer may well ask why Trilling, among critics of "The Kinsey Report," discussed it with balanced good sense, or without irritation, pedantry, heat, or coldness. A champion of Freud might approve its glance at sex, and pity its naiveté. Before Trilling, Arnold had ventured into sex in *Literature and Dogma* (1873) to discuss what was least expected of him: casual sexual relationships or adultery. The casual affair, Arnold had argued, "has an attraction for all of us." Who has not thought of having a sexual liaison outside of his or her marriage? But the English with their Puritan heritage seem unable to *think* about this: they develop the sexual person crudely, grossly, because on this topic they are irrational. France in contrast develops the sexual person "confidently and harmoniously," and so well as to attract us with casual sex: life in Paris is reasonable in arrangements. "All of us feel," Arnold adds about sexual affairs, "at some time or other in our lives, a hankering after the French ideal, a disposition to try it."

Arnold went to parties without his wife in the 1870s. He dined out in a milieu in which casual sex was so common as to bore gossipers. But biographical explanations of his frankness about sex, I think, will explain nothing if they do not account for the temper of his mind. In clearing himself of emotionality, he had rid himself of many (if not all) of the Victorian fears. Trilling, too, purged himself, and what he saw in turn was the emotional basis of most of our thinking, most of our answers and enthusiasms.

For the biographer, the lives of Eliot and Trilling will always be illuminated by Arnold's thought and career. It is a paradox that all three placed the highest value on feeling and spontaneity even though what Trilling, and Arnold and Eliot before him, located as one prime cause of grief in modern society is our confusion of rationality and impulse, scientific objectivity and emotionalism, which now and then is a contributing factor in the killing of six million Jews, a Vietnam war, or the murder of a Polish priest. Whether Arnold and Trilling misused their talents in showing that the same mistakes that result in false judgments of Shakespeare or Keats may be seen in British education reports or in analyses of sexual behaviour is, perhaps, debatable. But an emotional problem is at the root of the human dilemma and may always be expected to be, and those whom we call the great critics from Sidney, Dryden, and Johnson to Arnold, Eliot and Trilling continually refresh us because they manage to penetrate it.

Chapter Eighteen

HISTORICAL PRIVILEGE: EZRA POUND, ROBERT BROWNING, AND "KIT MARLOWE"

I

THERE IS no mention of Ezra Pound's essay "Landor (1775–1864)" in Mr. Humphrey Carpenter's rather large biography of a thousand pages, *A Serious Character: The Life of Ezra Pound* (published in 1988), though T. S. Eliot left this key piece out of his edition of Pound's essays and no one can be expected to comment on all that Pound wrote. I find Mr. Carpenter's biography helpful with personal detail, and not oblivious to the viciousness of Pound's sponsorship of fascism and the lunacy of his attendant ideas. George Steiner has been most lucid on that "crackerbarrel" aspect of Pound: "Pound's anti-Semitism produces lousy verse which looks and sounds as if it had been stuck on the body of his serious poetry," wrote Steiner in the *London Review of Books* (July 27, 1989). It may be impossible for any biographer in this century to see Pound clearly— since he was blind to matters of great moral urgency, however "crackerbarrel," populist, Midwestern American, and typical of the 1920s and 1930s Pound's lunacy was. However, it cannot be said that Pound was not intelligently at home with much of the past, or that he was not an artist. His racism stands well outside the periphery of his essential work as a lyric poet, and he does not appear to have been vicious or obtuse with individuals: "Even in the years of his all too overt Fascism in Italy," writes Steiner, he "sought to be of assistance to individual Jews." So though a biographer's moral revulsion over Pound's lunacy is quite justified, Mr. Carpenter's horror may prompt him to be a little too quick and cavalier with Pound's best verse, as when describing the *Cantos* as "a botch." (Pound at least liked that word, and in his last Venice years used to hand visitors a small card that read something like, "Forgive me if I do not speak; I have made too deep a botch of things.") Mr. Carpenter is not at ease with Pound's poetry but something has happened to impair the ear for poetry late in the twentieth century, and here we have the case of a biographer who makes up for unhelpful comments on an author's work by giving us much new data about an author's life. Pound himself has something to teach us about intimate representations of history, or about access to the personal past with which biographers are concerned. So, with Mr. Carpenter's help at first, with Pound's views of Robert Browning and of "Kit Marlowe" in focus, and with some help from the ne- glected "Landor" essay, too, I want to see what poets may have to tell literary biographers about access to history.

Mr. Carpenter reminds us of how cocky and footloose Pound was when, at twenty-two, fired from his teaching post at Wabash College, Indiana, because he had let a penniless burlesque girl sleep in his bed (when he slept on the floor), he found himself in Venice. Here he paid to have his poems *A Lume Spento (With Tapers Quenched)* printed. He was unsure of them, but they appeared in July 1908 and were full of allusions to his mentor Robert Browning, who had died nineteen years earlier at the Palazzo Rezzonico on the Grand Canal. Here we must leave Mr. Carpenter. Pound's admiration for the poet who wrote *Sordello* and *Men and Women* had in it a strain of hero worship. Browning had left the narrow, Puritan ethos of middle-class Victorian England and the restricted scene at suburban Camberwell, under skies of brass and iron, to live under Italy's blue dome at Pisa, Florence, and Rome as if in a time machine. Italy's streets, markets, churches, paintings, sounds, and colors were all gateways to her past, so that in Italy one had a chance to be intimate with history, and history in Browning's poetry is never a backdrop but a constituent of feeling and awareness. In a sense Browning even at Camberwell— with his Italian books and visits to the Dulwich Gallery—had grown up as an Anglo-Italian and had been learning to write of the English present and the Italian past simultaneously before his removal to Italy in the mid-1840s. He had a certain breadth and intimacy of vision, a clear overview of human life and a superb mastery of historical and psychological detail. So, in "Mesmerism," Pound gives him an Idaho hug—almost forgiving him for faults in diction and rhythm. "Master Bob-Browning" may be old hippety-hop o' the accents who is as wheezy as a head-cold long-tonsilled calliope, but he is still "Clear sight's elector!" Lyrics in *A Lume Spento* such as "Fifine Answers" and "Scriptor Ignotus" are relevant, and Pound's "Cino" is a brief compendium of Browning techniques. The troubadour poet Cino da Pistoia, with a wry, comic weariness not at all like that of the 1890s, brings history before us as he steps along an open road of the Campagna in 1309.

When engaged in the Imagist campaign, Pound continued to be Browning's advocate. Stendhal was quite right—Pound feels—to say around 1830 that prose has replaced poetry in England and Europe as the clearest means of conveying states of human consciousness ("le mouvements de coeur"), for had not Stendhal just behind him delicate examples of the prose of Prévost, Constant, Jane Austen, and others? (The implication is that you need only to read *Manon Lescaut, Adolphe,* and *Emma* to see what the Frenchman means.) France has only four poets since Stendhal's time who will withstand that wide condemnation of modern verse—and England has only one. England offers only Browning, who has no exact parallel anywhere, Pound assures us.

In the "Landor" essay (1917) Pound does, at any rate, offer an explicit reason for Browning's excellence. No doubt the poet of *Men and Women* had been able to look out of his own time and reach the exact standpoint of a past time; and the glory for that must go to that other English exile in Italy, Landor, whose enormous *Imaginary Conversations* Pound has been reading aloud with Yeats. (Not even Mr. Carpenter can tell us whose voice tired first.) Pound admits that Landor is prolix, but claims that Landor's technique with historical particulars gave Browning, the better poet, access to the past. In other words, Browning exploited what Pound implies is (and I shall call) historical privilege—an intimacy with history that demands that one treat the past unromantically or without distortion and represent its life—its tones, moods and outlooks—with psychological realism.

But even with Landor's help, how did Browning gain such intimacy? Pound, I think, would invite us to compare poets and epochs for an answer. His own Browningesque poem "Sestina: Altaforte" had put him in mind of "Kit Marlowe," and in the Landor essay he tells us that lines in Christopher Marlowe's Ovidian Elegies are the first to render in English the exact tone of a writer of the distant past.

II

Pound in his essays only darts back at the past; he does not say how a poet achieves biographical intimacy with history, or how Marlowe was able to see Ovid plain—or duplicate the tone of a writer who died in A.D. 18. In fact the *Metamorphoses* and *Art of Love*, though subject to censorship, cuts, rewriting or moralized emendment, were not unknown in late-medieval Europe; but shortly before Marlowe and Shakespeare were born Ovid was freed for the most part from modification by censors; humanists had given his works in more faithful editions and translations. One thinks of Shakespeare's use of Golding's version of the *Metamorphoses*. Formerly Europe had *Ovide moralisé;* then it had an Ovid made new again. The importance of what is "new," authentic, caught from history, is that it helps the mind to traverse time so that associated "old" or already known facts seem to become fresh, immediate, or "new" again themselves. The young Marlowe at Canterbury and at Cambridge responded to Ovid, and the past, with a freshness and exhilaration matched only by Shakespeare's: it can hardly be coincidental that in their twenties by 1592 both playwrights had passed far beyond the example of the stiff and lifeless chronicle play; both with astonishing confidence had brought historical intimacy to the popular stage and both had entered into the minds of English kings. Marlowe's *Edward II* and Shakespeare's tumultuous *Henry VI* plays seem to take us far from Pound's compliment to the Elizabethan poet who reached Ovid's "exact tone." But, I think, all of these achievements relate to the excitement and stimulus of the "new," or to that Elizabethan experience of having a great deal of the new and authentic from the past continually brought to light. A plentitude of new historical facts was made available by antiquaries, chroniclers, translators, and gazetteers in the reign, and William Lambarde's *Perambulation of Kent* (1576)—the first of the county histories, published when Marlowe was twelve—gives us a notion of a certain imbalance in it all. Lambarde's friend Thomas Wotton begins (in beautiful italic type) with the usual vague but suggestive Elizabethan reasons we should read history: it is useful for the training of gentlemen, or "profitable" and "delectable." After that Lambarde supplies (in black-letter pages) a flood of particulars on the local history of Kentish towns. It would seem that no religious, moral, or other sort of Tudor commentary was ever vast or detailed enough to keep pace with the new accretions.

Is it, then, the sheer, sudden availability of new facts that grants a poet intimacy with history? The less interpreted they are in one's own time, perhaps, the more seminal they will be for the poet? Elizabethans and Victorians have written the best history-poetry in English. There are parallels between the two times. When Landor and Browning were alive, there was a more perplexing rush of new facts and nothing integrated it all—not the work of Ranke, Michelet, and all of Europe's historians together. Sources of history had become legion and included the daily, weekly, and monthly press as well as sermons, biographies, encyclopedias, treatises, memoirs, collections of letters and of folksongs, even novels, poems, calendars and dictionaries.

Historians and *litterateurs* had added to the flood. As Eichhorn had opened up church and legal history, so Herder and Grimm had

opened up folk history, and Barthold Niebuhr—the Danish friend of
Dr. Arnold and of other English historians—had opened up the early
history of customs, social classes, and institutions. Mary Ellis Gibson's
perceptive study *History and the Prism of Art* (1987) shows how all of
this produced angst. Carlyle fretted over the "Chaos of Being" and
Arnold over the "multitudinousness." But it must be noticed that a
respect for the fact once again helps to produce a new art—besides
stimulating biography, historiography, and in one way or another
every branch of intellectual effort in the nineteenth century. Ms. Gibson might have rather more to say on the new concern with historical
sources, on the immense effort to determine the reliability of past
"facts." The historian John Adolphus had begun sifting and comparing primary documents on the French Revolution early in the century. John Wilson Croker used the medium of successive book reviews
to assess source material on the French Revolution—and this in the
1830s when Carlyle was writing his tempestuously well-balanced *The
French Revolution* and Browning was spending seven years with Italian
history to write *Sordello*.

A respect for the historical datum, then, the reliable fact unvar-
nished, is an item of Browning's poetic creed. Pound once wrote that
he admired the form of *Men and Women* and that it was superior to
the form of Ovid's *Heroides*—as if no higher praise of a modern poet
would be possible to give. But "form" in the dramatic monologues of
Browning's *Men and Women* is not built up out of a sequence of
verifiable historic particulars in what might be an historian's or a biographer's manner. Rather, the poet's immersion in facts of the past
seems to give him the authority to explain history by imagining its life
and blood, which dead records and a thousand discrete facts of the
past never have in them. This is the sense in which Browning uses the
word "explain" in a letter to his friend Miss Julia Wedgwood about
The Ring and the Book. He had been in a light flirtation with Miss
Wedgwood, who seemed in her comments on his villain Guido Fran-
ceschini to be rejecting Browning as well as his poem. His reply to her
is petulant and yet exact and careful, as if he knew she would save his
letter. "But here," he writes on November 19, 1868 at the age of fifty-
six, "—given the subject, I cannot but still say, given the treatment
too: the business has been, as I specify, to explain *fact*—and the fact is

what you see and, worse, are to see . . . Before I die, I hope to purely invent something—here my pride was concerned to invent nothing: the minutest circumstance that denotes character is *true:* the black is so much—the white, no more." We should be grateful for the volume of correspondence, *Robert Browning and Julia Wedgwood: A Broken Friendship as Revealed by Their Letters,* edited by Richard Curle (New York, 1937: see especially pages 143–144), for offering the clearest exposition of Browning's intentions as a writer of poetic monologues. Other statements about his art such as the discussion of objective and subjective poetry in his Essay on Shelley are more ambiguous, though he refers more than once to his (very Carlylean) respect for factuality.

Now to "explain" persons such as Edward II and Henry VI, their reigns and characters and actions, is also what Marlowe's play and the early history plays of Shakespeare appear to do. Elizabethans believed in a variety of things but not in our doctrines of fictional or historical realism, and it is of no consequence that playwrights of their time took liberties with what seemed to be the historical particularities of source material. In the writing of a history play or history poem at any time an exact fidelity to the supposed facts of a source must be a minor matter—which cannot add to the work's artistry or authenticity. What may count a great deal is the pressure of interest and imagination that animates the material; and Marlowe's tragedy *Edward II* and Browning's monologues such as "My Last Duchess," "The Bishop Orders His Tomb" and those in *Men and Women* all seem most alike in being responses to an impulse from history. The playwright and the monologue writer have felt, one might say, a pressure of interest in history, a pressure not really separable from a widespread fascination for the "new" in history that many of their contemporaries show. What seemed new, to Elizabethans and Victorians, helped to make old and familiar events and facts for them "new" enough in turn for art. Presumably because something was known and felt about kingship and the English past and a little about Edward's short, tragic reign, Marlowe could give his audience a wholly fresh, new intimacy, a close-up portrait in action of King Edward II and his Gaveston.

A historical privilege—for the poet—may depend then on being able to write at a time when an enthusiasm for history is general, when faith in the importance of the past is hardly disputed, or when the public *wills* that the writer should share the faith. But what then are the limitations of the privilege? We may have a clue to the necessary limitations in Ezra Pound's respect for Browning's mastery of "form" in the dramatic monologue. And it is possible, too, that Browning's other critics in the present century have been instructive about the limits of historical privilege just through the diversity of their approaches to his finest poems.

Pound, of course, had begun admiring his Victorian mentor when the Browning societies were in vogue. In response to their adulation, Pound's contemporaries began to call Browning a sham. By and large the New Critics of the 1930s did not know what to do with Browning's poetry, but after H. B. Charlton and W. C. DeVane had shown the intelligence of his texts a more perceptive criticism began to appear. Following Roma A. King's *The Bow and the Lyre* and Robert Langbaum's *The Poetry of Experience* in the late 1950s, it became possible to see that his difficulties—and his excellence—owe to subtleties in his technique and the necessary ambiguity of readings of historical monologues.

If we read Browning's "My Last Duchess" as a monologue spoken by a sixteenth-century Duke of Ferrara who has locked up or killed his first wife and is therefore reprehensible, we seem trapped by a text. Whom do we condemn, the guilt-free Duke who is untouched by our own feelings, or the society that produced him? If we sympathize with the Duke's svelte character glimmering through the brilliancy of his discourse, as we might momentarily sympathize with any monster who let us follow his pattern of thought and feeling, we must remember to hate and judge him, too. But no critic convinces us that there is a "right" way to read the poem. No statement as to what the reader's response to the monologue *ought* to be is valid. The difficulty with judgment in this case is that it is irrelevant; I cannot take my judgment into the time of the poem. And my sympathy is also defeated. Who asks me to sympathize with the Duke? If we neither sympathize nor judge, "My Last Duchess" may itself judge the Victorian present—in which wives are victimized in home or factory for causes less offensive than failure to appreciate a Duke's "nine-hundred-year-old name"—and this poem may judge our own time, when we lack the Duke's smart and appealing elegance and sense of decorum. On the other hand, it is not quite true that any decided reaction to the history poem may not enrich it. "My Last Duchess" in its indeterminacy seems designed to attract comment, while its speaker remains safe behind the beauty of his discourse.

Though I have discussed only one perfect example of Browning's use of historical privilege, that poem shows the limits of the privilege. A respect for history implies a respect for time. If a poet feels pressure to conjure up a particularized past, the imagined past must work out its own fate. We cannot enter into the past with any applicable approval or disapproval—until the past is seen to produce its result for the good or the bad. Just this troubled Browning, with his moral imperatives. In *The Ring and the Book*, he tried to conjure up the vast number of particulars which would give grounds for a judgment of his speakers and inserted the speech of a contemporary seventeenth-century Pope who could judge persons. Marlowe in *Edward II* leaves us with a final indeterminacy, a tragedy of a man who shows mettle in suffering, and may not be blameworthy in his preference for a favorite over a Queen so easily capable of adultery.

The importance of the severity of the historical privilege, I think, is this. Writers who have it—and use it—show us that the past is held off from us. It is inviolate. A poet may find or place into it almost anything he or she wishes, but must not violate it with overt moral judgments from the present if it is to *seem* to be the past itself. Ezra Pound understood this in the delicate and superb *Cantos*, where the past has its main meaning in the pathos and beauty of its removal. In the great Elizabethan history plays, the past judges itself in the flow and continuity of its own action. And so, one might add, in history and biography the retrospective method is always faulty and unconvincing. Only by giving the ongoing movement and presence of an historic life in its immediacy, with the future ahead and problems of the moment in view, can a biographer begin to suggest a past reality. And only by letting the past reveal itself in its own flow can the poet or historian judge it.

Chapter Nineteen

DAVID LODGE
BEFORE
CHANGING
PLACES

I FIRST MET David Lodge when he was a student at University College in London in the 1950s. I was a student myself and had just published a short story in the College's periodical, *New Phineas*. In fact at Catford, where I was trying to live on 56 pounds a month, I had opened an envelope that contained a little typed list of classic short stories by Turgenev, Hemingway, Katherine Mansfield, and others; the final typed name on this list was my own, followed by the title of my story in *New Phineas*, as I noted with awed surprise. A David Lodge was asking me to appear before his discussion group to answer questions about *my* story.

To answer his summons was the least I could do. Since the other classic authors were no longer able to answer questions, I would gloriously represent them as a living writer. But I might have been warned by Lodge's amusement when I arrived at the Bloomsbury flat where his group convened. In the course of the evening, I concluded that my name had been added to the select list of classics as a kind of ballast, because I had written the worst story any member of the group had been able to find. Enjoying the evening and the wine despite my flattened ego, I left with the feeling that Lodge's remarks had been sharp.

I saw him often after that. I thought of him as a future critic, though he mentioned fiction writing. One day he handed me a smudgy, tattered, disgraceful-looking novel in typescript called "The Picturegoers": he had been sending it round to London publishers and accumulating rejections. Then the unbelievable happened: an editor at MacGibbon & Kee accepted his novel and *The Picturegoers* was published in 1960.

As nobody had offered me a job I had left England; I returned on a permanent basis after nine years to teach in a room next to Lodge's tutorial room. He had continued to write and develop as a critic while flourishing as a novelist, and seemed to manage two writing careers very well in tandem. His most important critical work had appeared as *Language of Fiction* (1966). His fourth novel was soon published and it has seemed to me since then that his fiction writing career has fallen into two halves. From *Changing Places* through *Nice Work* of 1988, partly because his comic American professor Morris Zapp and his cigar loom so large, light satire prevails with comedy in Lodge's work, whereas the four novels before *Changing Places* tend to be serio-comic, and at least three have tragic elements. But that is not an adequate description of Lodge's early works, and I propose to look at a few features in these rather more exactly. The novels I have in mind are *The Picturegoers* (the least well known of his books), *Ginger, You're Barmy, The British Museum Is Falling Down*, and *Out of the Shelter*.

"I am admittedly schizophrenic about my novel-writing and my criticism," he has said disarmingly. As a critic Lodge displays a special concern for the novelist's style and rhetoric. The "schizophrenic" attitude does not keep that concern out of his fiction, since in the early novels he uses language with finesse to treat the British postwar experience. *The Picturegoers* introduces a young intellectual hero, Mark Underwood, and an omniscient but impartial narrator with a cameralike eye. Two typical experiences of South London life are examined from multiple viewpoints. There is the Saturday night showing of a sumptuous mammary epic from Hollywood (*While the Cat's Away*, starring Amber Lush) and the Sunday morning performance of Mass (by doddery Father Kipling in a church not far from a marmite factory). Both events attract Mark Underwood—who manages to be appropriately cynical until he understands them.

Mark is a rather restless media student. He yearns for the landlady's daughter Clare. In fact, he scribbles "On Hearing His Beloved's Urination" while she is in the loo:

> O gushing stream
> You bring sweet music to my troubled ear;
> And as I lie upon my restless couch,
> I fit a picture to each sound I hear.

Not far away in the cinema is Harry. He is a failed rapist:

> Harry pissed savagely into the wall behind her back. Seeing a
> block of camphor in the channel by his feet he directed his
> urine at it like a hose, but succeeded only in spattering his suede
> shoes.

But Harry responds to poetry too:

> Ten o'clock, eleven o'clock, twelve o'clock rock!
> We're gonna rock
> Around
> The clock
> Tonight!

And so does Fr. Kipling's wheezing flock:

> "Sursum corda."
> "Habemus ad Dominum."
> "Gratias agamus Domino Deo nostro."

> > "Sanctus,
> > > Sanctus,
> > > > Sanctus."

"On Hearing His Beloved's Urination" seems a tribute to Keatsian sensationalism. Urban poetry is a correlative of feeling—rising to throbbing words—when accompanied by the auditory formality of rock or the priest's mumble or the conjured sensations of the lavatory. Mark hardly needs to think of the poet Robert Browning to remind himself of the sensuousness of the Catholic Mass or of that "essential indecency behind the candles. . . . Christ risked making himself cheap by mass production." Indeed. Our Ford in Heaven knows as much.

Nevertheless the hour of Marshall McLuhan is at hand.

Mark sits beside Clare through the Technicolor glow of Amber Lush. The Hollywood star Amber is radiant on the screen in her well-filled brassiere, but he's at wit's end by the time the trailer for Next Week's Coming Attraction blares. Gamely he takes it in:

ADVENTURE: horse-riders galloped pointlessly through a copse . . . AGONY: a woman awaited the result of an operation on her lover. LAUGHTER: the comic relief fell backward into a pool.

In the roaring darkness a McLuhanite epiphany comes at the apex of Mark's frenzy. He glances round at the cinema audience, and perceives:

Like fish in a glass tank, their stupid, gaping faces were pressed to the window on a world they could never hope to achieve, where giant brown men stalked among big-breasted women, and where all events kindly conspired to throw one into the arms of the other. The hysterical affirmations of the trailer's commentary rolled easily off each person's saturated consciousness; yet perhaps only the assurance of this window on the ideal world, on the superlife, made the waking nightmare of their daily lives tolerable. It was in a way a substitute for religion—and indeed a fabulously furnished pent-house, and the favours of awesomely shaped women, offered a more satisfactory conception of paradise than the sexless and colourless Christian promise—the questionable rapture of being one among billions of court-flatterers.

The Picturegoers preceded *The Gutenberg Galaxy* by two years. Lodge makes the point that the film's message—though it does matter—matters less than the experience of a medium of such intimacy that "superlife" becomes, for the moviegoer, a personal possession. By portraying the affective texture of the inner lives of contrasting characters he also shows who needs Amber Lush, who doesn't, and why.

The Picturegoers and *Language of Fiction* alike celebrate the novelist's medium. To understand the methods of the novel—and of Lodge's others—we ought to attend to his ideas about contemporary fiction, I think.

He knows that the tide is running against the comic and moral, Fielding to Drabble tradition of realism in England. "Realistic novels continue to be written," he observes, but "the pressure of scepticism on the aesthetic and epistemological premises of literary realism is . . . intense." So much so "that many novelists are at least considering the two routes that branch off from the crossroads" into fantasy (or what Robert Scholes calls "fabulation") and into nonfiction or B. S. Johnsonian anti-fiction novels. Why stick to realism at all? Lodge can because he believes "the reality which realism imitates" exists ("History may be, in a philosophic sense, a fiction, but it does not feel like that when we miss a train or somebody starts a war.") and because he thinks realist conventions (such as consistency with the empirically perceived world and solidity of specification) help the writer to control and transform his material. Realistic fiction is made out of personal experience. This must be believed in, checked against objective facts as the fictive imagination shapes and adapts it rhetorically: "In the novel personal experience must be explored and transmuted until it acquires an authenticity and persuasiveness independent of its actual origins."

Lodge in "The Novelist at the Crossroads" welcomed nonfiction novels such as Capote's *In Cold Blood* and Mailer's *Armies of the Night* and such a comic-apocalyptic fantasy as Barth's *Giles Goat-Boy* because these use novelistic strategies. But he treated B. S. Johnson's anti-fiction confessional *Albert Angelo* with dry asperity. (He shouldn't like Johnson's *House Mother Normal* either. This is not an anti-fiction but, at least more nearly, an anti-prose novel using Eliot-like verse as a norm.) Though British, Johnson out-Americanized Americans in his tendency to shatter discourse and to exhibit language; whereas Lodge—though emphatic about the novelist's need for "linguistic resourcefulness" and eclectic in considering rhetorical modes in *Language of Fiction*—is deeply set against exhibitionism and "style." His dislike of bravura that shows off the novelist has usually been strong. "If the current malady of English fiction is the cult of unpretentiousness . . . the American novel is afflicted by the opposite—and on the whole more promising—symptom of pretentiousness, straining for effects, excessive indulgence in lyricism," he has declared. Though entranced and amused by modern American fiction, he finds American novelists of small use to him. He is assaulted by them:

> When I read most American novelists they seem to be rather battering me over the head, flexing their verbal muscles, and so on. . . . The English writer, though, is trying to get you into a conversation and starting to work on you rhetorically without your knowing it.

What the English writer is "trying" to do is what Lodge has usually demanded of his own prose.

But there is an obvious drawback to unobtrusive rhetoric and a conversational style that lasts three hundred pages. A transparent manner with language in realistic fiction is likely to result in a rather wearisome, expressive monochrome. Lodge (well aware of much "timid, inept" contemporary writing) avoids the danger in two traditional ways (practiced by Henry James, for instance). He places in the foreground of a novel a luminous "consciousness" that is capable—to cite *Language of Fiction*—of "a more sensitive and complicated verbalization of experience" than is usual in a "world in which the public language is imaginatively impoverished." This psyche is realistically limited. We have clever but fumbling Mark Underwood in *The Picturegoers*, Jon the troubled rationalist in *Ginger*, Adam Apple as manic thesis writer in frillies in *The British Museum*, and Timothy Young groping into the sexual world in *Out of the Shelter*. The point

is that they are sensitive enough to demand, as it were, of their creator
Lodge clever and interesting "verbalization" when he narrates from
their viewpoints. Then Lodge exploits the relieving linguistic bravura
of what characters say or write. The comic disintegration and fall of
Adam Apple in *British Museum*—struggling to finish a Ph.D. thesis
and not to fertilize his wife Barbara (again)—is marked by his own
attempts to complete a couplet for a furniture manufacturer's cash
prize. Adam sorely needs the money:

> I always use a Brownlong chair
> For laying girls with long brown hair,

he begins badly, and by midday is in grave psychic trouble:

> . . . pair, rare, scare, stair, ware, wear, yare.
> It's just like floating in the air
> Another chair I couldn't bear
> And then I sit and stare and glare
> Like a lion in his lair
> Or a tortoise crossed with hare
> Or a horse without a mare
> Or a man who's got no heir
> Or an heir who's got no hair
> Hypocrite lecteur! mon semblable, mon frère!

Bernie Schnitz, who wants to transport the British Museum to a Colo-
rado mountaintop, salvages Adam at last with an oddly practical job
offer. The novel comments on two writers whom an Oriental
postgraduate calls "C. P. Slow" and "Kingsley Anus"—one recalls
Amis's Grim Grin and Ifflin Voff—through its own quick wit and
bizarre mockery of luck; but the phantasmagoria applies realistically
only to the theme of ye-gods-she-isn't-preggers-*again*-is-she?

Lodge's manner with narrative viewpoints is often innovative. In
The Picturegoers the novelist's own camera—in that familiar maneu-
ver of impressionism—is set behind the characters' eyes. "Reality" is
perceived and felt by representative South Londoners. But the viewpoints are not developed in the showily imitative fashion of dialogue.
Instead there is a subtle shift between kinds of vocabularies as view-

points change. "Harry pissed savagely into the wall behind her back" is narratively transparent so that the reader attends to nothing but the fact. What seems to accrue and "stick" to our conception of Harry is the tactility of a verbal phrase which is vulgar without being (in the lexical context) patently vulgar. We feel why Amber Lush isn't enough for Harry—the visual and auditory appeals of the film correlate with some verbalizations in other viewpoints, but not with "pissed savagely." Nor do they correlate with Mark's verbal range, linguistic subtlety, wit, or fondness for the fleshy abstraction exhibited in "His Beloved's Urination" but equally felt in unobtrusive point of view phrases used for him: "saturated consciousness" . . . "awesomely shaped women" . . . "rapture of being" . . . "billions of court flatterers." We understand why Harry must swing in the aisle when he goes lackadaisically to see "Rock Around the Clock," and why Mark at considerable psychological cost prefers the essential indecency behind the candles. *The Picturegoers* is like a well-operated cinecamera in concealing what is most effective in its technique.

Postwar realists in England—for decades—have tried to cinematize the language of fiction so that varied "styles" cling to the thing represented. Kingsley Amis's telegraph key in *I Like It Here* has, I think, traveled most of the way from Joyce to cinematism:

ALL MY LOVE GOE SWITH YOU MY FARLINGS SEND
ALL NEWS AND KEEP PHOTOGRAPHICAL BUM TO
SHOW ON RETURN BON VOYAGE + MOTHER

But that is too perfect to be an accidentally garbled cable (as Amis knows, we know, and Amis's hero knows: "There is a God, Bowen thought"). Amis wrote it. In perfect cinematism the novelist is not linguistically on view at all. McLuhan's "multi-levelled gestures and resonances" of punning and lyricism are relegated to the level of what the characters appear to create. The author must *seem* to be no more important, particularly, than a Hollywood or BBC technician.

A passage from Lodge's novel *Out of the Shelter* will show us, however, what one cinematist owes to Joyce. A London boy grows up in Goering's blitz:

Timothy found a piece of shrapnel one morning on the way to
school. It was lying in the gutter, and when he picked it up it
was still warm. It was heavy in his hand and rough to the touch,
like the pumice-stone in the bath when it was dry. He went to
school with Joan Collins, who was older than he was and was
supposed to look after him because his mother was working at
the Town Hall on Ration Books. She tried to make him throw
the piece of shrapnel away, but he kept it even though she
pinched him. The piece of metal, warm and rough and heavy in
his hand, excited him strangely: a piece of war that had fallen
out of the sky. He began to collect shrapnel. You were supposed
to collect it to give to the Government to make new shells; but
Timothy kept the pieces he found, in a cardboard box under his
bed.

Since in *Shelter* nothing is bravura, I have hesitated to quote that
much—for the artificial bravura that anything takes on when we
quote it. But we can see that the limpidity, the naiveté and the symbolic quality of this owe, in part, to Joycean precedents in A *Portrait
of the Artist*. The difference is, I think, that "style" has disappeared.
The cinematist does not try to emulate the stylist whose finely wrought
prose exhibits, as it were, the artistic triumph of the writer—Joyce, for
instance, rather grandly paring his fingernails, as Baby Stephen De-
dalus's viewpoint unfolds in baby-like diction and syntax on the first
page. In cinematism language must not seem tailored to fit a viewpoint. The attempt is to write so as never to call attention to one's
English.

Every detail in the passage above is implicitly sexual. The warm
piece of shrapnel is an incident in Timothy Young's developing relations with his penis and, therefore, with the world. Language copies
life's symbolism but without excess. He finds his mother when she is
dressed in trousers and in his father's zip jacket ("for the raids") and
then his fat, mild, innocent, large-breasted sister Kate sexually focal
until he goes, after the war, to PX-ridden Germany for initiation into
the rites of Spring. Timothy does advanced masturbation in a
women's dorm. He hears—but cannot see—coitus and the failure of
coitus next door; later he sees—but doesn't touch—the "beard of vivid

ginger" between the terrifyingly spread legs of his available neighbor. This lady quotes Wordsworth's "Daffodils" in her seduction speech. The effect is neither bizarre nor ironic in *Shelter*, which explores— more convincingly than any other postwar novel, with a similar theme, that I know—the complex innocence of sexuality.

Yet *The Picturegoers, The British Museum Is Falling Down*, and *Out of the Shelter* all avoid—perhaps to their detriment—aberrant or neurotic experience. Lodge states that his view of reality is not apoc- alyptic. His Timothys and Adams seem as unpredictable, compli- cated, and (one must admit) appealing as normal young intellectuals tend to be. But, though it is an imperfect novel, his own *Ginger, You're Barmy* gains in having two extreme personalities at its center. Neither Jon, a squeamish pragmatic young man of "prudent fore- sight," nor his friend, an equally bright but violently romantic Irishman, Michael, resolves or explains the fictional theme of cru- cifixion. Jon "writes" about their brutal experience in the Twenty-first Royal Tank Regiment at Catterick and later at Badmore—narrating the first and last episodes of it, throughout, in alternate chapters. Em- phasis falls on the quality of an ordeal in which one conscript, Percy, is hounded to death, and another, Michael himself, is goaded into criminal and self-sacrificial rebellion.

> As the door closed he lifted his hands in a gesture of . . .
> . . . of what? Reassurance? Dismissal? Benediction? Would I
> ever know?

Well, if Christ's motive on the cross was pretty clear, Percy's and Mike's, I think, are not. Still the Christian story, without celebration, very movingly recurs. In *Ginger* the techniques of cinematic realism triumph over thematic vagueness. Lodge responds to "apocalyptic" ex- perience better than he admits, perhaps. In his best novels he "films" from normal interior viewpoints to explain in language finely adapted to character what Hollywood or the television camera can suggest, after all, only from surfaces. An amusing production of Lodge's novel *Nice Work*, first shown in England in September and October 1989, was based on a television script prepared by the author himself. As sensitive as Lodge's script was, the production reduced the effects of his interior "filming" and simplified a novel's comic art. But then, television is always likely to do much worse for a novel by, say, Martin Amis, who is closer to modern American experimental prose in his methods. Lodge's finest novels to date are *The Picturegoers, Changing Places,* and *Small World.*

Chapter Twenty

GINSBERG AND KEROUAC

S LIM, BEARDED, with slightly staring eyes but a pleasant face, Allen Ginsberg stood up in a San Francisco gallery in October 1955 to read "Howl." This was the beginning of the Beat movement in American literature. The poet had been a wayward Columbia University student, but his poem was to be as famous as any since T. S. Eliot's *The Waste Land*.

England has often been more hospitable than America to twentieth-century American poetry (Robert Frost printed his first two volumes in London), and the first edition of "Howl" was printed in England by Villiers, passed through U.S. Customs and published late in 1956 by City Lights Bookstore in San Francisco. However, Customs seized 520 copies of the second printing on March 25, 1957, and on April 3 the American Civil Liberties Union decided to contest the legality of the seizure, since it considered the poem not obscene.

A California court finally agreed "Howl" had cultural value and meanwhile interest in the obscenity trial made Ginsberg and the Beats famous.

A few months later, when Jack Kerouac's novel *On the Road* was published by Viking Press in New York on September 5, interest in the Beats became frenzied, and Jack Kerouac was made to explain to the press or television what "Beat" meant. He remembered Herbert Huncke of Chicago saying "Man, I'm beat"—and "I knew right away what he meant somehow," said Jack; but the word had the connotation of *upbeat*, and also, as Kerouac insisted, of *beatific*. "*Beat* is really saying *beatific*, see?" To one television interviewer who asked what he was looking for, Kerouac replied that he was waiting to see the face of God. With his enthusiasm for Thelonius Monk and Charlie Parker, he also insisted the word had a relation to jazz and bop. "And so Huncke appeared to us and said 'I'm beat' with radiant light shining out of his despairing eyes." It was a word, Kerouac admitted, "perhaps brought from some midwest carnival or junk cafeteria. It was a new language, actually spade [black] jargon but you soon learned it." In 1948 John Clellon Holmes had prodded him to characterize his attitude and Kerouac had spoken then of young hipsters in Times Square walking down the street, watchful, catlike, in the street but not of it, and he felt the hipsters expressed his own and his generation's "beatness—I mean, being right down to it, to ourselves, because we *really* know where we are—and a weariness with all the forms, all the conventions of the world. . . . It's something like that. So I guess you might say we're a *beat* generation." Holmes had picked up the term in writing "This is the Beat Generation" for *The New York Times* in 1952, and so the media had the word "Beat" to conjure with five years later when Ginsberg and Kerouac were being interviewed.

What had influenced Ginsberg and Kerouac?

Both young men at Columbia University had known two of the finest professors alive, Lionel Trilling and Mark Van Doren. A subtle, questing liberal humanist in the tradition of Matthew Arnold (the subject of his first book), Trilling in the 1940s was arguably the most skillful literary critic in America. He was touched and bewildered to have among his students a young Jewish homosexual, Allen Ginsberg, who struck up a personal relationship with him: Ginsberg would show his poems to Trilling, ask for advice, and boast of antics. Lionel and Diana Trilling as Jews were shocked and mystified, for example, when Allen got into trouble with the Dean by writing "Fuck the Jews" on his Hamilton Hall window. Allen claimed his cleaning lady disliked Jews, and he'd hoped the phrase would get his windows cleaned. Columbia's dean was not amused; nor were the Trillings.

Even odder than Allen Ginsberg of New Jersey (where he was born in 1926) was his lover, confederate, and fellow writer Jack Kerouac, a handsome young man born in 1922 in Lowell, Massachusetts, to parents with French-Canadian roots in Quebec. Kerouac came to Columbia before the war on an athletic scholarship, drifted back, and was conceded to be the best student in Professor Mark Van Doren's Shakespeare course. Van Doren gave him an A, listened to him, read his typescripts, and told Harcourt Brace to publish his novel, *The Town and the City*. He was horrified, however, to find Kerouac banned from campus after his arrest as a material witness to a murder. Even so, when an official burst into Ginsberg's room in Hamilton Hall to complain about the window writing, he almost caught Kerouac in bed with Ginsberg.

English teachers should never have a Keats, Christopher Smart, Ginsberg, or Kerouac alive in class, and Diana Trilling's essay "The Other Night at Columbia" reminds us of the problem. Trilling and Van Doren were kindly and tolerant, but the nation's ethos was violent and fractured. In the Depression of the 1930s and during the war Americans had drawn together, but the war years had changed the social structure. In 1939 the United States had only four million taxpayers; in 1945 no less than 45 million were filing taxable returns (in a population of 140 million) as many laboring people had risen into the middle class. Suddenly these people lost their sense of cohesiveness and purpose that even the shortages, dislocations, and sacrifices of war had given. In the late 1940s vicious strikes began. Life became a nervous quest for status and security, whatever the cost, in a lonely crowd. Truman's Fair Deal seemed bumbling and unfair. One heard the pun "To err is Truman." And, after forty-four months of anxieties of war, President Truman had released an untested uranium bomb (not even the implosion-type plutonium bomb tested at Alamogordo) experimentally on Japan and seemed to have little sense of what he had done. *The New York Times* of August 11, 1945, had found Truman's remarks on the bomb weird, incredible, disturbing, as if the President were stunned because "the gruesome fantasies of the 'comic' strips were actually coming true."

Then, in a speech that *The New York Times* printed in full, Stalin, on the eve of Russian elections in February 1946, declared that the cause of the war had been "monopoly capitalism" and that the U.S.S.R. was encircled by enemies. A month later Churchill, in Fulton, Missouri, made his memorable comment that "from Stettin in the Baltic to Trieste in the Adriatic, an iron curtain has descended across the continent" and that Warsaw, Berlin, Prague, Vienna, Budapest, Belgrade, Bucharest, and Sofia were enslaved. "Last time I saw it all coming," said Churchill as he compared the Soviet threat with Hitler, "and cried aloud to my own fellow countrymen and the world, but no one paid any attention." Inside America, as the poet Archibald MacLeish wrote in the *Atlantic Monthly* in 1949, the Russian conquest of the American people had begun. MacLeish meant Americans were now guided by Russians in offering a bitter opposing policy, a mirror image, to nearly anything the Soviet Union did or proposed.

It was in this atmosphere that General Eisenhower, or Ike, became president of Columbia University and then of the nation. An ironical fate had sent him to a place where Ginsberg and Kerouac had been. When told there were exceptional physicists and chemists on his staff, Ike asked if they were also "exceptional Americans." Don't send him a long note, people at Columbia said, or his lips will get tired. "Dear Eisenhower," Kerouac wrote with a friend, "We love you—You're the great big white father. We'd like to fuck you." Ferlinghetti wanted to impeach him (and wrote a poem on the subject), but Ginsberg and Kerouac wrote dream sketches with Eisenhower as the hero—and Kerouac explains that one *must* love Eisenhower if one is a child. However, if Ike's scorn for technocrats and love of America were appealing, his ineffectuality was more important. He took office as president in 1953 during Senator McCarthy's witch hunting of supposed Communists. When McCarthy attacked a teacher at Columbia University, Ike did nothing and indeed kept silent when McCarthy tried to defame Eisenhower's own friend and former companion at arms, General Zwicker. Army officers might have been seriously demoralized, but Ike stated that he would "remain aloof" since he would not compromise the nation's executive power. But what was that power, then, if it let a McCarthy with the instincts of a Hitler do what he wished to people? McCarthy was supported by Len Hall, chairman of the Republican party, and by senators such as Dirksen, Jenner, Knowland, and Bridges. And the great white father, formerly president of Columbia and then of the nation, did nothing and said nothing to check McCarthyism.

Eisenhower became a profound symbol for the Beat writers. A good and capable man, the invader of Europe, he presided over a smugly opportunistic, spiritually weak America which had lost its way and become mechanical and inhuman.

"Howl" was at once a roar of protest against Eisenhower's America and a deeply moving, loving poem, in tears and beyond tears and directed against an ethos that kills or outlaws the spirit. It was meant to be recited. Ginsberg, in his performances, said its lines with gusto, gesticulating, screaming, begging, urging, and at least once after taking off his clothes. His hipsters in their dreams and drugs, who "cut their wrists three times successively unsuccessfully" or who went to asylums—as his friend Carl Solomon did—were images of the soul in reaction to Hiroshima and the Cold War and the materialism of a modern, technological society. If Moloch possesses the "mind" and science turns nearly every creed or illumination into "bullshit," then the beleaguered soul may thrive among the eccentric or crazed—or with Carl Solomon, the Jewish reader of Dostoevsky whom Ginsberg met in the Columbia Psychiatric Institute. Ginsberg was waiting to be assigned a bed when he heard Solomon mention "repentant mystics" and told him, "I'm Myshkin" (a reference to Dostoevsky's holy idiot) to which Solomon replied, "I'm Kirilov" (the nihilist in *The Possessed*).

> Carl Solomon! I'm with you in Rockland
> where you're madder than I am.

Ginsberg and Kerouac saw themselves not as political agitators, but as writers devoted to art, to technique. Kerouac spent months with Stendhal's *The Red and the Black* and Dostoevsky's *The Brothers Karamazov*, studying methods scene by scene. When reading Hart Crane's *The Bridge* he and Ginsberg walked to the Brooklyn Bridge to compare its engineering with Crane's art. They discussed individual lines from Shakespeare, such as "This is the Forest of Arden": where should the emphasis fall, what did it mean in dramatic context? With the wealthy, drug-taking William S. Burroughs they also explored the self. They had "Dostoevskian confrontations" in which they criticized their feeling and its expression. Kerouac, who was bisexual, lived in Manhattan apartments shared by six or fifteen other people, went to bed with two or three others at the same time. Though edgy about "love," a commitment, and sometimes annoyed by Ginsberg's advances, he believed that bodies were to be used freely.

Burroughs had friends among con men and gangsters, who stored guns or stolen goods in Kerouac's flat, but he knew all sides of New York. Kerouac accepted Bill Burroughs as part of a Balzacian education in the city. Drugs and alcohol were to be used not just for kicks but to discover new weird states of consciousness, and indulgence was to be paid for by a steady battering at one's typewriter, whatever one's head felt like. Kerouac typed so fast his machine sounded like static on the radio, a blur of sound resulting in heaps of words that came too quickly for sheets of paper; he began to write on scrolls of teletype paper. His subject was America; he compared himself to Thomas Wolfe of *Look Homeward, Angel* and learned from Wolfe's sensuous gigantism. His subject was importantly America *then*, with its House Un-American Activities Committee witch hunts, regimentation of the average person, censorship of artists and filmmakers, and the Cold War (soon to be a hot war in Korea and Vietnam). "The Cold War is the imposition of a vast mental barrier on everybody," Ginsberg later told the *Paris Review*. "A hardening, a shutting off to the perceptions of desire and tenderness which everybody knows," and this makes for "a self-consciousness which is the substitute for communication with the outside" and a "fear of total feeling, really, total being."

Ginsberg and Kerouac saw the worst obscenity as "God is dead," and forgave friends for all faults but that of not being "serious." They themselves wasted time on alcohol and drugs, and lacked sleep and quiet routines, but two benefits accrued from their behavior. Unlike many contemporary writers, including Lowell, Mailer, and Bellow, the Beats functioned as a group; Ginsberg and Kerouac prolonged their undergraduate days and benefited from mutual encouragement, intelligent talk, and debate. Since they were mild and receptive in manner—at least before fame made Kerouac uncharacteristically boastful some nights, though even then he alienated few of his friends—they added other writers to their informal group besides Burroughs. Out at Berkeley, Ginsberg attached himself to a circle of San Francisco poets. He met Lawrence Ferlinghetti, a Sorbonne-educated seaman and poet who ran City Lights Bookstore and had a good sense of French and American literature. Ginsberg also renewed his friendship with Philip Lamantia, a poet born in San Francisco, though he had moved to New York, where he helped to edit the surrealist magazine *View*. Lamantia brought Caribbean mambo, Afro-Cuban rhythms, and the importance of jazz fully into the reckonings of Beat writers, who imitated jazz in verse rhythms and in moods and patterns of their prose. Ginsberg met the poets Robert Duncan, Chris MacLaine, Gerd Stern, and Leonard Hall, the Tibetan Buddhist scholar, but more important to him was a run-in in New York with a young, cherubic, prankish Italian-American and ex-criminal, Gregory Corso, who had sheaves of poems. Corso at that time was twenty-one. (He had been an inept robber, it seems, too pleased with his plan to chat with his gang by walkie-talkie and had spent three years on a robbery charge in Clinton Prison—a blessing, as it gave him time to write.)

First, then, their easy camaraderie helped the Beats to know their nation. Second, it helped them to rid themselves of untested beliefs of that nation's culture. They tried to get *outside* America while living and observing *in* it, and studied the loving, detached Walt Whitman, Thoreau of Walden Pond, and Henry Miller alive at Big Sur. Nelson Algren, who was to telegraph his praise of *On the Road* to Kerouac, had shown in his own novels and stories an implicit patriotism with a severe criticism of city life and he had gone *outside* Chicago by diving into its drug-pushing lower depths (depicted in his novel *The Man with the Golden Arm*). When I published an essay on Algren in Chicago's *New City* in 1964, the novelist J. T. Farrell was furious: the article, he wrote, "seemed to me good until I thought about it. It is not criticism but a personal expression . . . about Nelson Algren," and

Algren furthermore was only a novelist with a "pretty good talent for blasting" (*New City*, March 1, 1964). But it was blasting in combination with his love for Chicago that made Algren palatable to the Beats, who valued writing that was clearly "personal expression" and who felt that all they wrote had to come from what they had lived through. Their works are autobiographical because the only trusted viewpoint in Beat writing is an "I." No other voice can be honest enough to report the truth. Kerouac's heroes are not simply like Kerouac but, deeply, *are* Kerouac, as Sal Paradise is in *On the Road*. The voice speaking in Ginsberg's poems examines Ginsberg: he adopts no role, shelters behind no substitute, and examines himself directly or indirectly in every poem he writes. So too the language in Beat works includes four-letter words since the authors used these words in talk. They used images that had impressed themselves on their minds, and did not try to seek for artificial pictures.

All is to begin with the self and yet, as in Whitman and Emerson, the self is a point of religious raying-out. For the Beats each person is born to wonder, dream, guess, and hope, to relate to the cosmos through truths of ancestors; and Zen Buddhism, if a rich way, offers only one of the multiple interlacing truths of the spirit. Christian, Jewish, Hindu, Muslim, and Zen ideas confirm one another with interchangeable symbols, so that Ginsberg, the Jew, finds the cross valid. But the cross is a beckoning image. Beyond the cornices of New York buildings, as Ginsberg and Kerouac felt in Times Square when neon advertising signs suffused the night sky with red, there was a holy architecture out in space asking them for a "panoramic awareness"— but *that* implied looking at America itself. Though Beat writing is usually religious and mystical it is freed from any religious or mystical certainty in doctrine. It is Transcendental exactly in the New England sense of Emerson and Thoreau, since illuminations are to come from looking at the here and now, in this case, at the streets and geography of America. Fortunately in the 1950s, as a San Francisco renaissance in jazz and poetry overtook Greenwich Village in New York, Ginsberg and Kerouac had been having America interpreted for them by a young man who was "on the road" and one of the best drivers alive— Neal Cassady.

Young men bummed across America in the late 1940s and 1950s, as my brother and I did. We never met Neal Cassady, though we wish we had, but we met young thugs who talked about America's beauty out in the desert or at Denver near the Rockies. To be on the road as we were in a 1925 Dodge car, or riding in boxcars, was to see and hear about that beauty. Even old jailbirds on railway-repair gangs could wonder aloud over America's landscape, and Neal Cassady had a good feeling for landscape. Raised by a drunken father in Denver, Cassady had been in and out of reform school; starting at age fourteen he had stolen some five hundred cars, and had earned a reputation as Denver's greatest "cocksman." When Kerouac met him in the 1940s Cassady had been reading Schopenhauer, Nietzsche, Dumas, and Proust to impress girls—but he wanted to write. He seemed as handsome as a movie cowboy, a Gene Autry, with a slim build and rugged but well-cut features. He talked to seduce and his comments on writing were good, as when he told Kerouac that one should write as if one were the first person on earth and was "humbly and sincerely" putting down what one felt and saw, with sorrows and desires and "passing thoughts."

He was cool, easy, and generous, until he became restless; he let his wife Carolyn sleep with Kerouac for a time in a ménage-à-trois. And he was sublime behind a wheel. Swerving round a truck at 110 miles per hour and turning his head, smiling and exulting, Cassady as Dean Moriarity becomes in *On the Road* more than an archetypal American: he is a saint of freedom who values experience, movement, and the beauty of loose, easy readiness. He is on a quest back and forth across America, in which questing itself is the goal. Even in real life this man's actions seemed symbolic: as Cassady risked all in the flick of a finger on the steering wheel, so in the instant of quick spontaneous writing the Beat poet throws his life into a phrase. And, since Kerouac and Ginsberg kept drifting back to bohemian intellectual New York, Cassady blew through that "dragged-out end of the Columbia scene like a fresh wind from the West," as Joyce Johnson remembers in *Minor Characters*. American academies were choked by intellect and science. Poetry and novel writing seemed to be in the hands of academically trained writers obsessed by taste, irony, innuendo, attenuated feeling and *New Yorker* niceties of style, so stifled they could not see how lifeless their own work was. (The only intellectual to be trusted, the Beats felt, was one who valued feeling over reason.) Cassady was saved by instinct, boyish grace, impulse—moving and free like a latterday Huck Finn. Kerouac saw himself and Ginsberg and Cassady as a creative triangle, with Cassady perhaps as its apex—its guide, at least, from the West. Rivers, plains, deserts— over three thousand miles of westwardness had made the American experience; the American mind responds to geography; and so Cassady (and *On the Road*) symbolized a terrain and its sources of renewal for the spirit.

Ginsberg recalls him best in "The Green Automobile," and Kerouac, after *On the Road*, portrays him convincingly as Cody Pomeray in *Big Sur*, showing us a mellow hero after Cassady had served some time in prison on a minor drug charge. John Clellon Holmes, a New England novelist four years Kerouac's junior (their birthday, March 12, was the same), in turn depicts Cassady as Hart Kennedy in the Beat novel *Go*, although Holmes found Cassady's outlook less stimulating than Kerouac's "special view of the world." But for all his excess of charm, Cassady lacked self-discipline to survive for long, as man or writer: in 1968 he died of exposure on the railway tracks. A year later Kerouac's self-indulgent love for drink killed him at forty-seven.

If Neal Cassady was the hero of the Beats, was there any place for a heroine? In attacking the Beat Generation in the late 1950s, *Time*, *Life*, and other American journals chiefly had males in mind. As Fred McDarrah in *Saga* (August 1960) noticed, for *Time* magazine Jack Kerouac was a depraved spokesman for young men, or the "latrine house laureate of Hobohemia." Can women be hoboes even if bohemians? In a Negro magazine, America's typical "beatnik" (an unpatriotic word taking its suffix from the Russian Sputnik) is a "pseudo-intellectual" who smokes reefers and lives "in protest of something or other." Had groups of women, since the suffragettes, often been known to "protest"? *Life* doubted that "pad-sharing" females could be many, but still some women, even nice, educated ones, were dropping out, going to live in Greenwich Village. The magazine looked into this phenomenon, and, to McDarrah's surprise, it ran a photo essay showing a "beat chick dressed in black" in her pad. Nearby were "naked light bulbs, a hot plate for warming [the] expresso coffee pot and bean cans, a coal stove for heating baby's milk" and "drying [the] chick's leotards." To complete this forlornly truthful view, *Life* showed a "beat baby who has gone to sleep on the floor after playing with beer cans."

This particular photo essay may have been faked, but women un- questionably were sharing their lives with bohemians. Artists and would-be's from San Francisco, attracted to New York because the scene was livelier and survival easier, had invaded Greenwich Village. They included poets, painters, photographers, dancers, and jazz musi- cians, living in the East Village near warehouses and factory lofts and Fourth Avenue bookshops. In her vivid memoir *Minor Characters*, Joyce Johnson—who was then Kerouac's young lover—recalls the women. Their men took no jobs but felt it was all right for a wife or girlfriend to work for wages since women had no creative endeavors to be distracted from; and, says Joyce, "women didn't mind, or, if they did, they never said—not until years later."

Kerouac and Ginsberg had powerful, claiming mothers, despite the fact that Ginsberg's mother spent many years in an asylum; Kerouac's beloved "Mémère" took precedence over each of the three women he married. Beat women could be muses, angels, whores, or typists of the Great Male Work, but the only way they rose to fame was usually by spectacular death, as when Burroughs accidentally shot his wife, Joan, in Mexico City. Ginsberg in 1954 recorded a "dream letter" from Clellon Holmes with the words, "The social organization which is most true of itself to the artist is the boy gang," to which Ginsberg added in his journal, "not society's perfum'd marriage." For a woman, a relationship with a Beat writer was likely to be disastrous.

Joyce, in her black sweater, black skirt, and black stockings and hair hanging down over her shoulders, waited in her apartment for Jack Kerouac. After making love, he liked to sleep alone. He was "brotherly," and she listened when Jack and his friends talked. Always the voices of men, only the men, would fall and rise as beer glasses collected, she recalls. Cassady's wife, Carolyn, who slept with her two men, similarly had been very grateful when a man asked her opinion. Mostly, "Beat" women were as useful as robots might be, as visible as nondescript furniture, obedient as collies. One night Jack took Joyce to a Bleecker Street poetry recital; in a coffee shop a neat, trim- bearded black man was reading an "academic" poem, with a few hip touches. Later he introduced himself: he was LeRoi Jones. Proud of Hetty Cohen, his girlfriend, he did the nicest possible thing and instead of talking about metaphors LeRoi graciously said, "This woman over here is Hetty. . . ." That was enough; Hetty and Joyce were noticed, and in public could expect little more.

Their impasse was that a woman's notion of her selfhood was fixed by what men thought, and Kerouac had not examined that sort of oppression. Yet the Beats encouraged a change in at least two ways. They greatly valued feeling and spontaneity or a full, easy voicing of the self, and opposed all notions of social rank and race and ideas of hierarchy, including the idea that God is somehow privileged or above us. If presidents and generals were to be seen as ridiculous and Eisenhower was only to be "fucked" (literally and perhaps joyfully), the *next* idol to topple might be the American male. Beat writing did speak for equality and honesty, and Jack did not mislead Joyce, though he hardly treated her well; he stumblingly tried to be her "friend" or "brother"; he did not try to shut her up. She behaved in his company as a nice Jewish girl from upper Manhattan might be expected to do in marriage, but was wiser when she left him.

Disliking marriage (though sometimes remarrying), Beat writers saw friendship as preferable—a way of relating without claims. They condemned all static relationships and felt that in a muddying, blinding world playing with war and nuclear bombs, social connections were suspect. The self, the soul of each person must be heard; the body tells us about ourselves; masturbation is truthful and pure, not obliging. One's sexual partner ought to be chosen casually. In denying notions of obligation, the Beat writer implies that women have as much to gain from a new truth to self as men do. The Beat discovers that we are truly tender and gentle, not beings of violence, which is caused by a social order (under capitalism or communism) which represses wonder and love and viciously exalts technology and material values. In emphasizing the holy nature of the body, the Beat is not especially "male" and would liberate us all; and a poet such as Sally Stern found it natural to write in a mode similar to that of other Beats. But although the Beat message was potentially liberating, in reality, the female hipster was not liberated. Most of her views were not greatly different from those of a Bronxville High School girl—and the subur-

ban debutante became a "beat chick" often enough to face rather gen-
teel poverty in the Village. Still, many years later, and after the
insights of feminism, one feels that some Beat attitudes about the self
anticipated the future.

The Beats were certainly to affect the literature of subsequent decades just as they had themselves drawn inspiration from earlier writers, especially from mainstreams in British and American poetry.
Whitman above all is a beloved spirit for the Beats, as Ginsberg's
"Supermarket in California" shows in content and form. Whitman's
free-verse line, his generous egotism, moral sensuality, interest in colors, textures, surfaces, and sounds of New York all echo poignantly in
the California poem. Emily Dickinson's spontaneity and delicacy set a
mark for Corso. The deceptively casual "Autobiography" by Ferlinghetti—a poem for jazz accompaniment—is a fine, deft sketch of a
man who is defined with the help of Twain, Melville, and Thoreau,
as well of course as Pound, Yeats, Eliot, and others. Moreover,
Ginsberg for one is attentive to the rhythms of English prophetic
verse, so that, for example, the cadences of Christopher Smart's
Jubilate Agno

> Let Noah and his company approach the throne of Grace,
> and do homage to the Ark of their Salvation . . .

may be heard faintly in "Howl":

> angelheaded hipsters burning for the ancient heavenly
> connection to the starry dynamo in the
> machinery of night.

Ginsberg, indeed, says that he was influenced by Smart, Blake, and
others, but that he wrote "Howl" mainly to satisfy Kerouac's sense of
sound.

Kerouac's sound is determined by bop. In jazz a player improvises
from the musical metrics of the instant; a syncopated melodic beat
carries the musical improvisations up from level to level—as in Louis
Armstrong's jazz. But bop, exemplified by Charlie Parker, frees jazz
from the monotony of boring melodies, and moves up from level to
level on sheer improvisations alone. Bop avoids meaning and fosters
movement, free creation, and spontaneity. "I'm the Bop writer," says

Kerouac's hero in *The Subterraneans*, and for Ray Smith-as-Kerouac in *The Dharma Bums* Charlie Parker is king and "founder of the Bop generation." As bop frees itself from theme and exists in improvisation, so *On the Road* departs from conventional "theme" and exists as movement, a movement between six cities or a mad tour with Sal Paradise saying "Yes, he's mad" or "Yes, he's my brother" as he clings to Dean Moriarty (Cassady) in a swing from New York to New Orleans, Mexico City, Denver, San Francisco, and back to Chicago and New York.

Ginsberg and other Beats also admired the spontaneity of bop improvising. Ginsberg battered out the first part of "Howl" in a mad rush to give it the flow "Kerouac would like the sound of"; he took peyote to write the "Moloch" passage. He drugged himself on amphetamines, morphine, and Dexadrine to write "Kaddish"—a failure—and left off drugs in despair, to return to them later. But Beat writers were not always high when they wrote, nor did they often compose whole works at one sitting. Good phrases such as "hydrogen jukebox" do not usually come easily. Most of the good Beat poems seem to have been composed on the principle of John Keats and Wilfred Owen: the draft is written quickly, perhaps with the help of notes, and then very carefully revised. But the bop inspiration is usually there.

Ginsberg's best poems have a strong, compelling social urgency, as though the fate of American society (perhaps of the globe) depended on whether one American, at last, could tell the truth about himself. An effect of improvised phrasing combines with delicacy in cadence in Ginsberg's "Under the World," a poem as religious as Donne's Divine Sonnets or Hopkins's so-called Terrible Sonnets. Religious, too, is "The Lion for Real," Ginsberg's tribute to his teacher Lionel Trilling. "Death to Van Gogh's Ear!" is an important poem in that it elucidates Ginsberg's views of the political and economic present and the cultural past, even if its technique is not as fine as that in "Supermarket," "Under the World," "Mescaline," "The Green Automobile," or his relatively early "Paterson."

Gregory Corso's tonal range is greater, although his discoveries in sound are less important than Ginsberg's. He is almost conventionally lyrical in "Horses" and "Marriage"—good poems to read aloud to those new to the Beats—and even in these there is a "bop" quality of seemingly free improvisation. "The Thin Thin Line"—typically Beat in exploring a personal experience (the simple, humdrum, and yet bafflingly strange act of falling asleep)—and in contrast the wittily grand "Ode to Old England & its Language" together suggest Corso's suppleness and variety as a poet. "Columbia U Poesy Reading—1975" amusingly shows what time has given the Beats: fame, respect, less hair (at least in Ginsberg's case), self-doubt, perhaps more humility in thinking of forebears such as "Emily D," Shelley, Southey, Chatterton, Coleridge, and De Quincey, and a wry (but not very serious) sense of failure with renewed self-love and pluck. Success hurts Beats—and its results are best explored in Kerouac's deeply honest *Big Sur*. (Ginsberg is badly served by his own *Collected Poems*, since he has written too many works in which sentiment and self-indulgence replace passion; only a small number of his poems are excellent.) Gary Snyder is the best poet of the lesser Beats, fresh and deft in exploring moods of his recollecting of recent experience, and Philip Lamantia is an authentic Beat in regarding the lyric as a means of spiritual quest.

Subsequent writers were influenced by these precedents. Through their jazz friends and poets such as LeRoi Jones, the Beats in the 1950s were in the vanguard of anti-racist feeling, which helped to spark off Civil Rights movements a decade later. They quickly influenced songwriting, and journalism. Protest songs carry the Beat note often. The New Journalism of Tom Wolfe in *The Electric Kool-Aid Acid Test* or Hunter Thompson in *Fear and Loathing in Las Vegas* has a "Beat" spontaneity in effect. Robert M. Pirsig's *Zen and the Art of Motorcycle Maintenance* owes much to Kerouac's locating of meaning in movement. Journalism and semi-autobiographical works may respond much more quickly to influences than do the conservative genres of biography and history. But the Beat influence has helped us to question our reportage on, and accounting for, the human past. We no longer think it absolutely truthful to account for past lives or events in a wholly retrospective way, as though, in the past, the future were already known, fixed and settled, or as though unpredictability, emotional experience, and the "feeling" of anyone's living through a day ought not to concern any historian. It seems significant that journalism, which records history of the present, on occasion took a new form in reporting the Vietnam War: piece after piece on Vietnam brought home to Americans the moods and immediate sensations of patrols in combat, and often in a prose deeply indebted to Kerouac. The Beats have brought literature closer to the texture of life, and their influence has not ended.

Kerouac's unusual sensibility has become clearer to us over the years. We perceive, for example, how each of his heroes determines the syntax and tone of each novel. We feel the difference between the nervous lucidity of *On the Road*, the long meandering "bop"-style sentences in *The Subterraneans* that are attuned to its hero, Leo, the notes of wonder and quest in the manner of *Dharma Bums* with its splendid landscapes and dialogues, and the elegiac, graphic, troubled, and yet often lyric manner of *Big Sur*. At their best Kerouac and Ginsberg are as artful as any other writers of the 1950s and 1960s and so we may feel that just as the Beat movement has affected our ways of reporting on experience it has refreshed art itself, while producing more than one exciting American classic.

Chapter Twenty-One

KERMODE ON
SAINT MARK

FRANK KERMODE is one of our most astute and flexible critics. He came to maturity with his book *The Sense of an Ending* (1966) and discovered there his natural topic—which is the nature of literary fictions. Rather like Matthew Arnold and Lionel Trilling he has learned much from continental thought; he is an agile comparatist, a wide reader alert to French and German critical developments and lacking in matey insularity (the bane of many critics in England and America). He has found much to inspire him in William Carlos Williams, and especially in Wallace Stevens (about whom he has written a book); he takes notably from Stevens the idea that—if there is no Supreme Fiction—fictions are consolations in an age of unbelief. There is a "jovial hullaballoo" aspect of Stevens that is missing in the decent, witty angst of Kermode's critical personality; and this angst, this yearning for certainties together with what Kermode himself calls a clerkly scepticism about all beliefs and schemes, lies at the heart of his two best books, *The Sense of an Ending*, and his study of the gospel of Saint Mark, *The Genesis of Secrecy: On the Interpretation of Narrative* (1979).

Kermode ranges far outside a biblical text in the latter book, but Saint Mark is the focus of discussion and *raison d'être*; and with interest in his remarks on nonfiction narratives and his use of structuralist ideas, I want to comment on what he says in *Genesis of Secrecy*, particularly on what he implies about biographical interpretation.

We assume "the interpretive inadequacy of our predecessors," Kermode claims, and so long as any narrative creates hermeneutic pressure and begs to be interpreted, it remains alive. All narratives must be obscure, since none is transparent on reality. It follows from this that narrative obscurity involves two branches of interpretation. First, there are problems of genesis and genre: when, how, and by whom was the narrative composed and for what purpose or as what kind of work? Second, semantics: what was the meaning of the work originally, or what has it come to mean, or (most difficult of all) what is its meaning?

The genesis of the Gospels is wrapped in an obscurity complicated by the fact that they were composed with the help of midrash or midrashim—to an extent hard to determine. Midrash, in Saint Mark's time, was a Jewish censorship that pruned a text, or fleshed it out with material from Scripture to make it look and sound right, or to make it conform with what was felt to be truth. The earliest gospel to survive is Mark's. Using a missing ur-gospel plus midrash, he may have invented the character of Judas, for example, out of the idea of betrayal. Matthew and Luke, as they wrote, used Mark's text plus midrash. John, the last writer, used a text similar to but not identical with Mark's; and by the time John wrote (as Kermode believes) the fictional Judas already had generated new narrative, so that John's gospel adds fictional material to the original chronicles about Jesus.

Now it is clear that Kermode uses midrash too freely as a license, since there is no historical evidence Judas is fictive. No ur-gospel exists to show what Mark censored or invented; and, since Mark's narrative had to seem true to early Christians and came into being less than a lifetime after Jesus died, he may have invented little. M. D.

Goulder tells me that the meaning of "Iscariot" has not been traced; it has no proved root in any Aramaic word for "betrayal," and even if it did, the Aramaic meaning would have been lost on Mark's readers. But, by bringing midrash into secular criticism, Kermode illuminates the psychology of interpretation. Interpreters in one sense are censors hungering for inner logic in stories; hermeneutic anxiety causes us to melt, combine, or adjust details in a narrative, even to misread, suppress, reject, or cease to inquire, just to make things "truer" or to see coherencies.

Consider two details in Arnold's life—for a moment. We need a coherent story of it, and so Trilling in *Matthew Arnold* (1939) makes Arnold die one day too early while leaping a low fence in joy over his daughter's arrival on "the 14th of April." (There is something nearly midrashic in Trilling's research, which led him to "almost no unpublished material," but we need not dwell on errors resulting from that practice.) Two hours' work in a newspaper library would have shown him that Arnold, having leapt the fence, did not die, but took a walk, dined, slept, rose, breakfasted, went to church near Liverpool, lunched, and died just before 3:00 P.M. on April 15, 1888. But the death-in-joy idea looked and sounded right; and later scholars, once the "midrash" notion of Arnold's death in the joyful leap of April 14 got into the "story," repeated and fleshed out the notion. Again, it looks right to imagine young Arnold in a sexual romp with a French chambermaid named Marguerite in a hotel bed at Thun. Generations of critics give life to Marguerite. Arnold seems to meet her in the Alps in scholarly notes to the Longmans edition of his poems; and Iris Sells, in an evangelical manner, makes fictive history more vivid by telling us of the lovers' strolls against an alpine backdrop.

Literary competence is no check on midrashic developments in interpretation. A sophisticated interpreter may try to make historical facts, details in a novel, or almost any sequence of data in a narrative coalesce into manageable wholes when there is no such whole. Trilling was guilty of this; and so is Kermode, who invents a fictive Judas to get the genesis of the synoptics to look and sound right. The interpreter has an in-built misreader; the clever misreader, sensing that narratives fail to be transparent on reality, finds relief from hermeneutic anxiety the more he or she can get out of the semiotic codes in the work into an extraneous fictive construct giving an illusion of coherence. Once you imagine that Horatio is a woman (as someone has done in the *Yale Review*), *Hamlet* gains a new logic with troublesome details marshaled and in order. Once you believe that *King Lear* was meant to satirize primogeniture, Lear's madness and his daughters' behavior enter a new scheme of coherence. We may be prey to reductive interpretation and illusions of coherence until we get what A. J. Greimas in *Semantique structurale* meant to offer, and what Jonathan Culler calls, "a scientifically rigorous way of characterising the meaning of a text."

Assuming that Mark's Gospel is not wholly fictive and has some basis in ur-chronicle, how do we interpret it? Kermode's strategy—more complex than my resumé will suggest—has two aspects. He calls Mark's narrative not chronicle, but "history with a literary structure" that has been subject at the composing stage to literary pressures—not wholly unlike some of those Henry James faced. Influenced by Greimas and especially by Vladimir Propp's *Morphology of the Folktale*, Kermode posits that Mark's narrative may be treated as an action, and that the persons in it may be considered actants "with no being except in relation to a plot." This enables him to comment on Mark's architectonic problems, and rather acidly, if justly, on "the remarkable naiveté of professional exegesis when confronted with problems of narrative." But Kermode, though suggestive, neglects something in narrative which modern Biblical exegetes, some of them aware of structuralist methods, have been alert to: namely the strong sense of a portrait (Jesus's) as it accrues from a reading of the text. Here, "character" is an element of "followability." Mark's pre-Passion chapters are as occult, disjointed, and achronological as Kermode suggests (there is, by the way, no reason for us to assume that Mark cared much for being chronological), but the sense accruing of a "person" helps to make them intelligible. More than this, disjunctions may be a necessary element in this kind of portrayal.

Mark's narrative is person-centered to a degree that few modern accounts of lives ever are; nothing counts as significant in any other way than as a reflector of the principal figure, Jesus, whose "story" is strangely told. The pre-Passion chapters show what Erich Auerbach calls "horizontal disconnection" in the extreme. But the "greater the separateness and horizontal disconnection," Auerbach says of Old Testament stories, the stronger is a "general vertical connection. God chose and formed these men. . . ." (*Mimesis: The Representation of Reality in Western Literature*, 1957, 14). Discontinuities in the oracular style suggest control beyond the teller's, and they are appropriate and functional in sacred texts used as lectionaries—that is, when the "story" is relatively unimportant. The lectionary is a list of portions of scripture appointed to be read aloud and meditated upon. In the New Testament narratives, as well as in those of the Old, deity is seen to control narrative, slicing away comforting suggestions of sequence, place, temperament, gesture, or other trivia to suggest the moral profundity of what is unfolding—and, in Mark, Jesus's character is the agent of that profundity. He must impress us (and has impressed readers for two millennia) even in short passages. Mark's narrative even in early Christian times was certainly used as a lectionary.

But who is the Jesus of Mark? No other gospel is starker, darker, less moralistic or more suggestive of a lonely, secretive exorcist, misunderstood, and feared by friends and family but understood by demons. This Jesus does not become more intelligible when viewed as an actant, "with no being" apart from what he gets from the plot. Kermode does suggest that we might come to fresh interpretations of what Mark's narrative can mean (if never quite to what it meant in Mark's time), on the basis of a systematic, extremely complex linguistic analysis, in which all of the text would have to be seen as a mass of constituents for its key portraits—that of Jesus and of Mark, the narrator.

But would even this illuminate what one exegete calls "the greatest of all literary mysteries"—or Mark's narrative ending? Kermode discusses the problem but offers no solution. The mystery, at the simplest level, involves grammar, semantics, style, structure, and Mark's persona. We can be confident that the last verse of Mark's is 16: 8. Verses 16: 9–20 were added by a later author, who may have been as baffled by Mark's ending as we are. If none of Mark's gospel is lost, and if it is unlikely that he died or was imprisoned suddenly after writing 16:8,

then he meant to end his book with a weak Greek enclitic in the
phrase *ephobounto gar*, "for they were afraid"—a practice with few
parallels in Greek sentences and none in contemporary Greek books.
Grammatically, this is nearly as unusual, Kermode suggests, as the
endings of *Ulysses* and *Finnegans Wake* in "Yes" or "the." Mark's
ending is powerful, but in a modern way, and it is hard to imagine
him as a very advanced litterateur. The meaning of the ending may
reflect Mark's fondness for verbs meaning "astonish," "amaze," "ter-
rify," and the like, or disconcerting features in a book offering "good
news." Three women enter Jesus's tomb to annoint his corpse, and
Mark signs off with this account (16: 5–8, Revised Standard Version):

> And entering the tomb, they saw a young man sitting on the
> right side, dressed in a white robe; and they were amazed. And
> he said to them, "Do not be amazed; you seek Jesus of
> Nazareth, who was crucified. He has risen; he is not here; see
> the place where they laid him. But go, tell his disciples and
> Peter that he is going before you to Galilee; there you will see
> him, as he told you." And they went out and fled from the
> tomb; for trembling and astonishment had come upon them;
> and they said nothing to anyone, for they were afraid.

If the women's astonishment is holy awe and the Resurrection is
promised, we do not see Jesus risen; and the final note—which is
more than odd—is that of confusion, nervous trembling, and terror.
No amount of semantic analysis of signs in relation to a plot, I think,
will tell us whether Mark meant to end this way; or if he did, why at
least three Greek words in his last sentence signify fear and confusion.
But an analysis of the narrator's persona—based on principles we have
yet to develop—may tell us, some day, what fear, confusion, mystery,
loneliness, misunderstanding, and what one critic calls *esseulement*
mean to Mark; and why he, so much more than other evangelists,
emphasizes these things in the story. Psycholinguistics may be one of
many tools to be used in reconstructing, in a reliable system, Mark's
persona. Any hermeneutic scheme which short-circuits or reduces
"character" in narrative will tell us little about Mark's text.

Why, in interpretation, must we withdraw from our data and schemes? Kermode says that the only way to gain access to some secrets in oracular narrative is by "sensory failure." This seems to me a very suggestive insight. It isn't by any means out of weariness or in complaint that a biographer may notice two separate phases in his or her interpretive act. One phase has to do with the system or systems enabling one to amass facts and reports about a person; interpretation adjust itself to incoming facts, little by little, and gathers from the mass (thanks to whatever help one's systems, outlines, or other organizing means may give). But another interpretive phase begins, it often seems, in discouragement or desperation, when one begins to remember how to forget—or when one has gone through the same data so often that some of it, somehow, submerges. Some comes into light. One becomes aware that the cadence of a phrase is an interpretative element; one is trying, then, to render into narrative a sense, held or lurking in one's mind but not yet in "words," of some truth formed from dozens or hundreds of pieces of evidence. One's style becomes interpretative—and in one's revisions one hopes for that intensity, economy, or suggestiveness that will realize, in a way, a fraction of an intuition. What does one conclude from such an experience, which one repeats again and again? First, it is complex. The final, intuitive stage in interpretation involves a right remembering and a right forgetting; one would like to get to it quickly—but one finds no shortcuts. Similarly, the interpretation of one narrative seems to prepare one in no necessary way for another narrative. Second: it may be a peculiarity of our ethos, with its elaborate methodological systems, that we cannot do without the systems. Intuitive interpretations of persons or texts need to have the backing of a great deal of data to have value; in human relationships we take in that "great deal of data" and computerize swiftly and efficiently. In assessing the historical text (fictive or factual), we have the midrashic misreader within to mislead us. We need all of the information about the text that we can get, and rigorous systems to organize the information. We must be organizers before we can be diviners, or dull plodders with exacting paths to follow before we can begin to forget, or as Kermode says, before we can benefit from "sensory failure."

Few critics have begun to discuss the state of mind for adequate interpretation of narrative. Mark's text purports to contain words of God; but its secrets are no more accessible, today, to believers than to secular critics. Western society removes most of us equally from the evangelists' real ethos and world. This is one reason why scientific techniques in a scientific age help the exegete: they can be used to help re-create the fullest, particular sense of the past. Kermode publishes no charts, no results of elaborate analysis—but his first strength lies in his openness to, and familiarity with, the ideas and insights of expert interpreters with specialized information. This secular critic relies on clerical help; and, in general, the good interpreter (even of Mark) surely gains less from meditation, pious living, retreat, or isolation, than from reading as widely as possible out from the center of his or her interest and gathering in every relevant insight and piece of data. This—and the processes of organizing the data—will begin to prepare the historical critic or biographer for the interpretive act. The intuitive stage of interpretation, with its right remembering and forgetting, may follow. At that stage compassion and other spiritual qualities have what effect they may in tempering and refining the interpreter's sensibility.

However, there is to be found in biblical studies since the beginnings of the Higher Criticism (with J. G. Eichhorn in eighteenth-century Germany) a paradoxical lesson for relatively well-informed interpreters. Two hundred years ago, the *Aufklärung* in Germany guided biblical study in new directions. Through the last century the textual study of New Testament narratives, aided by linguistic and historical work of Max Müller, Baur, Ewald, Renan and others, did reduce theological naiveté and seemed to promise much. But none of this work, one must say, has helped Kermode (or anyone else) to understand the characters of either Mark or Christ with convincing certainty. Modern insights into persons in the New Testament are no better than those of St. Francis de Sales, or those of the German mystic Johann Tauler, and seem inhibited by our familiarity with the texts we would interpret. Hence intuition into persons may be dependent on those who help us to see by defamiliarizing textual evidence. Victor Shklovsky, the Russian formalist, has pointed to the functions of *ostranenija*, defamiliarization, restoring strangeness as in this case to what *was* once sensed as awesome or new and puzzling. Kermode's touching puzzlement itself is thus suggestive. In settling nothing, but in directing us to historical mysteries, he refreshes the textual evidence and clears a way for new interpretations of the brief, dazzlingly complex narratives of Christ and possibly for a better understanding of the person of Saint Mark.

PART FOUR

TAILPIECE

Chapter Twenty-Two

SHAKESPEARE'S LIFE

INVITED TO discuss problems that confront a Shakespeare biographer at Birmingham University's Shakespeare Institute in England on December 3, 1987, I felt that a dialogue on the topic might be useful and amusing. My speakers Eric and Betty are imaginary, but I wanted them to think freshly about research, interpretation, form, and traditions in Shakespeare biography. I have learned to respect Eric's scholarly common sense and belief in the value of facts, but Betty's outlook is odd. My speakers teach at Oxford. I was in a tree recording bird songs when Eric and Betty sat down nearby with a picnic hamper. (I transcribe what I recorded on tape when I was hidden, that late summer day at Oxford, by green foliage.)

ERIC: That Mouton-Rothschild is fantastic, a lot better than your filthy Bourgueil. . . . Darling, at the end of that *Troilus* lecture I'm working up for next term I'm going to ask the students to read Sam

Schoenbaum's *Documentary Life* of Shakespeare, oh, and his funny and glorious book *Shakespeare's Lives*, the one about the failures of all the biographers.

BETTY: Poor boy, to no avail.

ERIC: What do you mean, "to no avail"?

BETTY: Why don't you ask your students if they care about Shakespeare's life to read Nicholas Rowe, or Malone, or E. K. Chambers, Edgar Fripp, M. M. Reese, or Muriel Bradbrook along with Schoenbaum?

ERIC: Well, I might do that.

BETTY: To no avail, to no avail. Have *any* of you at Balliol, at any time, given five minutes' thought to the problem of biographical form *and its limits*? Have you thought about biographical research? What do you suppose biographers should be looking for? What *is* important, Eric, in your life and mine?

ERIC: I love you when you talk that way.

BETTY: Shut up and listen—and *stop that* because someone may be watching us. None of the Shakespeare lives tells us all that can be known about him.

ERIC: But so few facts *are* known about Shakespeare.

BETTY: Name three.

ERIC: He was born at Stratford, had plays produced in London, and his wife gave birth to a girl and then twins—a boy and a girl.

BETTY: Don't you see, Eric? Those facts are valuable. I am glad to know he was born at Stratford so we won't have more theories about the sea's influence on his formative life as we might if he had been born at Portsmouth! But those facts, out of which the biographies are made, are not very *telling*. Your friend John Dykes was born at Stratford, my friend Veronica has had plays produced in London, and our poor old friend Honan—

(Here I rattled the branches of the tree I was sitting in.)

—has a wife who gave birth to a girl, then to twins, a boy and a girl, just as Mary Shakespeare did and a few million other mothers have done too. And so, Eric, none of those facts is very distinguishing. But Shakespeare revealed himself in his plays, sonnets and long poems, so that we know more about him than about almost any other literary figure of the British past.

ERIC: But how can you *extract* him from his works? Caroline Spurgeon tried, you know, in her book *Shakespeare's Imagery* of 1935 and told us that he was disgusted by spaniels and greyhounds at dinner table because he hated dogs who licked the sweets! Not much to know, even if we accept it as gospel truth.

BETTY: Agreed. But you seem to be locked into the false mindset of your time, Eric, and you forget history.

ERIC: Oh, Shakespeare was much influenced by history.

BETTY: He was not influenced at *all*: *that's* one of the troubles with biographers: they assume that individuals are influenced by history whereas history is ourselves. How can you be influenced by something you *are*? From some remote, impartial view in the universe the atomic bomb at Hiroshima—and that leaf that just fell from the trembling branch up there—are one and the same: two events of change. Change goes on and on in our universe. But I am history—yes, I, Betty. *I* discriminate, and history is only discrimination. I say that Hiroshima exists in my mind as important, and is *not* just one more change, Eric. I am made up of Hiroshima. The falling leaf is important, but I don't take it in especially, and it isn't part of me. If you and I consist of history—I mean *are* history, and are not just being influenced by this or that—then this has implications for biography. Shakespeare was different because the history that was part of his being was different from yours or mine.

ERIC: Shakespeare *is* history you say?

BETTY: Yes: your view of the Reformation and Renaissance cannot be Shakespeare's. He was made up of the Renaissance and the Reformation; you just look back on them. He was a part of those things himself.

ERIC: All right, but how does this affect biography? What is a biography?

BETTY: A biography is a work that gives the fullest evidenced truth about a person.

ERIC: So it might describe the auricles and ventricles of Shakespeare's heart?

BETTY: If there were evidence.

ERIC: Oh, Betty, really. Surely we can take *some* things for granted?

Shakespeare was born with two eyes and one nose in a house at Stratford, where sometimes it rained.

BETTY: How often did it rain?

ERIC: How many children had Lady Macbeth? How often did it rain? This is a rainy isle—haven't you noticed?

BETTY: But Stratford gets only twenty-four to thirty-five inches a year since it's protected by the rain-shadow of the Welsh Hills, whereas it rains up to a hundred inches a year in the British Isles, and up to forty elsewhere in the West Midlands. I haven't seen that discussed in a biography.

ERIC: Be thankful you haven't.

BETTY: Well, it may not be important that Stratford's days are mild and dry, I mean by comparison. But can't you see? A biography involves the earth, soil, climate, roads, and then the farming and commerce of a region.

ERIC: Mmmm—all that's background.

BETTY: No, Eric, it's part of a human being's identity. A biography should never have a sentence in it about background but should be about one living person.

ERIC: Why do you say "living"? Isn't Shakespeare dead?

BETTY: Yes, he is, but if you write about his life, he is living in your exposition, with the unknown future ahead of him. All of the biographies, through their bad form, make it look as though he always knew he'd be a great success, and that the Elizabethans were totally confident, knowing they were existing at a grand time, secure with their Queen, serene about the future, proud of their religious martyrs under Mary Tudor's reign, and earning enough to be jolly. We ought to have a realistic sense of history's unfolding present, and I haven't read a life of Shakespeare that gives it. Have you?

ERIC: But then the history of Shakespeare's own family is a blank. What do we know about his mother, Mary Arden?

BETTY: Male biographers tell us little enough about her. Is that what you mean? Is it illegal to think about her? She had a child as late as 1580, so she couldn't have been born before 1539 or 1540. She was seventeen or eighteen then when she married the Stratford glover John Shakespeare. And this is interesting: her father, Robert Arden of Wilmcote, had made Mary one of his two legal executors, despite her youth. Since Robert's will was Catholic in phrase and form, Mary can hardly have been an extreme Protestant. It's very *unlikely* that she would have had her father's trust if her religion had been different from his.

ERIC: So Shakespeare's mother was young, and probably a believer in the old faith. What does that tell us about *him?*

BETTY: Nothing. I'm interested in *her.* In 1564 Mary had lost her second and perhaps her first child. The second, Margaret, you know, was buried in April 1563. The first child, Joan, can't have been alive in 1569 when the parents christened another child Joan, and the only months when she was likely to have escaped being entered in Stratford's burials register were in 1559 and 1560. See for yourself, Eric. The register has great gaps in it and was very badly kept in those months—in between the tenures of the Catholic vicar Dyos and the Protestant one, Bretchgirdle. Eric, do I sound pedantic?

ERIC: Yes. You're telling me that Mary Shakespeare, a young mother, had lost two children by the time William was born in April 1564.

BETTY: That's what the evidence would suggest, Eric. The plague that April was north of London and known to be moving north, and in July when the vicar recorded the words *hic incepit pestis* it struck Stratford with terrible effect. The fear of *any* young mother then would have been evident (infants were the most likely to die) and the fear of a mother already knowing infant death, alarmed for her first-born boy, very considerable. We need no psychological theory to believe that mothers care for infants. You see, the facts suggest the *likelihood* of Mary's special or unusual concern.

ERIC: Mary Shakespeare, then, had a deep and special concern for her infant William? Ho hum.

BETTY: And can't we look ahead? Shakespeare the man lacks a nervous egotism. He has a long and relatively peaceful career in the theater, without Ben Jonson's kind of embroilments, or Marlowe's. It's as though he had no ego to assert, or that he was fairly content within himself. To judge from his work he has a calm fine control of emotive materials with great power. His sonnets, after all, are distinguished for their emotional structures. If then, in early life, he was not emotionally deprived, but just the reverse, isn't it likely that a pattern of special care for this child survived the plague? We can't say how that care was affected by the birth of two sisters and three brothers who followed William; but we do know that *he* flourished.

ERIC: All right. We needn't neglect his mother. And we know his father John Shakespeare was a rogue with all those illegal wool dealings! Now that is something I find truly interesting.

BETTY: Yes, the Public Record Office isn't to blame for telling us that John Shakespeare broke the law. He was accused of illegal wool dealing under an Act of 1552. But biographers of his son, William, haven't noted that towns such as Norfolk and Halifax were declared exempt from the Act, or even that respectable citizens often ignored the laws affecting *economic* life. John is brash or heedless only if we separate him from the whole context of his life, just as the Shakespeare biographers usually do. Professor Schoenbaum gives us documents with almost no context, little of the Reformation or Renaissance, or of John and the fellow glovers of Stratford . . .

ERIC: Oh, but biographers have combed through *all* the documents—and chosen what to tell us. Isn't there much about people we can take for granted?

BETTY: Yes. People still fall in love, fear death, worry about money, go to school, look for work. But none of these things is quite the same in Tudor times as now. With delicacy and care, Eric, we ought to be able to conclude more from the Tudor documents than we do at present.

ERIC: Oh, dear, I'm getting bewildered. But let me try to sum up what you've said. I think Schoenbaum's life of Shakespeare is fine; you're dissatisfied. You complain about the way biographies are structured and written. First, you don't want to treat history as "background," but as a part of anyone's individuality. You'd hold that we neglect some aspects of history which, in a sense, must have been a part of a Tudor person. Second, you say that even normal aspects of environment—roads or rainfall—may belong properly to identity. Third, you say that biographies falsify history of being backward looking in their manner, whereas they should give a continual sense of a whole verifiable present unfolding before us. Or a sense of time as it was lived through, with an unknown future problematically ahead.

And then you want a biographer to be more humble with persons, a little more attentive to various aspects of individuality—

BETTY: A little less stupid about women.

ERIC: —or more cunning with the documentary evidence. But, with Shakespeare, aren't you avoiding the nitty-gritty? What would you do about the mythos, Betty? I mean those dubious legends about him dating from the late seventeenth century. You remember that E. K. Chambers in *William Shakespeare: A Study of Facts and Problems* listed about fifty-eight early comments on Shakespeare, and I don't suppose that's a complete list, is it?

BETTY: *No*, dear boy. Chambers, in 1930, used the heading "The Shakespeare-Mythos," put Aubrey and Rowe in that category, left out useful remarks by Theobald and others, and kept us from thinking delicately enough for the next fifty or sixty years about seventeenth- and eighteenth-century evidence. Schoenbaum took over Chambers's phrase, Shakespeare Mythos, in *Shakespeare's Lives* . . .

ERIC: And wrote pretty well, admit it, about poor William's early marriage to Anne Hathaway. Sex in the hayfields, I suppose! Schoenbaum thinks Anne was growing "a bit long in the tooth for the marriage market," by the standards of her time. Now if that's accurate, then Anne at twenty-six appears to have trapped William into marrying her when he was only eighteen. At any rate, a lady "long in the tooth" sounds ominous to me. A friend of mine says it must have been a "shotgun" or a "longbow" wedding, alas poor Will!

BETTY: But, Eric, the earliest biographers don't hint that the marriage could have been a mistake. Rowe in 1709 said that the playwright when very young had seen fit to marry in order to settle down in a family manner. Theobald, a little later, said that Shakespeare was moved either by a force of inclination or by "circumstances of convenience." By neatly dismissing these fairly early reports as the Shakespeare Mythos we can see Anne as a monster! A trapper. Little matter that the families of Hathaway and Shakespeare had had a sound connection dating back to the time of William's infancy.

ERIC: All right, you don't want to throw out the whole Shakespeare Mythos. You want to believe in it.

BETTY: No. But why can't biographers work with it? Why should they stop thinking about it?

ERIC: But what about vast gaps in our knowledge of Shakespeare which the mythos doesn't touch—whole seas of questions about what he was doing at a given time, to whom he wrote the sonnets, whether people and feelings in the sonnets are fictive or factual? Look, darling lovely girl, I have a tutorial to get to—and I'm a respecter of tradition.

BETTY: But so am I. Your last word illuminates the mythos and sonnets.

ERIC: My last word?

BETTY: Tradition. After all, despite everything that people say about the failure of the Shakespeare biographies, their traditions must be respected. *They* save us from eccentricity . . . not from work. Don't you think?

ERIC: *That* sounds a little more sensible.

BETTY: Eric, do you know, a biographer's worst fault is the Coriolanus one, pride, lack of humility. Oh, Eric, a biographer *is* faced with "fierce methodological problems," sifting truth from legend, the probable from the possible . . . Don't step on my dress . . . and there is so much to think of, I know. But we *can't* go on supposing that a document of four hundred years ago has the same meaning it would have today, or that history doesn't affect people, all they say and do. We can't suppose that his unfolding time had no effect on Shakespeare; we don't have to see him in a false, retrospective way. We don't have to think his mother, his wife, his friends, Ben Jonson, and the others meant nothing to him, as biographers who treat them all so distantly almost suggest. The changing events of Elizabethan England were part of his life, but you hardly hear of them in accounts of his life. You'd never know the Elizabethans were a religious people, or that recent changes in the national religion had some effect on the temper of the times, to judge from our biographies. You'd never know that green England, nature, the soil, and the climate had much to do with the man, or that he ever studied human character at Stratford or anywhere else. You'll be late, Eric; you're standing on my dress. Yes, I love biographies, but *still*, one ought to question the way we write about authors' lives. . . .

INDEX

Wotton, Thomas, and rationale in
    1576 for history-study, 215
Wyatt, Sir Thomas, 161
Wymer, Norman George, 41

Yeats, W. B., 69; reads Landor with
    Pound, 214

Zen Buddhism, 238
Ziegler, Philip, 42, 47–48
Zwicker, Ralph, 235